101

QUESTIONS & ANSWERS
S E R I E S

LAND LAW

101
QUESTIONS & ANSWERS
SERIES

LAND LAW

ALLAN COOMBES
LLB, Senior Lecturer in Law (Holborn College)

OLD BAILEY PRESS

OLD BAILEY PRESS
200 Greyhound Road, London W14 9RY

First published 2000
Reprinted 2001

ISBN 1 85836 368 3

British Library Cataloguing-in-Publication Data

A catalogue record for this book is available from the British Library.

Printed and bound in Great Britain.

Contents

Foreword

This book is part of a series designed specifically for students studying at undergraduate level and is based on the syllabus of the London University (External) LLB examinations. The questions are drawn in the main from past papers, but also include some prepared by the author.

The suggested answers are longer than could be written within the time constraints imposed by the examination. While seeking to provide the basis for answering questions in the examination room, the author has also been concerned to use the answers as a teaching vehicle for a subject which many students regard as a difficult area of law. Hence the expanded length of the answers, which are also designed to provide an exposition of the law so as to enhance the students' understanding of it, which will in turn better facilitate analysis of the questions and application of the law to the issues they raise.

Each chapter consists of a short Introduction, Interrograms and Examination Questions. The Interrograms and answers deal with fundamental concepts and these should be mastered before embarking on the Examination Questions. Thus, it is intended that students should work through the Interrograms and Examination Questions before checking their knowledge against the suggested answers.

The law is as stated on 31 March 2000.

Acknowledgement

Our thanks are extended to the University of London for their kind permission to use and publish questions taken from the University of London LLB (External) Degree examination papers.

Caveat

The answers given are not approved or sanctioned by the University of London and are entirely our responsibility.

They are not intended as 'Model Answers', but rather as Suggested Solutions.

Table of Cases

1

Basic Concepts of Land Law

Introduction

This chapter deals with fundamental concepts of land law and the 1925 property legislation on which modern land law is based. The importance of this chapter cannot be stressed too strongly as it forms the foundation for the rest of the syllabus. Candidates should therefore aim at a thorough grasp of the material, both in the Interrograms and in the three substantive questions. Unless this material is mastered candidates will experience difficulties as they work through the remainder of the syllabus.

Questions

INTERROGRAMS

1 What is an estate in land?
2 What is an interest in land? How does it differ from an estate?
3 Define tenure.
4 What is the meaning of the term 'freehold'?
5 What is a legal right in land?
6. What is an equitable right in land?
7 What is the doctrine of the bona fide purchaser?
8 What was the legislature's objective in enacting s1(1)–(3) LPA 1925?
9 Explain the meaning of the expression 'fee simple absolute in possession'.
10 What is a term of years absolute?
11 What are the most important land charges in the Land Charges Act 1972?
12 What is the meaning of the term 'estate contract' as defined by the Land Charges Act 1972?
13 What is the effect of registering a land charge under the Land Charges Act 1972?
14 What is the effect of non-registration of a land charge under the Land Charges Act 1972?
15 L gives a written lease for five years to T and then later sells his freehold to P. Does P take subject to, or free from, the lease?
16 What is overreaching?
17 Give examples of equitable interests which are neither overreachable nor registrable under the Land Charges Act 1972. What is their effect on third parties?

QUESTION ONE

a   'There are thus two fundamental doctrines in the law of real property ... tenure answers the question "upon what terms is it (land) held"?; estate answers the question "for how long"?' (Megarry and Wade, *The Law of Real Property*).
    Explain this statement.

b   What interest, if any, is created by the following transaction:

A conveys Blackacre to B in fee simple imposing covenants and reserving a right of re-entry on breach of covenant.

University of London LLB Examination
(for external students) Land Law June 1985 Q1

QUESTION TWO

Examine the ways in which the 1925 property legislation sought to simplify conveyancing. What subsequent alterations have been made by legislation?

Prepared by the author

QUESTION THREE

'The case is plain. The Act is clear and definite. Intended as it was to provide a simple understandable system for the protection of title to land, it should not be read down or glossed; to do so would destroy the usefulness of the Act': per Lord Wilberforce in *Midland Bank Trust Co Ltd* v *Green* (1981) referring to the Land Charges Act 1925.
    Explain Lord Wilberforce's statement and assess the efficacy and fairness of the statute. How does the statute's treatment of equitable interests compare with that of the Land Registration Act 1925?

Prepared by the author

Answers

ANSWERS TO INTERROGRAMS

1   The doctrine of estates was described in *Walsingham's Case* (1573):

'The land itself is one thing and the estate in land is another. For an estate in land is a time in the land, or land for a time; and there are diversities of estates which are no more than diversities of time; for he who has a fee simple in the land has a time in the land without end; and he who has land in tail has time in the land for as long as he has issue of his body; and he who has an estate in land for life has no time in it longer than his life.'

It is essential to note the contrast made between land and the estate in that land. An estate is an abstract concept and as such allows different persons to hold different estates in the same plot of land at the same time. Thus, in the case of leaseholds the landlord holds or 'owns' the fee simple in the land, while the tenant holds or 'owns' a different estate in that same plot of land, namely a term of years absolute. Both estates subsist at the same time. As *Walsingham*'s *Case* indicates, an estate is 'a time in the land, or land for a time'. The size of an estate is measured by its duration and the differences between estates are no more than 'diversities of time'.

Walsingham's *Case* does not mention leasehold estates as it is only dealing with freehold estates, ie those held on a free tenure. Leasehold estates grew up outside the freehold tenural system and are described as estates less than freehold. Whereas the freehold estates all share the common characteristic of being of uncertain duration, the leasehold estate is for a fixed period whether it be granted for a fixed term of years, eg seven years, or takes the form of a periodic tenancy, eg a yearly tenancy.

An estate measures the quantum or size of the holder's interest in land in contrast to his tenure which describes the terms on which he holds the land.

2   An interest in land denotes a right in someone else's land, eg an easement or the benefit of a restrictive covenant. It is to be contrasted with the 'ownership' of land, which an estate confers, albeit in varying degrees. A fee simple absolute in possession endures forever; a term of years confers an 'ownership' of limited duration.

3   Tenure derives from the Latin verb tenere 'to hold'. It has never been possible in English law for an individual to own land. The sole owner of land is the Crown. After the Conquest in 1066 King William I granted land to his followers as tenants-in-chief. These grants were not outright gifts but grants of land to be held by those tenants in return for rendering to the King specific and defined services. Most of the services were of a military nature: knight service. For example, a tenant might be obliged to supply the king with ten knights for a fixed number of days per year. Where land was granted to the Church it was in return for services of a spiritual nature, eg to say mass for the King. The tenants in chief in turn sub-granted (subinfeudated) to under tenants in return for services, thus giving rise to a system of land-holding in the shape of a pyramid with the King at its apex. Neither tenants-in-chief nor their sub-tenants could be said to have owned the land since their rights to hold the land were conditional on the performance of their services. The word 'tenure' described the type of services in return for which the land was held. It is not necessary to describe the various types of tenures and their subsequent decline in any detail.

As a result of changing social and economic conditions, tenures were commuted to money payments and by the Tenures Abolition Act 1660 all free tenures were converted into socage tenure, which was a form of agricultural tenure and which by that date, like the other tenures, had been converted into money. It is the only remaining tenure and its existence is a reminder that land is still held by the Crown and not owned absolutely. The tenure is of course only theoretical but it still exists in law.

The statue of Quia Emptores 1290 forbade the creation of new tenures. It also permitted tenants in fee simple to freely alienate their lands without their lord's consent, but stipulated that any such alienation must be by substitution instead of subinfeudation. This meant that the alienee did not become a sub-tenant of the alienor but would instead take his place and 'hold the same lands or tenements of the chief lord of the same fee by such service and customs as his feofor (alienor) held before'. The statute remains one of the foundations of modern land law. Where a vendor, who is in theory a tenant of the Crown holding a socage tenure, sells his land to a purchaser, the latter becomes the new tenant of the Crown for that land holding it on socage tenure.

4   Originally the expression 'freehold' referred to free tenure and a man holding on free tenure was called a freeholder. In mediaeval times tenures were divided into two groups: free tenure and unfree tenure. Examples of the former were military tenure; socage tenure (which is the only surviving tenure); and spiritual tenure (frankalmoign). The services due under the free tenure were defined and fixed. In the case of military service the tenant would be obliged to supply the King with a fixed number of knights for military service for a defined number of days per year.

An unfree tenure was called villeinage but later became known as copyhold tenure. The services due under copyhold tenure were not fixed. As time passed, the services, in common with those of free tenure, were converted into monetary payments. Copyhold tenure remained until its abolition by the 1925 property legislation. In modern times the term 'freehold' still survives but is generally used to distinguish land held in fee simple absolute in possession from leasehold land.

5   Here the word 'right' is used to describe both an estate and interest in land. It was a right recognised and enforced by the old common law courts as opposed to a right recognised by the Court of Chancery. Legal rights were rights 'in rem', that is to say enforceable against the whole world. Recognition of the existence of rights by the common law courts would only be granted if the rights were created by the appropriate formalities, eg a deed. The modern law still reflects this approach. The s52 LPA 1925 enacts that a legal estate or interest in land must be created by deed. There are exceptions to the rule, one of the most important being contained in s54 LPA 1925 which enables legal leases not exceeding three years to be created without any formalities at all. The definition of a legal easement in s1(2)(a) LPA 1925 should also be noted.

6   An equitable right is one recognised or created by equity. Equity is a system of rules and doctrines developed by the old Court of Chancery and came into being to remedy and ameliorate the rigidity of the common law, as well to provide for situations which the common law did not. The Judicature Acts 1873 and 1875 abolished the Court of Chancery and the common law courts and transferred their jurisdiction to the newly created Supreme Court of Judicature. The administration of law and equity was fused, but the rules of common law and equity were not. It has been said that 'after the Judicature Acts the waters of law and equity now flow in the same channel but their waters do not mingle'. The distinction between legal rights developed at common law and equitable rights created by equity remains and is fundamental to land law.

Equity originated and was developed on an ethical basis by the mediaeval chancellors who, until the dismissal of Cardinal Wolsey in 1529, were high-ranking clerics whose training and ethical outlook heavily influenced their work.

The most outstanding contribution of equity was in the field of trusts and an examination of that contribution also provides an illustration of how the common law courts and Court of Chancery differed in their approach and produced the dichotomy between legal and equitable rights. If S conveyed land to T (a trustee) to hold that land for the benefit of B, common law would only recognise the trustee's ownership. As far as common law was concerned the ownership had been transferred to T and the land was his to do with it as he wished. He was the owner at law; his rights were legal rights and good against the whole world. The obligation imposed upon him by S was regarded as a purely moral one of which the common law took no cognisance.

Equity took a different view and while recognising the trustee's ownership at law, was prepared to compel the trustee to observe the terms of the trust because he was under a moral obligation to do so. The dictates of conscience demanded it. Hence, the Court of Chancery's later label as a 'Court of Conscience'. Equity would act against the person of the trustee to compel him to discharge his duties towards B. Equity acted 'in personam'. In so doing equity conferred upon B a corresponding right and, since that right was created by equity, it was regarded as an equitable right in the land. Equity regarded B as the true owner of the land which, in substance, he was. Although the legal fee simple estate was vested in T, B enjoyed the fee simple in equity: he therefore had an equitable fee simple.

This equitable right was originally only enforced against the trustee but equity was obliged to consider whether B was entitled to enforce his equitable right against T's successor in title, eg his heir or his grantee. That depended on whether that successor's conscience was affected by knowledge or notice of B's rights. Equity gradually extended the class of persons against whom it would enforce B's rights until an equitable right became similar to a legal right in rem - one enforceable against the whole world - but with one exception: the 'bona fide purchaser of the legal estate in the land for value without notice' who is sometimes known as 'equity's darling'. This exception was a serious defect in an equitable right and one which was potentially addressed by the Land Charges Act 1925.

Finally, notice that the s25 Judicature Act 1873 provided that where there is any conflict between the rules of law and the rules of equity, the rules of equity shall prevail.

7   The fundamental weakness of an equitable right in land is that it binds the whole world except the bona fide purchaser of the legal estate in the land for value, without notice. There are a number of points to be made.

a   A purchaser cannot claim to be a bona fide purchaser if he has acted in a dishonest or irregular way. It can be linked to the absence of notice in the sense that such absence of notice must be genuine and honest, but it is not inevitably so linked. In *Pilcher* v *Rawlins* (1872) James LJ regarded the requirement of good faith as an independent requirement. Thus, even if a purchaser genuinely had no notice of the equitable right he was still obliged to prove his good faith. See also the judgment of Lord Wilberforce in *Midland Bank Trust Co Ltd* v *Green* (1981).

b   The word 'purchaser' bears a different meaning from that found in everyday use. It means someone who acquires land by an act of the parties as opposed to the operation of law. Thus, a beneficiary under a testamentary disposition will be a purchaser even although he has given no value. If the beneficiary inherits under an intestacy, since his acquisition is by operation of law, he will not be a purchaser.

c   The purchaser must give value and this can consist of money, money's worth or marriage. In the case of money or money's worth it is immaterial that the value is nominal. It will still suffice. A beneficiary under a will, although a purchaser within the definition of that word, will not fall within the definition of a bona fide purchaser since he has given no value.

d   The purchaser must acquire the legal estate in the land. It will not be sufficient if he acquires only an equitable interest.

e   There are three types of notice:

   i   *Actual notice*: This means what it says. It covers the case where the purchaser actually does know of the existence of an equitable right in the land he is buying.

   ii *Constructive notice*: A purchaser who has no actual knowledge of an equitable right may nevertheless be regarded by equity as having constructive notice if he could have discovered its existence by reasonable and diligent enquiries. A purchaser should always inspect land he is proposing to purchase since occupation is constructive notice of an occupier's rights: *Hunt* v *Luck* (1902).

   iii Imputed notice: Where a purchaser's agent, eg the solicitor acting for him in the purchase, has either actual or constructive notice of an equitable right in the land, such notice is imputed to the purchaser: see *Kingsnorth Finance Co Ltd* v *Tizard* (1986).

8 Section 1(1)–(3) LPA 1925 provides:

'(1) The only estates in land which are capable of subsisting or of being conveyed or created at law are –
(a) An estate in fee simple absolute in possession;
(b) A term of years absolute.
(2) The only interests or charges in or over land which are capable of subsisting or of being conveyed or created at law are –
(a) An easement, right, or privilege in or over land for an interest equivalent to an estate in fee simple absolute in possession or a term of years absolute;
(b) A rentcharge in possession issuing out of or charged on land being either perpetual or for a term of years absolute;
(c) A charge by way of legal mortgage;
(d) Any other similar charge on land which is not created by an instrument;
(e) Rights of entry exercisable over or in respect of a legal term of years absolute, or annexed, for any purpose, to a legal rentcharge.
(3) All other estates, interests, and charges in or over land take effect as equitable interests.'

The objective behind this section is to reduce the number of legal estates and interests in land which may subsist at law. A legal estate or interest in land binds a purchaser whether he knows of it or not, even if there are no means by which he could have discovered it. Such legal rights can be considered as mines concealed in a field, the existence of which the purchaser only discovers when they unexpectedly explode after he has purchased the land. The hazards presented by the rule have not been removed entirely but they have been reduced by s1. Thus a considerable number of estates and interests which could have existed at law before 1 January 1926 can now only exist as equitable interests: s1(3). Notice that the wording of the section is permissive. It does not say that the two estates and five interests listed in s1(1), (2) must be legal but that they are the only ones which may be legal.

9   This is a term originating in medieval times. The word 'fee' denotes that the estate was one of inheritance which meant that the tenant could not alienate the land so as to deprive his heirs. In the thirteenth century that restriction disappeared, thus depriving the word of much of its meaning, although the heirs would still inherit if he did not alienate.

The term 'simple' denoted the class of heirs entitled to inherit, ie the general heirs as opposed to the descendant heirs as was the case with the fee tail estate. Again the word has lost much of its practical meaning, although it continues to distinguish the fee simple estate from the fee tail.

The word 'absolute' is of greater significance. It denotes that the fee simple is subject to no provisos or conditions which can prematurely determine it. In consequence it lasts for ever with the result that the holder of a fee simple absolute enjoys the equivalent of absolute ownership. The fee simple absolute must be compared with the modified fees. Examples are the determinable fee simple and the fee simple defeasible by condition subsequent. The modified fees can now only exist in equity (s13 LPA 1925), although the Law of Property (Amendment) Act 1926 has produced some unexpected results as regards conditional fees.

The term 'in possession' is defined by s205(xix) LPA 1925 to mean that an estate is in possession if it is immediate, not in remainder or reversion, and includes the receipt of rents and profits and the right to receive the same.

An owner of land who has granted a lease to a tenant does not have physical possession of the land because it is the tenant who enjoys physical possession. Nevertheless, by virtue of the definition the landlord is regarded as being in possession because he is entitled to receive rent from the tenant. Were that not the case, he would not have a fee simple absolute 'in possession' and his fee simple would not qualify to be a legal estate under s1(1) LPA 1925.

10 A term of years absolute, commonly known as a legal lease, is defined by s205(xxvii) LPA 1925:

> ' "Term of years absolute" means a term of years (taking effect either in possession or in reversion whether or not at a rent) with or without impeachment for waste, subject or not to another legal estate, and either certain or liable to determination by notice, re-entry, operation of law, or by a provision for cesser on redemption, or in any other event (other than the dropping of a life, or the determination of a determinable life interest); but does not include any term of years determinable with life or lives or with the cesser of a determinable life interest, nor, if created after the commencement of this Act, a term of years which is not expressed to take effect in possession within twenty-one years after the creation thereof where required by this Act to take effect

within that period; and in this definition the expression "term of years" includes a term for less than a year, or for a year or years and a fraction of a year or from year to year.'

It is one of the two estates which can subsist at s1(1) law: LPA 1925. Rent is not a necessary ingredient of a term of years absolute as the definition indicates. The word 'absolute' is superfluous. It neither adds to, nor subtracts from, the definition. The word 'absolute' appears in the definition 'fee simple absolute in possession' and in that context indicates the fee simple is not liable to premature determination as is the case with the modified fees, eg the determinable fee simple. It therefore lasts in perpetuity. Clearly the word 'absolute' cannot have that meaning for the term of years absolute since the definition of the latter contains provision for its determination 'by notice, re-entry, operation of law.'

The definition was discussed by the House of Lords in *Prudential Assurance Co Ltd* v *London Residuary Body* (1992). 'A demise for years is a contract for the exclusive possession and profit of land for some determinate time. Such an estate is called a "term"': per Lord Templeman.

A lease must be for a term certain and a lease granted for an indefinite time, eg 'for the duration of the war' is void for uncertainty: *Lace* v *Chantler* (1944), confirmed by *Prudential Assurance Co Ltd* v *London Residuary Body*.

Lord Templeman made reference to *Say* v *Smith* (1563): '... every contract sufficient to make a lease for years ought to have certainty in three limitations: viz in the commencement of the term, in the continuance of it, and in the end of it; so that all these ought to be known at the commencement of the lease'.

Dealing with periodic tenancies Lord Templeman affirmed the principle of *Lace* v *Chantler* – that a term must be certain, applied to all leases and tenancy agreements – but pointed out that a tenancy from year to year (and all other periodic tenancies) were saved from being uncertain because each party had power to determine by the appropriate period of notice. In the case of a yearly tenancy for example, the term continued until determined as if both parties made a new agreement at the end of each year for a new term for the ensuing year. He pointed out that in the case of a yearly tenancy if no-one had power to determine the lease, or if only one party had power to determine, then neither position is consistent with a yearly tenancy.

11 The most important land charges are:

a   Class C(i): This is a legal mortgage not protected by a deposit of title deeds. This means that the mortgagor (the borrower) has not deposited the title deeds with the mortgagee (the lender) and this will generally be because there already is a first mortgagee who has the title deeds.

b   Class C(iii): A general equitable charge and which includes an equitable mortgage not protected by a deposit of title deeds.

c   Class C(iv): An estate contract. This is one of the most important of the land charges and candidates should study it with care. Basically it is a contract to create or convey a legal estate in land but it includes an option to purchase and an option to renew a lease. An equitable lease falls within the definition.

d   Class D(ii): Restrictive covenants created on or after 1 January 1926. Restrictive covenants made before that date are subject to the doctrine of the bona fide purchaser.

e   Class D(iii): Equitable easements. An equitable easement is one that does not fall within the definition of a legal easement in s1(2)(a) LPA 1925. It is registrable as a land charge if created on or after 1 January 1926. If created before that date it is subject to the doctrine of the bona fide purchaser.

f   Class F: This charge was not included in the LCA 1925 but is now included in the LCA 1972. A discussion of this right properly belongs to family law but it may be described here as the statutory right of a spouse to occupy the matrimonial home. A spouse who has no legal or equitable right in the property may register a Class F land charge as may a spouse who has only an equitable right arising, say, from a contribution to the purchase price. In the latter case the statutory right of the occupant is quite independent of any rights enjoyed by virtue of the equitable interest.

12   An estate contract is a land charge Class C(iv) which is defined by s2(4)(iv) LCA 1972 as:

> '... a contract by an estate owner ... to convey or create a legal estate, including a contract conferring ... a valid option to purchase, a right of pre-emption or any other like right.'

An estate contract falls within Law of Property (Miscellaneous Provisions) Act 1989 and must be made in writing, contain all the terms of the contract and be signed by all parties.

An agreement for a lease (ie an equitable lease) is an estate contract.

An option to purchase is within the definition and is sometimes found in leases in the form of a tenant's right to purchase the landlord's reversion.

The effect of an option to purchase is to confer upon the grantee an equitable interest in land: *London and SW Railway* v *Gomm* (1882). There has been much debate about the conceptual classification of an option to purchase. On the one hand it has been regarded as a conditional contract, while another school of thought has regarded it as an irrevocable offer by the grantor. In *Spiro* v *Glencrown Properties Ltd* (1991) Hoffmann J regarded it as falling in neither category preferring to describe it as a relationship 'sui generis'.

In that case the applicability of the Law of Property (Miscellaneous Provisions) Act was considered. The grant of the option itself satisfied s2. The grantee gave written and signed notice of his intention to exercise the option but then decided not to complete the purchase. The vendor sued him for damages and the grantee argued that the written notice could not constitute a contract because, since it was not signed by the vendor, it did not comply with s2 which required signature by all parties. If an option to purchase is classified as an irrevocable offer then the contract only comes into existence when it is accepted by the grantee. If that be the case then a written notice of intention to purchase would constitute the acceptance but would not satisfy the requirement of s2 because it did not contain the vendor's signature. If an option to purchase is regarded as a conditional contract then the grantor of the option to purchase itself must comply with s2. Hoffman J held that strictly speaking the grant of an option to purchase was not a conditional contract in the conventional sense but was analogous to it, and therefore it was the grant of the option, as opposed to its exercise, that was caught by s2. In the instant case the grant satisfied the requirements of s2 and the purchaser was held liable.

A right of pre-emption is sometimes known as the right of first refusal. The grantor is undertaking to the grantee that if he decides to sell his land he will offer it to him first. In *Pritchard* v *Briggs* (1980) Templeman LJ pointed out that with an option to purchase the initiative lies with the grantee. It is he who decides whether to exercise the option and if he does the grantor is bound. In the case of a right of pre-emption the position is reversed. The initiative lies with the grantor and until and if he decides to sell the grantee has a mere 'spes' (hope). In *Pritchard* v *Briggs* the Court of Appeal held that that right of pre-emption did not confer an interest in land until the grantor decided to sell the land. Stephenson and Templeman LJJ held that it could nevertheless be registered as a land charge before the grantor decided to sell land to a third party, and then a third party would be bound. Goff LJ took the view that a right of pre-emption could never be an interest in land which could bind a third party even if it was registered.

13 The effect of registration 'shall be deemed to constitute actual notice … to all persons and for all purposes … as from the date of registration': s198(1) LPA 1925. Thus, a purchaser who does not search the register will still be bound by any land charge which has been registered.

14 The effect of non-registration depends on the class of land charge. The LCA 1972 provides that:

a   A land charge Class C (except Class C(iv)) shall, if not registered, be void against a purchaser of any interest in land. A s4(5) LCA 1972 'purchaser' is defined in s17 as 'any person (including a mortgagee or lessee) who for valuable consideration takes any interest in land'. Valuable consideration includes marriage.

b   'An estate contract [C(iv)] and a land charge Class D created on or after 1 January 1926 shall be void as against a purchaser for money or money's worth … of a legal estate in the land charged with it, unless the land charge is registered in the appropriate register before the completion of the purchase': s4(6) LCA 1972.

c   'A land charge Class F shall be void as against a purchaser of the land charged with it, or of any interest in such land, unless the land charge is registered in the appropriate register before the completion of the purchase' s4(8) LCA 1972.

It shall be noted that these provisions apply even if the purchaser is aware of the interests concerned: *Midland Bank Trust Co Ltd* v *Green* (1981).

15 This question is designed to illustrate a formula for dealing with a standard situation in land law problems where title to the land is unregistered. It consists of a number of stages:

a   *Stage 1*: Whether P is bound or not depends on whether the lease is legal or equitable. Section 1 LPA 1925 provides that a lease (term of years absolute) *may* be capable of being legal. The section is permissive.

b *Stage 2*: Is this particular lease legal? A legal estate in land may only be created or conveyed by deed: s52 LPA 1925 (but note s54). This lease is not by deed and does not therefore comply with s52.

c *Stage 3*: Does this lease come within the dispensation provided by s54 LPA 1925 which provides that a legal lease may be created without any formalities provided that certain conditions are satisfied and particularly that the lease does not exceed three years. The answer is in the negative because this lease is for five years.

d *Stage 4*: Since it is not legal is it equitable? Equitable recognition is not automatic. Equity will regard the transaction as a contract to create a legal lease providing all the ingredients of a valid contract are present and the contract is one which equity will specifically enforce. Being a contract for the disposition of land it falls within s2 Law of Property (Miscellaneous Provisions) Act 1989 and so must satisfy the requirements of that statute. We are not told the contents of the written lease and so we cannot be certain if it satisfies the statute. We do not know if the tenant has signed the lease and the signatures of both parties are required. If s2 is not complied with the contract is void and there can be no equitable lease.

e *Stage 5*: If the requirements of the statute are satisfied then there is a valid contract to create a legal lease. Provided it is one which equity will enforce by specific performance, equity will go one stage further by applying the maxim 'equity looks on that as done with ought to be done' and treat the parties as in the relationship of landlord and tenant, ie there is an equitable lease. The contract is registrable as a land charge Class C4.

f *Stage 6*: We are not told whether the tenant has registered it and we must therefore argue in the alternative.

g *Stage 7*: If it has been registered, registration constitutes notice to the whole world (s198 LPA 1925), and P is bound even if he has no actual knowledge of the lease's existence.

h *Stage 8*: If the lease is not registered then P takes free from it if he is a purchaser of the legal estate in the land for money or money's worth (s4(6) LCA 1972) and this is so even if he knows of the lease: *Hollington Bros Ltd* v *Rhodes* (1951).

16 Overreaching is a device whereby beneficial interests under a Settled Land Act settlement, a trust for sale and a trust of land are converted from being interests in land to interests in money (the proceeds of sale), with the advantage to a purchaser that he acquires the legal estate to the land free from the beneficial interests which, before his purchase, existed in the land. The provisions are contained in s2 LPA 1925 as amended by the Trusts of Land and Appointment of Trustees Act 1996, Sch 3 para 4. To operate the provisions it is necessary for a purchaser to pay the purchase money to two trustees or a trust corporation.

If in the case of unregistered land payment is only made to one trustee no overreaching occurs and the purchaser takes subject to the equitable beneficial interests, unless he can establish that he is a bona fide purchaser.

In the case of registered land if the beneficial interests arising under a trust for sale fall within s70(1)(g) LPA 1925 they will be overreached (*City of London Building Society* v *Flegg* (1988)) if payment is made to two trustees.

17 Restrictive covenants and equitable easements created before 1 January 1926 are not registrable as land charges under the LCA 1972. Nor are equitable rights of re-entry: *Shiloh Spinners Ltd* v *Harding* (1973). Equitable rights of estoppel are not registrable: *Ives (E R) Investments* v *High* (1967).

These types of interest are miscellaneous in nature and fit neither into the registration, nor the overreaching, provisions. They constitute a residual class. The doctrine of the bona fide purchaser still applies.

The altered position of bare trusts should be noted. They too were neither registrable nor overreachable. They have now been embraced by the Trusts of Land and Appointment of Trustees Act 1996 and have become subject to overreaching.

SUGGESTED ANSWER TO QUESTION ONE

General Comment

A question to remind the candidate that all examinations are based on a syllbaus and the examiner is entitled to select questions from any part of that syllabus. Part (a) emerges from the first substantive paragraph of the syllabus and is a welcome encouragement to those tutors who advise students that an understanding of land law is always helped by an appreciation of fundamental areas such as this.

Part (b) is a trap for the unwary and relates to rather an obscure point in connection with a modified fee simple and which was covered b the Law of Property (Amendment) Act 1926.

Key Points

a • Describe tenure: quality of holding – feudal pyramid – forms of tenure – tenures today
  • Describe estate: quantity of the holding – types of estate before 1926 – the legal estate today (s1(1) LPA 1925) – conclusion
b • Reservation of a right of re-entry – effect of Law of Property (Amendment) Act 1926 on s7(1) LPA 1925.

Suggested Answer

a This statement of Megarry and Wade summarises the rules which formed the basis of land law. Tenure answered the question 'upon what terms' was the land held. This described the quality of the holding and, in particular, referred to the early rules of subinfeudation by which the grantee held 'land' in return for services. This concept of subinfeudation emerged after the Norman Conquest and represented the rewards given by the King to those who had supported him. This created a form of holding which acquired the title of the feudal pyramid because all 'land' was held either directly or indirectly through intermediaries, from the King himself. This may be represented by the following diagram of freehold tenures:

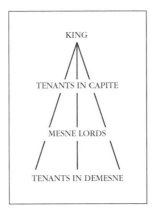

Thus each intermediary would grant an interest in land in return for some service and in this way the fabric of feudalism was created. It did not last for many years in that it became much easier to pay for services than provide them directly. As a consequence the doctrine of subinfeudation was brought to an end by the statute Quia Emptores in 1290. The major effect of the statute was to replace subinfeudation by substitution. This is described in Megarry and Wade (6th edn) at p29:

> 'Quia Emptores marked the victory of the modern concept of land as alienable property over the more restrictive principles of feudalism. For no new tenures in fee simple could thenceforth be created except by the Crown.'

This is concluded on p30 by a suitable epitaph to the feudal pyramid. After 1290 the feudal pyramid began to crumble. The number of mesne lordships could not be increased, evidence of existing mesne lordships gradually disappeared with the passing of time, and so most land came to be held directly from the Crown. In the words of the statute itself:

> 'Our Lord the King ... at the instance of the great men of the realm ... ordained, that from henceforth it shall be lawful to every freeman to sell at his own pleasure his lands and tenements, or part of them; so that the feoffee shall hold the same fee by such service and customs as his feoffor held before.'

The forms of tenure may be described as the quality of the holding. This quality was varied by the nature of the services to be provided by the grantee. A popular diagram of the forms of tenure is as follows:

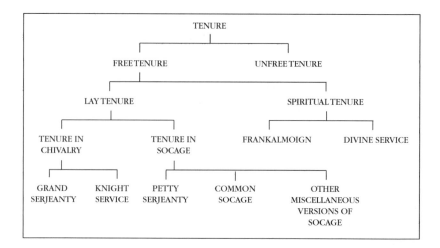

Of these forms of tenure the most significant was, probably knight service. This contained many incidents which formed the basis of the tenure and included relief, escheat, wardship and marriage. Most of the forms of tenure had ended by 1660 with the passing of the Tenures Abolition Act 1660. Some, including frankalmoign, the honorary incidents of grand and petty serjeanty, survived until 1925. From 1 January 1926 the only surviving form of tenure is socage now known as freehold tenure. The consequence is neatly summarised in *Cheshire and Burn's Modern Law of Real Property* (15th edn) at p25:

> 'The result is that though the general theory of tenure is still a part of English law in the sense that all land is held by a superior and is incapable of absolute ownership, yet the law of tenure is both simpler and of less significance than it was before 1926. It is simpler because there is now only one form of tenure: namely socage. It is of less significance because all the tenurial incidents (including escheat) which might in exceptional cases have brought profit to a mesne lord have been abolished ... We can, in fact, now describe the theory of tenure, despite the great part that it had played in the history of English law, as a conception of merely academic interest. It no longer restricts the tenant in his free enjoyment of the land.'

Estate deals with the duration of interest and describes the quantity of the holdings. It is, again, possible to demonstrate this by way of diagram in which it will be noted there are two major categories of estate: the freehold and the less than freehold estate. Unlike tenures the concept of estates remains with us today and formed the essential part of s1(1) Law of Property Act (LPA) 1925. The types of estate that existed before 1926 may be shown diagrammatically as follows:

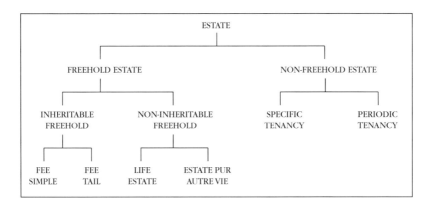

Of these estates the fee simple and the non-freehold estate remain as legal estates under s1(1) LPA 1925. They are now, respectively, the 'fee simple absolute in possession' and the 'term of years absolute'. The fee tail and the life estate also continue but are now equitable interests known, respectively, as the entailed interest and the life interest. A feature of the estate is that several could exist concurrently and this is retained by s1(5) LPA 1925: 'A legal estate may subsist concurrently with or subject to any other legal estate in the same land'. The effect today is the existence of the fee simple, leases and sub-leases all being separate estates in the same land.

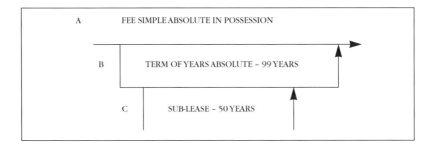

It will be seen that estate is not the land itself. The estate is a conceptual matter which has been separated from the land. It is the estate that is the subject of conveyance, lease or assignment whilst the land itself remains in the ownership of the Crown as a further reminder of the feudal origins. *Cheshire and Burn* define 'estate' at p33 as 'the right to possess and use the land for the period of time for which it has been granted.'

Most authors recognise the unique quality of the estate and the right of seisin which represents the present right to enjoy the possession of the land by an owner of the freehold estate holding for freehold tenure. A fitting conclusion is provided by *Cheshire and Burn* at p33:

'In conclusion, it may be said that this doctrine of the estate has given an elasticity to the English law of the land that is not found in countries outside the area of the common law.'

b   A holds the fee simple absolute in possession in Blackacre and he conveys it to B. The conveyance includes covenants which mean that A will retain an interest as covenantee and will be able to enforce the covenants, whether they are positive or negative, as a matter of contract against B. The question which arises is whether B has an 'absolute' fee simple when A may re-enter if any of the covenants are broken. This clearly is a restriction on the 'absolute' nature of the estate as the word 'absolute' is defined in general usage. This problem was recognised, belatedly, by the draftsmen of the 1925 legislation and the following words were added to s7(1) LPA 1925 by the Law of Property (Amendment) Act 1926, ie 'and a fee simple subject to a legal or equitable right of entry or re-entry is for the purposes of this Act a fee simple absolute.' The effect of this addition to s7(1) is that B does hold a 'fee simple absolute in possession', a legal estate, even though A has a right of re-entry if any of the covenants are broken.

SUGGESTED ANSWER TO QUESTION TWO

General Comment

A question which invites an overall view of the reforming property legislation of 1925 with the inclusion of subsequent legislative changes and in particular the Trusts of Land and Appointment of Trustees Act 1996 as it relates to settlements and trusts for sale. The material represents the foundation on which modern land law is constructed.

Key Points

*   Legal and equitable rights in land before 1926
*   Difficulties for a purchaser
*   Treatment of legal estates and interests in land by s1 LPA 1925
*   Equitable interests after 1925 – three groups:
    -   Land Charges Act 1925 (now LCA 1972)
    -   overreachable equitable interests under the Settled Land Act 1925 and trusts for sale under the LPA 1925
    -   equitable interests in neither group still subject to the doctrine of the bona fide purchaser
*   Changes made by the Trusts of Land and Appointment of Trustees Act 1996
*   Registration of title – Land Registration Act 1925

Suggested Answer

Before coming to the legislation it is first necessary to consider the pre-1926 law and its implications for conveyancing. The purchase of land is more complicated than that of chattels because land may be subject to a considerable number of rights in favour of third parties, eg a right of way over the land (an easement) in favour of a next door neighbour's land. A purchaser will be concerned to know whether, when he acquires the land, he will take subject to, or free from, those rights which could affect the land's value or its use.

The position may be stated in broad terms: if the right is legal, ie one recognised at common law, he automatically takes subject to it whether he knows of it or not and even if it is not capable of discovery. Legal rights bind to the whole world.

As regards equitable rights, ie those recognised by the old Court of Chancery, the rule is that equitable rights bind the whole world with one exception: they do not bind 'a bona fide purchaser of the legal estate in the land for value without notice'. For a purchaser to claim the dispensation he has to prove that he comes within that description and that is not always easy to establish. The position of a purchaser claiming to be a bona fide purchaser was described in *Pilcher* v *Rawlins* (1872):

> 'Such a purchaser, when once he has put in that plea, may be interrogated and tested to any extent as to the valuable consideration which he has given in order to show the bona fides or mala fides of his purchase, and also the presence or absence of notice.'

The reason for the bona fide purchaser's immunity was described by F W Maitland in his series of lectures on equity: 'Equity cannot reach him, because, to use the old phrase, his conscience is unaffected.'

It will be appreciated that a purchaser could not always be sure that he would be able to prove that he came within the privileged category and his position was frequently attended by a degree of uncertainty.

We may now turn to the legislation to see how it dealt with the position which has been described, and we begin by an examination of s1 Law of Property Act 1925 which is fundamental to the reforms effected by the legislation as a whole. Section 1(1)-(3) relating to legal estates and equitable interests provides as follows:

> '1(1) The only estates in land which are capable of subsisting or of being conveyed or created at law are –
> (a) An estate in fee simple absolute in possession;
> (b) A term of years absolute.
> (2) The only interests or charges in or over land which are capable of subsisting or of being conveyed or created at law are –
> (a) An easement, right, or privilege in or over land for an interest equivalent to an estate in fee simple absolute in possession or a term of years absolute;
> (b) A rentcharge in possession issuing out of or charged on land being either perpetual or for a term of years absolute;
> (c) A charge by way of legal mortgage;
> (d) Any other similar charge on land which is not created by an instrument;
> (e) Rights of entry exercisable over or in respect of a legal term of years absolute, or annexed, for any purpose, to a legal rentcharge.
> (3) All other estates, interests, and charges in or over land take effect as equitable interests.'

It will be noted that what these provisions do is to reduce the number of estates and interests which can exist at law, and the advantages to a prospective purchaser are immediately obvious. While some legal estates and interests still remain they have been drastically reduced in number. The implications of s1(3) should be noted. Any estates or interests not falling within s1(1) and (2) take effect as equitable interests. Thus, a number of what before could have been either legal or equitable estates lost their identity as estates as well as being able to subsist henceforward only in equity. For example, life estates, entailed estates, modified fee simples, as opposed to absolute ones, can now only be equitable interests.

Section 1(2) limits the number of legal interests which may subsist in land to five, and the definition of a legal easement in s1(2)(a) should be recalled when easements are studied later in the syllabus. An easement not falling within para (a) will take effect as an equitable easement.

Finally, the provisions should not be misunderstood. The provisions are permissive: only the two estates and five interests listed may be legal. They may also subsist in equity.

Having dealt with the treatment of legal rights consideration must now be given to that of equitable rights. After the 1925 legislation equitable rights fell into three groups:

1   those registrable under the Land Charges Act 1925 (later the Land Charges Act 1972);
2   those taking effect behind a trust and subject to the device of overreaching;
3   those falling into neither group.

They will be considered in turn.

The Land Charges Act 1925 (later the Land Charges Act 1972)
This has now been repealed and replaced by the Land Charges Act 1972 but the provisions are substantially the same. The 1925 Act provided for five separate registers to be kept at the land registry. Here we are only concerned with one: the register of land charges. These were divided into classes and identified by an alphabetical letter with each class being subdivided numerically. The most important ones were C(i), C(iii) and C(iv), and D(ii) and D(iii). Class F, introduced by the Matrimonial Homes Act 1967, was included in the 1972 Act. They will be discussed in more detail in the question based on the Land Charges Act as we are only concerned here with the overall picture. The Act provided a party entitled to an equitable interest in land, registrable as a land charge under the Act, with a means of protecting it against purchasers. He could do so by registering it in the Land Charges Register and under s198(1) LPA 1925 registration 'shall be deemed to constitute actual notice ... and of the fact of such registration, to all persons and for all purposes connected with the land affected, as from the date of registration ... and as long as the registration continues in force.'

Thus, a person entitled to a registrable interest in land was provided with a facility he did not have before. He could protect his interest against the whole world by the simple act of registering as a land charge. What is the position, however, when such a person does not take advantage of that facility? The effect of non-registration varies according to the land charge in question. Classes C(i), C(iii) and F are void against a purchaser of any interest in the land for valuable consideration (now s4(5) and (8) LCA 1972). Classes C(iv), D(ii) and D(iii) are void against a purchaser of the legal estate in land for money or money's worth: s4(6) LCA 1972. These provisions apply regardless of the state of a purchaser's knowledge of the equitable interest: *Midland Bank Trust Co Ltd v Green*

(1981). For example, suppose that land owned by O is subject to an equitable lease in favour of T. T can register that lease as a land charge class C(iv). If he fails to do so and if O subsequently sells the land to P then P, providing he is a purchaser of the legal estate in that land and has paid O money or money's worth, will take free of the lease even though he knew of its existence or even if he had agreed to purchase the land subject to the lease: *Hollington Bros Ltd* v *Rhodes* (1952). Thus, where an equitable interest is registrable as a land charge, the doctrine of the bona fide purchaser is no longer applicable. He has been replaced by the purchasers defined by s4(5), (6) and (8) LCA 1972 above. No longer is it necessary to consider whether a purchaser is in good faith or has notice. These factors were eliminated to introduce a certainty into conveyancing which did not exist before.

Equitable interests taking effect behind a trust and subject to the device of overreaching: ss2 and 27 LPA 1925 as amended by the Trusts of Land and Appointment of Trustees Act 1996

Only the interests listed in the LCA 1972 may be registered as land charges, which leaves a number of interests which are not embraced by the Act. Included in these are equitable interests arising under a trust. Under the 1925 legislation they existed either as settled land under the Settled Land Act 1925 or as interests behind a trust for sale under the Law of Property Act 1925.

To take settled land first, this was defined by s1 of the SLA 1925. Section 1 included the various interests which were capable of being legal estates before 1926 but can now only exist as equitable interests under s1 LPA 1925 and which now, being only equitable interests, must exist behind a trust, eg life interests, entailed interests, modified fee simples. A perusal of s1 reveals that, with two exceptions, land is settled where it is limited to persons in succession. The most common form of settled land is a life interest.

There is a succession of interests in the case of a life interest because either a reversioner or a remainderman will succeed to the land at the determination of the life interest. The policy behind the Act can be illustrated by reference to a life interest.

The life tenant has an equitable interest which is he is free to deal with as he wishes. In addition, he is also invested with the legal estate in the land, usually the fee simple absolute in possession.

Although he holds the legal estate, having been invested with it either by a vesting assent or deed, he is not free to deal with it as he wishes. His powers of dealing with it are limited to those conferred by the trust instrument and by the SLA 1925. The most important statutory powers are powers of sale (s38); powers of leasing (ss41 and 42), and powers of mortgaging: s71. Any capital monies arising out of these transactions are payable not to him but to the trustees of the settlement. He cannot dispose of the legal estate in the land for whatever sum he wishes. Section 39 SLA 1925 imposes on him an obligation to secure the best price reasonably obtainable.

These powers effectively enabled the tenant for life to manage and dispose of the land. He is not required to obtain the trustees' consent to the exercise of his powers although he must give them written notice of his intention to exercise them: s101 SLA 1925. Any clause in the trust instrument purporting to inhibit him from exercising his powers, is void: s106 SLA 1925. He must have regard to the interests of the other beneficiaries when exercising his powers (s107 SLA 1925) but the courts have shown considerable reluctance to apply the section strictly: *Wheelwright* v *Walker* (1883).

The Act does simplify conveyancing from the purchaser's point of view. A purchaser wishing to buy settled land will want to purchase the legal fee simple absolute in possession unencumbered by the equitable interests, eg those of the life tenant and the remaindermen. It is to one person alone to whom the purchaser has to look to acquire the legal fee simple – the tenant for life, whose title is proved by production of the vesting assent or vesting deed. He pays the purchase monies not to the tenant for life but to the trustees of the settlement and, providing he pays those monies to two trustees (or a trust corporation), the equitable interests created by the settlement are overreached, ie the equitable interests are detached from the land so that a purchaser takes free of them, and they are attached instead to the proceeds of sale in the hands of the trustees who then hold them on trust for the beneficiaries. These interests are therefore converted from land into money. The life tenant will receive the income from those monies for life and on his death the remainderman will be entitled to the capital.

The Settled Land Act 1925 is still in force but since 1 January 1967 no new Settled Land Act settlements can be created: s2 Trusts of Land and Appointment of Trustees Act 1996. The limitations in s1 SLA 1925 now take effect behind a trust of land as defined by s1 of the 1996 Act.

We may now turn to interests under a trust for sale. In contrast to Settled Land Act settlements in the case of the trust for sale, the legal estate is vested in the trustees and it is they who manage the land and decide whether or not it is to be sold. Their powers were defined in s28 LPA 1925 as being those of a tenant for life and Settled Land Act trustees under the SLA 1925. A trust for sale was defined in s205 LPA 1925 as:

'"Trust for sale" in relation to land, means an immediate binding trust for sale, whether or not exercisable at the request or with the consent of any person, and with or without a power at discretion to postpone the sale ...'

But the Trusts of Land and Appointment of Trustees Act 1996 amended the definition so that it now reads as:

'Trust for sale, in relation to land, means an immediate trust for sale, whether or not exercisable at the request or with the consent of any person ...'

The trust for sale is a flexible device that can be used to cover a number of situations. It can be used instead of the SLA to cover situations where the land is given or devised to persons in succession. Unlike settled land, where because of s106 the tenant for life cannot be restrained from selling the land, the trustees for sale powers of sale can be fettered by a stipulation in the instrument of creation that they must not sell until they have obtained the consent of nominated persons. In that respect it was a more suitable device for keeping the land in the family than settled land. In cases of co-ownership the courts took the view that if the land was not conveyed to the co-owners on an express trust land for sale then one would be implied under ss34 and 36 LPA 1925 or in some instances under SLA s36(4). See for an example of the latter *Bull* v *Bull* (1955).

To better appreciate the benefits conferred upon a purchaser by a trust for sale consider his position before 1925 when he was purchasing land from co-owners who held as tenants in common. Tenants in common hold land in undivided shares, ie each has a separate title. Nor do the rights of survivorship operate on the death of a tenant in common. Thus, if one of the original tenants in common died and bequeathed his share to his five children then the number of co-owners of the land would have increased. If, for example, there were four tenants in common and one died, his share would not accrue to his surviving co-owners, thus diminishing the numbers, but would pass to his five children, each obtaining a fifth of his individual share. In order to take title to the land the purchaser would have had to acquire the shares of the surviving tenants in common, together with shares of each of the individual children.

The conveyancing complexities and the costs involved are obvious. Had the co-owners been joint tenants the position would have been easier. On the death of one joint tenant his share would have passed automatically to his surviving joint tenants by right of survivorship with a corresponding reduction in the numbers.

The structure of the trust for sale established by the LPA removed those difficulties. With a trust for sale the legal estate is vested in not more than four trustees: s34 Trustee Act 1925 and ss34 and 36 LPA 1925. They must hold the legal estate as joint tenants: ss34 and 36. Section 1(6) LPA 1925 abolished legal tenancies in common. Moreover, that legal joint tenancy cannot be severed, ie converted into a tenancy in common: s36 LPA 1925.

Thus, a purchaser, in acquiring the legal estate, has to deal with no more than four trustees. As they hold as joint tenants they hold one title since a joint tenancy is characterised by the four unities. The purchaser will want to acquire the legal estate unencumbered by the equitable interests of the beneficial owners under the trust for sale and he achieves this by activating the same overreaching device as operates under the Settled Land Act. Providing he pays the purchase price to two trustees overreaching occurs, which enables the purchaser to take the legal estate from the trustees for sale free of the equitable interest subsisting behind the trust for sale.

The Trusts of Land and Appointment of Trustees Act has made certain alterations to the law relating to trusts for sale. Apart from the alteration to the definition to which reference has already been made, the most important alteration has been in respect of implied or statutory trusts for sale which used to arise under ss34 and 36 LPA 1925 and the s36(4) SLA 1925. No longer is it possible to have an implied trust for sale as these sections have been amended by the 1996 Act to produce a trust of land without a duty to sell the land. Sections 34 and 36 LPA 1925 have been altered by s5 of the 1996 Act and its second schedule, where the altered wording is to be found. Moreover, the second schedule makes the alterations retrospective. The third schedule alters s36(4) SLA 1925 again to produce a trust of land instead of a trust for sale, but it makes no mention of any retrospective operation which is curious.

Section 25 of LPA 1925 implied into every trust for sale a power for the trustees to postpone sale unless a contrary intention was expressed. In order to exercise that power of postponement they had to be unanimous: *Re Mayo* (1943). That section has been repealed by the Trusts of Land and Appointment of Trustees Act 1996 and replaced by s4 of that Act which implies into a trust for sale 'created by a disposition' (ie an express trust for sale) a power to postpone sale with the provision that the power of postponement cannot be excluded.

The doctrine of conversion has been abolished retrospectively by s3 of the 1996 Act in so far as it applied to trusts for sale. The doctrine, based on the maxim 'equity looks on that as done which ought to be done', resulted in equity treating the interests of the beneficiaries under a trust for sale as being interests in money rather than land because it anticipated the sale which the trustees were under a duty to make. In 1925 this may have made sense when domestic home ownership was comparatively rare, but with the steady increase of co-ownership of domestic property over the years its application became increasingly artificial and irrelevant. The courts recognised this and began to acknowledge that the beneficial interests under a trust for sale constituted interests in land rather than money: *Bull* v *Bull* (1955); *Williams and Glyn's Bank* v *Boland* (1981). Section 3 of the 1996 Act, in formally abolishing the doctrine as it applied to trusts for sale, did little more than follow judicial practice.

The third group falling into neither category
These comprise equitable interests which remain untouched by the 1925 legislation in that they are neither registrable as land charges nor do they arise under a trust for sale or a SLA settlement with the consequence of being subject to overreaching. In the result they remained subject to the doctrine of the bona fide purchaser. Examples are equitable rights of re-entry (*Shiloh Spinners Ltd* v *Harding* (1973)); equitable licences by estoppel: *Ives (E R) Investments Ltd* v *High* (1967).

The doctrine of the bona fide purchaser continued to apply where in the case of SLA settlements and trusts for sale, a purchaser, say in the case of an implied trust for sale of which he was unaware and with only one trustee, paid the purchase money to that one trustee. In that case overreaching did not apply because of payment to a sole trustee and the purchaser then acquired the land subject to the beneficial interests unless he could establish that he was a bona fide purchaser.

The discussion so far has related to unregistered land and consideration must now be given to the Land Registration Act 1925 which extended the principle of registration of title. This represented a major step forward in the process of simplifying conveyancing, in that it sought to provide a simpler and faster method of proving and transferring title, as well as providing more efficient protection of equitable interests in land against purchasers.

In 1925 it was anticipated that registration of title would be extended at a much faster rate than actually proved to be the case, and it was not until 1 December 1990 that finally all of England and Wales became subject to compulsory registration of title. Under the system of registration of title, title is registered in the name of the registered proprietor (the owner) in the land registry for his area and his register of title replaces the title deeds to the land, he being supplied by the registry with an office copy of the register called the land certificate. Thus, a purchaser of registered land is concerned only to examine the register of title as opposed to deducing title from the title deeds as is the case in unregistered land. Moreover, he has the guarantee that the title has been investigated by the land registry and is thus assured that the vendor has a valid title.

The Land Charges Act 1925 (now the Land Charges Act 1972) had no applicability to registered land and third party rights in the land are dealt with on an entirely different basis.

The five legal interests in s1(2) LPA 1925 are registrable although this is rarely done.

Apart from these five legal interests, third party rights are divided into two groups – overriding interests and minor interests. The former are defined by the LPA 1925 in s3(xvi) and listed in s70(1), while the latter are defined by s3(xv). Basically, a minor interest is an interest in land which is not an overriding interest. Minor interests therefore are a residual class of interests which is wider than the specific list of interests contained in the Land Charges Act 1972. A minor interest should be the subject of an entry on the registered proprietor's register of title and as a general rule a purchaser will only be bound if such an entry has been made: s20(1) LPA 1925. However, this is something of a generalisation because there are four different types of entry; for example, a restriction is entered on the register not to ensure that a purchaser will be bound but that an equitable interest under a trust will be overreached.

As in the case of the Land Charges Act, the purchaser's actual knowledge is irrelevant. It is the state of the register that matters.

Overriding interests do not appear on the register of title but nevertheless bind a purchaser and as such constitute a difficulty for him, necessitating careful inspection of the land and assiduous enquiries to discover their existence. The most important overriding interest is contained in s70(1)(g) LPA 1925 with which all land law students must make themselves familiar.

The reforms embodied in the legislation were ambitious and far reaching in their attempts to simplify conveyancing and there can be no doubt that, by and large, they have met with a considerable degree of success. Perhaps not surprisingly difficulties have emerged as the years have passed. It had been assumed that the registration of titles in England and Wales would have progressed at a steady rate to replace unregistered titles, but the advent of the second world war seriously impeded progress. This gave rise to problems in connection with the Land Charges Act 1925 from the mid-nineteen fifties onwards, and those problems remain since a very large number of titles remain unregistered. These problems are discussed in more detail in the next question.

The system of registration of title has given rise to problems in respect of notice. There still seems to be a difference of judicial opinion as to whether s70(1)(g) LPA 1925 is based on the doctrine of notice, but there can be no doubt as to the contribution that the system has made to the simplification of conveyancing.

The Trusts of Land and Appointment of Trustees Act 1966 has recognised the need to change the law relating to settlements and trusts for sale and has now provided it with a rational basis more in keeping with modern requirements.

SUGGESTED ANSWER TO QUESTION THREE

General Comment

The question requires the candidate to explain the purpose of the statute which formed a fundamental part of the 1925 property legislation in its efforts to simplify conveyancing. The candidate is required to go beyond a mere descriptive approach and attempt a critical evaluation of its operation in practice. Further, a comparison is made with the Land Registration Act 1925.

Key Points

- Pre-1926 – equitable rights in land
- The difficulties of the doctrine of the bona fide purchaser
- The scheme of the Land Charges Act 1925
- The effect of registration – s198 LPA 1925
- The effect of non-registration – LCA 1972 – abolition of the bona fide purchaser and notice: *Midland Bank Trust Co Ltd* v *Green*
- The system of registration is 'name based' and the passage of time has created difficulties for a purchaser
- Difficulties aggravated by LPA 1969
- Not all equitable interests can be registered under the LCA 1972
- Contrast with LRA 1925 – minor interests form a residual group
- An unprotected minor interest may be protected as an overriding interest under s70(1)(g) LPA 1925 – no equivalent in unregistered land
- Survey of defects of the Land Charges Acts

Suggested Answer

The Land Charges Act 1925 (now LCA 1972) to which Lord Wilberforce was referring, was intended to replace the doctrine of the bona fide purchaser of the legal estate for value without notice as far as certain equitable interests were concerned.

Before 1926 the rule was that equitable interests were binding on the whole world except the bona fide purchaser, the onus of proof being on the purchaser to prove he came within that description.

The doctrine was based on the equitable concept of conscience and for its application it was necessary to investigate the purchaser's state of mind: did he, or should he have had, notice of any equitable rights in the land he was purchasing? Moreover, was he entitled to the description 'bona fide'? Clearly, it was difficult to predict the outcome of those enquiries and that uncertainty was disadvantageous both to the person entitled to the equitable right and to the purchaser himself. The former could never feel that his right was secure. If the land to which it was subject passed into the hands of a bona fide purchaser it was lost forever. Further, there was no way in which he could notify the world of his equitable right. The latter, on the other hand, could not be certain that he could establish that he was a bona fide purchaser. If he could not, he was bound by the right. The position was unsatisfactory for both.

The Land Charge Act 1925 dealt with the situation by providing a facility for certain equitable interests to be registered as land charges in a newly opened central Land Charges Register to be kept by the Land Registry. This is currently situated at Plymouth and covers England and Wales. The effect of registration is set out in s198(1) Law of Property Act 1925: it shall 'be deemed to constitute actual notice ... to all persons ... so long as the registration continues in force'.

Once a registrable interest is registered by the person entitled to the equitable interest any prospective purchaser is bound by it. The prudent purchaser will search the register first but if he does not he will still be bound.

The consequences of non-registration were set out in the 1925 statute and they are now to be found in the Land Charges Act 1972, which replaced the 1925 Act. These provisions will be described later.

It is proposed to deal only with those land charges with which candidates will be concerned and they are as follows:

Class C(i)   Puisine mortgage which is a legal mortgage not protected by a deposit of title deeds
Class C(iii)   General equitable charge which includes an equitable mortgage not protected by a deposit of title deeds
Class C(iv)   Estate contract
Class D(ii)   Restrictive covenants created on or after 1 January 1926
Class D(iii)   Equitable easements created on or after 1 January 1926
Class F   The right of a spouse to occupy the matrimonial home

Class F was not in the 1925 statute. It was introduced by the Matrimonial Homes Act 1967 and was incorporated into the 1972 Act by s2(7).

It will be noticed that the land charge C1 is a legal interest but has been included because of the technical rules relating to priority of mortgages.

The effect of non-registration varies according to the class of land charge and is as follows:

If land charges C(i), C(iii) and F are not registered they are void against a purchaser of any interest in the land: s4(5) LCA 1972. The phrase 'any interest' means a legal estate or equitable interest in the land. 'Purchaser' is defined in s17(1) as any person (including a mortgagee or lessee) who has provided valuable consideration for the purchase. Valuable consideration includes marriage.

If land charges C(iv), D(ii) and D(iii) are not registered, they are void against a purchaser of the legal estate in the land for money or money's worth: s4(6) LCA 1972.

Thus for a purchaser to take advantage of non-registration and regard himself as not being bound, he must establish that he is within an appropriate category.

It will be noticed that no reference is made to the bona fides of the purchaser nor is there any mention of notice. Neither of these elements play any part in the application of the Act. The uncertainties produced by the doctrine of the bona fide purchaser have been eliminated and replaced by a system which produces certainty for both parties alike.

However, the removal of the bona fide purchaser has also removed the ethical concept on which that doctrine was based, as illustrated in *Hollington Bros Ltd* v *Rhodes* (1951) and *Midland Bank Trust Co Ltd* v *Green* (1981). In the latter case a farmer gave his son an option to his farm. The option was registrable as a land charge, Class C(iv), but was not actually registered. The farmer later repented of his decision and sought to defeat the son's option by transferring the farm to his wife for what was in effect nominal consideration. The intention was to make the wife a purchaser of the legal estate in the farm for money or money's worth. The wife could hardly be described as bona fide and she obviously knew of the option. The House of Lords was asked to rule the statute ought not to be construed so as to allow the device to succeed but it refused.

Its approach was expressed in Lord Wilberforce's words contained in the quotation: 'The Act is clear and definite'. There was no requirement in the Act that for its application the wife had to be in good faith nor that she should be without notice to take advantage of the non-registration of the option. Dealing with the argument that the wife had only provided nominal consideration, Lord Wilberforce observed that she had provided money or money's worth. There was nothing in the Act to exclude nominal consideration. In coming to its decision the Lords were clearly giving effect to the legislature's intention.

It must be conceded that the desire to simplify conveyancing has taken precedence over ethical considerations, but it must be remembered that this type of problem arises only when a person entitled to register a land charge fails to do so. Although there is no obligation to register, prudence dictates the advisability of doing so.

That the Act has succeeded in simplifying conveyancing there can be no doubt, but the passage of time has revealed defects. The principal defect has arisen from the fact that the system of registration is 'name based'.

When a land charge is registered, it is registered against the name of the estate owner for the time being. It follows that when a prospective purchaser searches the register he must search against the name of that estate owner to discover it. Registration has been possible since the LCA came into force on 1 January 1926. The purchaser, therefore, needs to search against the name of every estate owner since that date and the land will have no doubt changed hands many times since then. The names of the estate owners will be in the chain of title deeds which the purchaser will examine when investigating the vendor's title. Armed with these names, he will then be able to make the necessary searches against them. There has, however, always been a limit set as to how far back a purchaser is entitled to go when investigating the vendor's title. Since 1926 and up to 1969, the rule was that he could investigate back as far as a good root of title, eg a conveyance, at least 30 years old. Up to the mid-1950s a purchaser therefore, was able to go back to 1926 and was thus able to search against any estate owner against whom land charges may have been registered from that date onward. After the mid-1950s purchasers, because of the 30-year rule, began to find that they were obliged to accept a good root of title which was executed after 1926 which meant that they were unable to discover estate owners who held the land between 1926 and the date of the root of title. There was a gap, and the gap widened with each year that passed. Deprived of the opportunity to discover the names of the estate owners who owned the land in that ever-widening gap, purchasers were unable to conduct searches against them to see if any land charges had been registered. Even although purchasers were unable to discover their existence they were nevertheless bound by them because of s198 LPA 1925.

In 1925, when the legislature was debating the legislation it had anticipated that in something like 30 years time most titles would have become registered under the Land Registration Act 1925 thus rendering the Land Charges Act, which only applied to unregistered land, substantially redundant. That anticipation proved widely optimistic and the Land Charges Act (now LCA 1972) is still in operation.

The problem has been aggravated by the passing of the s3 Law of Property Act 1969 which reduced the 30-year rule to 15 years. However, the Act did introduce a system of compensation for purchasers adversely affected by undiscoverable land charges. The problem will remain until the extension of registration of title is complete.

The name-based system has also given rise to difficulties where registration has been effected against an incorrectly spelt name or where a search has been made using a name incorrectly spelt. If registration is made against an incorrectly spelt name which could be regarded as a usual variation of that name the registration will be valid: *Oak Co-operative Building Society* v *Blackburn* (1968). The same case also indicated that if a purchaser searches against a wrong name he will be bound by any interests registered against the correct name.

A criticism that has been levelled against the land charges system is that not all equitable interests, other than those which are overreachable, are registrable as land charges. For example, interests arising under a bare trust (it should, however, be noted that these interests are now overreachable under the Trusts of Land and Appointment of Trustees Act 1996); equitable estoppel rights (*Pascoe* v *Turner* (1979) and *Ives (E R) Investments Ltd* v *High* (1967)); equitable rights of re-entry (*Shiloh Spinners* v *Harding* (1973)); pre-1926 equitable easements; and restrictive covenants).

These equitable interests remain subject to the doctrine of the bona fide purchaser.

The limited list of equitable interests contrasts with the treatment of equitable interests in registered land. In registered land (registrable interests apart) interests are either overriding or minor. A minor interest in land is one that is not overriding. Minor interests form a residual group of interests in contrast to the limited list of registrable interests in the Land Charges Act 1972. Moreover, an unprotected minor interest (one which has not been the subject of an entry on the title of the registered proprietor) may be re-classified as an overriding interest under s70(1)(g) LRA 1925 which protects rights of occupiers. Thus, an equitable lease is a minor interest and should be protected by a notice entered on the landlord's register of title. If it is not so protected, if the tenant is in occupation, it may be protected and bind a purchaser as an overriding interest under s70(1)(g). No corresponding safety net exists in unregistered land. In that case the equitable lease is an estate contract, land charge class C(iv).

If it is not registered it is void against a purchaser of the legal estate in the landlord's land for money or money's worth. The fact that the tenant is in occupation which was apparent to the purchaser will not help him. The lease will be lost. Care should be taken not to conclude that s14 LPA 1925 is applicable:

'This part of this Act shall not prejudicially affect the interests of any person in possession or in actual occupation of land to which he may be entitled in right of such possession or occupation.'

Section 14 only applies to Part I of the LPA 1925. It has no application to the Land Charges Act 1925, nor its successor.

The Land Charges Act 1925 introduced a much needed element of certainty in conveyancing in place of the doctrine of the bona fide purchaser. It has been criticised on the grounds that this has been at the expense of the ethical basis of the doctrine of the bona fide purchaser but it should be remembered that the uncertainty inherent in that doctrine can produce injustice to the parties as well as provoking litigation. It is the responsibility of the holder of a registrable interest to use the facility provided by the statute, which did not exist before, to protect that interest and the consequences of his not doing so are clearly spelt out in its provisions.

This application results in the destruction of the equitable interest beyond hope of revival, regardless of the purchaser's knowledge of it and there is no equivalent of s70(1)(g) LRA 1925 to provide a safety net. As has been explained s14 LPA 1925 has no application and the holder of the equitable interest cannot invoke it. There is a sharp contrast between the two systems.

Name based registration has also been criticised but the alternative, namely registration against the land itself, would clearly be impractical. The major defect has arisen through the passage of time and has resulted in purchasers being unable to discover the names of the estate owners going back to 1926. In consequence purchasers have been unable to search against these names and have sometimes found themselves bound by registered land charges which the law itself has precluded them from discovering. These difficulties were increased by the LPA 1969 when the 30-year period for the investigation of title was reduced to 15 years, although the statute did introduce a provision for monetary compensation out of public funds. However, money will not always adequately compensate for the subjection to a land charge of which the purchaser was unaware and which may have affected his decision to purchase if he had known of it. The position is unsatisfactory for a purchaser and it was not a situation contemplated by the legislature in 1925 which anticipated the future redundancy of the Land Charges Act before the problem arose. The problem will not disappear until all titles become registered under the LRA 1925.

2

Registered Title

Introduction

Registered title cannot be studied in isolation as its provisions can apply right across the syllabus where its impact can vary considerably. Therefore, the student when concentrating on any given area of land law must always question how the registered title provisions affect that area.

Examination questions may be confined exclusively to registered title and the two essay questions here are good examples. Alternatively, they may require a knowledge of other areas of the syllabus, for example, resulting and constructive trusts. One area which particularly lends itself to this combined treatment is adverse possession.

Sometimes a question is set in the context of unregistered land but concludes with the question: 'Would your answer had been different if title to the land was registered?' This type of question requires a knowledge of the unregistered land and registered systems if it is to be fully answered, as well as an appreciation that the application of the two systems can produce different results. Very frequently the results are different because of s70(1)(g) LRA 1925. Knowledge of this paragraph is very strongly advised, although at the same time the examiners' reports have pointed out a tendency of examination candidates to bring it into their answers even when it has no relevance.

Questions

INTERROGRAMS

1   Compare and contrast a notice and a caution.
2   Compare an absolute leasehold title with a good leasehold title.
3   What is a restriction?
4   What is a possessory title under LRA 1925?
5   What are the differences in treatment of possessory titles in unregistered and registered land?

QUESTION ONE

'The great advantage of registered conveyancing is that the register operates as a "mirror" reflecting all the facts relevant to a given title. It provides protection to encumbrances and purchasers alike.'

Explain this statement and consider the extent to which it is accurate.

London University LLB Examination
(for external students) Land Law June 1998 Q1

QUESTION TWO

'The system of registration of title is intended only to simplify conveyancing; it should not affect substantive rights.'

Discuss

London University LLB Examination
(for external students) Land Law June 1996 Q5

Answers

ANSWERS TO INTERROGRAMS

1   A notice is an entry made in the charges register of the register of title and its effect is described in s52(1) LRA 1925: 'A disposition by the proprietor shall take effect subject to all estates, rights and claims which are protected by way of notice on the register at the date of registration or entry'.

Section (2) states: 'Where a notice of a claim is entered on the register, such entry shall operate by way of notice only, and shall not operate to render the claim valid'.

Examples of minor interests protected by a notice are estate contracts and restrictive covenants. Included in the former are agreements for leases (ie equitable leases). Difficulties, however, can confront someone seeking to enter a notice on the register. To effect an entry he must produce to the registry the land certificate of the land to be adversely affected and this can only be done if the registered proprietor agrees. Since he would be co-operating to impose a burden on his land he may well be disinclined to do so. An equitable tenant should refuse at the outset to take up the lease unless the registered proprietor (the proposed landlord) agrees to co-operate.

Failing the co-operation of the registered proprietor it is always possible to enter a caution instead, which does not require production of the land certificate or the consent of the registered proprietor.

The caution imposes on the Registrar an obligation to warn the cautioner that an application has been made to register a transaction. It is then for the cautioner to take such steps, if any, that he can to protect his interest against an impending purchaser. The provisions dealing with cautions are to be found in ss53–56 LRA 1925. Section 55 imposes the obligation on the registrar and s56 provides for compensation against a cautioner who lodges a caution without reasonable cause.

2   A lease cannot be registered with a substantive title of its own if it is granted for 21 years or less. It will take effect instead as an overriding interest under s70(1)(k) LRA 1925. To come within this paragraph it must be legal: *City Permanent Building Society* v *Miller* (1952).

A leasehold may be granted with an absolute title or a good leasehold title. By s8(1)(b)(i) LRA 1925 'Where an absolute (leasehold) title is required the applicant … shall not be registered as proprietor until and unless the title both to the leasehold and to the freehold … is approved by the registrar'. Registration of an absolute title guarantees that the landlord had power to grant the lease and that it was properly granted.

Section 9 LRA 1925 enacts that the lessee is invested with possession of the leasehold interest together with all the rights attached to it and '(a) subject to all implied and express covenants obligations … incidental to the registered land; and (b) subject to the incumbrances and other entries (if any) appearing on the register.'

An absolute leasehold title cannot be granted if the registrar is not satisfied with the landlord's title. If the freehold title is registered there will be no problem but if it is not, and the applicant cannot produce satisfactory documentary evidence of it, then he will have to make do with a good leasehold title. The landlord is not obliged to produce proof of his title although the parties may contract that he should do so.

A good leasehold title does not guarantee that the lease was properly granted.

3   Section 58 LRA 1925 entitles a proprietor of registered land to apply for a restriction to be entered on the register of title. Its effect is to prevent any dealing with the registered land until some condition is complied with. It is entered on the proprietorship register of the registered title. A good example of its use is to be found in trusts of land to ensure that overreaching takes place. The restriction will be worded to the effect that no disposition of the registered land shall be registered unless the purchase money is paid to X and Y (two trustees). Production of the land certificate is necessary for entry of a restriction. From the purchaser's point of view it has the opposite effect of a notice. Entry of the latter ensures that he is bound. The restriction ensures that the equitable interests under the trust will be overreached and that he will take free of them.

4   A person may claim to have acquired title to someone else's land as a result of adverse possession under the Limitation Act 1980. In registered land he does not become it owner until his title is registered and he does this by applying for a possessory title. In the case of freehold land he may do so under s6 LRA 1925; in the case of leasehold land under s11 LRA 1925. Under those sections the registered proprietor with a possessory title takes subject to rights against the land at the date of registration of the first registered proprietor of the land.

5   In unregistered land the claimant of a possessory title has to establish 12 years' adverse possession under the Limitation Act 1980, with the result that the owner's title becomes statute-barred and extinguished. The difficulty is that the new owner will have no title deeds when he comes to sell. Although this is not necessarily an insurmountable obstacle it does cause considerable problems for an intending vendor as he has to prove his title by other means.

In registered land, once the 12 years' adverse possession has elapsed, the squatter may apply to the Land Registry to be registered with a possessory title which will supply him with the necessary document of title. Until registration occurs his title in the meantime is protected as an overriding interest under s70(1)(f) LRA: 'rights acquired or in the course of being acquired under the Limitation Act'.

Under s1 LRA 1986 a possessory title may be upgraded to an absolute freehold or, if the title is leasehold, to a good leasehold title. The registrar must upgrade on the application of the proprietor if either the registrar is satisfied with the title or the land has been registered with possessory title for at least 12 years and the proprietor is in possession.

SUGGESTED ANSWER TO QUESTION ONE

General Comment

The question requires the candidate to make a critical examination of overriding interests and their practical applicability in order to test the validity of the two assertions in the question. Does the register mirror all the facts of the title and does it provide equal protection for encumbrancers and purchasers. Section 70(1)(g) LRA must attract the most discussion but three other overriding interests must also be considered: s70(1)(a), (f) and (k). Paragraph (f) will only receive a mention since time does not permit a discussion of adverse possession.

Key Points

- Registration of title replaces title deeds with one document
- The purchaser is concerned to discover encumbrances affecting the land
- Overriding interests: definition and an examination of s70(1)(a), (f), (g) and (k) with particular reference to para (g)
- Paragraph (g):
    - two limbs
    - rights under para (g)
    - licences
    - is para (g) based on notice?
    - enquiries
- Conclusion as to validity of statements in the question

Suggested Answer

Despite its title, the Land Registration Act 1925 did not provide for the registration of land but for registration of titles. The purpose of the statute is to simplify conveyancing by replacing the old system whereby the purchaser was obliged to investigate the vendor's title deeds to ensure that he owned the land which he had contracted to convey with a system under which titles are registered in the land registry for the area. The title, having been investigated by the Land Registrar, is guaranteed by the State and is contained in one document, the register of title, retained in the registry. A copy called the land certificate, is given to the new owner, called the registered proprietor.

The register replaces the title deeds and thereafter a purchaser need only examine one document, the register. On transfer, the vendor's name is removed from the register and the purchaser's name substituted in its place.

However, a purchaser is not simply concerned with the vendor's title; he also needs to know what, if any, encumbrances, affect the land. The phrase 'mirror' principle, which is sometimes used to describe the basis of registered land, suggests that the register reflects all the interests which affect the land but this is not, and cannot be, the case and the legislature in 1925 recognised that. The 'mirror' principle is only partly applicable.

This recognition found its expression in the concept of overriding interests. These are defined in s3(xvi) LRA 1925 as 'all the encumbrances, interest, rights and powers not entered on the register but subject to which registered dispositions are by the Act to take effect'. Thus, although they do not appear on the register they nevertheless bind a purchaser. The holder of an overriding interest may therefore rest secure in the belief that he cannot be deprived of his interest, except where overreaching applies. A purchaser by contrast, may find himself bound by an interest of which he knew nothing.

There is an obvious conflict of interests between the person entitled to an overriding interest who wishes to keep it intact and a purchaser who would like to see it disappear. Somehow the law has to strike a balance between the two. The existence of overriding interests means that a purchaser cannot confine his investigations to the register. He will discover protected minor interests, but not overriding interests. To discover these he must inspect the land and make enquiries of the vendor and any occupiers.

It is now necessary to turn attention to s70(1) LRA 1925. It is clear that a number of interests can be excluded from consideration, namely s70(1)(b), (c), (d), (e), (i), (j) and (l). The key paragraphs which must be examined are 70(1)(a), (f), (g) and (k), although most of the discussion will centre of para (g).

Section 70(1)(a)
This includes legal easements and, according to *Celsteel Ltd* v *Alton House Holdings* (1985), some equitable easements, namely those which are enjoyed openly. The reasoning of Scott J in that case received the approval of the Court of Appeal in *Thatcher* v *Douglas* (1995).

Section 70(1)(f)
These are rights acquired or in the course of being acquired under the Limitation Acts. If a squatter on registered land has enjoyed adverse possession for 12 years this of itself does not give him title (compare this with the situation in unregistered land). To acquire title he must apply to be registered with a possessory title. Until this is done his rights are protected as overriding under para (f).

Section 70(1)(g)
This is the most important of all overriding interests and its provisions must be examined in some detail. It will be noticed that it does not refer to specific interests unlike the other overriding interests in s70. It simply refers to 'rights' which gives its application a very wide scope.

It consists of two main limbs. The first affords protection to the rights of an occupier and those of a person in receipt of rents and profits against a purchaser. The second limb provides a purchaser with a way of escaping from being bound by those rights. Thus, the paragraph is attempting to balance two conflicting sets of interests.

The key word in the first part is 'rights'. It is these which constitute overriding interests *not* occupation. These rights must subsist in reference to the registered land: s70(1). The observations of Lord Wilberforce in *National Provincial Bank* v *Ainsworth* (1965) make clear that the rights must constitute rights in land and not personal rights.

Examples of the rights which have been held to come within this paragraph are: an option to purchase a freehold enforceable by specific performance (*Webb* v *Pollmount* (1966)); and the rights of a tenant to make deductions from his rent to cover the cost of repairs where the landlord is in breach of his repairing covenant (*Lee-Parker* v *Izzet* (1971)).

One of the most important cases decided under s70(1)(g) is the House of Lords' decision in *Williams* v *Glyn's Bank* v *Boland* (1981). In that case a husband and wife decided to buy the matrimonial home. The wife contributed to the purchase price but title was conveyed only to the husband who became the registered proprietor. Later, without informing his wife, he mortgaged the house to the bank. The bank made no enquiries of either party as to whether the wife had any interest in the house. Her contribution gave her an equitable half share in the house as a tenant in common. The bank claimed possession of the house; the wife claimed that she was in occupation and that her equitable interest was overriding under para (g). The House of Lords found for the wife. It held she was in occupation and that her equitable rights were capable of coming within para (g). Although her equitable interest was a minor interest which could have been the subject of a caution entered on the register, her occupation converted it into an overriding interest under para (g). Since the mortgage monies were paid to only one trustee, the husband, no overreaching had occurred.

If a restriction had been entered on the register of title the Registrar could not have registered the disposition to the bank unless he had first ensured that the mortgage advance money had been paid to two trustees.

Notice from this case that a minor interest can change its identity and become an overriding one. Paragraph (g) provided a safety net for the wife's interest; a role it frequently plays. Had the title been unregistered the answer would have been different. A purchaser would have been bound by the wife's equitable interest unless he could have established that he was a bona fide purchaser for value of the legal estate without notice.

It is not clear if licences arising by proprietary estoppel are encompassed by para (g) and the complexities of the issue cannot be examined here. The authorities are not clear and the position is uncertain. The position will be examined in more detail later in this book. A claimant to a licence by estoppel cannot be certain that his claim is based on a sound foundation nor, if he has one, of its extent. That will only be known when the court decides. In the meantime perhaps he can protect his interest by entry of a caution on the register. A notice would present difficulties of wording since the licence would be inchoate and the registered proprietor would hardly be likely to co-operate in producing the land certificate necessary to enter a notice.

Once the court had given a favourable decision and defined the terms of the licence there seems no reason why it should not fall within para (g) and bind a purchaser. Such a licence it seems can bind a purchaser in unregistered land with the exception of the bona fide purchaser: see *Inwards* v *Baker* (1965); *Ives (E R) Investments Ltd* v *High* (1967).

What is meant by 'actual occupation?'

This is a matter of fact and not of law. The apparent simplicity of this phrase is deceptive. It is tempting to think that the rationale of s70(1)(g) is based on notice. In *Strand Securities* v *Caswell* (1965) Lord Denning certainly thought so. He stated: 'He [a purchaser] must take subject to whatever rights the occupier may have. Such is the doctrine of *Hunt* v *Luck* (1902) for unregistered land. Section 70(1)(g) carries the same doctrine forward into registered land.'

In *Hunt* v *Luck* it was said 'a tenant's occupation is notice of all that tenant's rights', but in *Williams & Glyn's Bank* Lords Wilberforce and Scarman rejected that view in no uncertain words. Counsel had sought to limit the application of para (g) in the light of the doctrine of notice, but, said Lord Wilberforce, 'this would run counter to the whole purpose of the Act', pointing out that in unregistered land the purchaser's obligations depended on notice, actual or constructive. 'In the case of registered land, it is the fact of occupation that matters ... no further element is material.' And Lord Scarman observed that 'the statute has substituted a plain factual situation for the uncertainties of notice, actual or constructive, as the determinant of an overriding interest.'

However the Court of Appeal in the later case of *Lloyds Bank* v *Rosset* (1989) expressed different views. Here a husband and wife decided to buy and restore a farmhouse which was in need of substantial repair. The vendor agreed that repair work could commence before completion and gave permission for the builders to move in six weeks before completion was due. The wife supervised the builders and undertook extensive decorating work. Completion took place on 17 December with the husband being registered as sole proprietor. This was at the insistence of the husband's family trustees who were providing the money for the project from family trust funds. Without telling the wife, the husband mortgaged the property to the bank to raise a loan. The transfer and charge were registered in the following February. The husband defaulted on the mortgage payments and the bank sought possession. The wife claimed she had an equitable interest under s70(1)(g) as she was in occupation prior to completion and at completion.

Purchas and Nichols LJJ thought the wife was in actual occupation and the former expressly stated that, in his view, s70(1)(g) was based on notice. He stated that 'the provisions of s70(1)(g) clearly were intended to import into the law relating to registered land the equitable doctrine of constructive notice'. It is clear that both Lords Justices regarded 'actual occupation' as being possible without the necessity for living on the premises. However. Mustill LJ did not think that as a matter of fact the wife was in actual occupation. Her presence was too intermittent. But on appeal to the House of Lords the occupation point was not discussed since it was decided there that the wife had no equitable right in the property to come within s70(1)(g).

The views of the Court of Appeal are certainly not consistent with those expressed in *Williams & Glyn's Bank* v *Boland*.

The Law Commission has rejected the idea that notice has a role to play in registered land: see *Property Law: Third Report on Land Registration* (1987) (Law Com No 158); *Land Registration for the Twenty-first Century* (1998) (Law Com No 254).

If the doctrine of notice was applicable to s70(1)(g) it would mean that the paragraph was only applicable if the nature of occupation was such as to put a purchaser on enquiry. That would represent a return to the doctrine of notice and provoke litigation on the nature of the occupation. The current conflict of judicial views is not satisfactory and hopefully the House of Lords will in due course provide much needed clarification.

From the purchaser's point of view, *Williams & Glyn's Bank* presents considerable problems where someone is in occupation but whose presence is temporarily invisible: see *Chhokar* v *Chhokar* (1984).

(Note the decision in *Abbey National Building Society* v *Cann* (1990). The relevant time for occupation under s70(1)(g) is the time of completion of that purchase.)

Consider now the phrase 'or in receipt of the rents and profits thereof'. This part of s70(1)(g) certainly presents problems for a purchaser since such a person will not be in occupation, but a purchaser will nevertheless be bound by his rights. Notice has no part to play here which lends support to the view that notice is not relevant to the occupier's position either. It would be somewhat inconsistent if notice was applicable to one part of the paragraph but not to another. A purchaser should of course make enquiries of the vendor but if he receives misleading replies he will still be bound by the rights of the person in receipt of rents and profits.

It appears that this provision is only applicable where the person entitled to receive the rents and profits actually receives them: *E S Schwab & Co Ltd* v *McCarthy* (1975).

The wording of the second limb reads as follows: 'save where enquiry is made of such person and the rights are not disclosed'. Whereas the first part of s70(1)(g) protects the occupier's rights against a purchaser, the second limb enables a purchaser to avoid them. It must be stressed however that the purchaser must direct his enquiry to 'such person', ie the person in actual occupation or in receipt of rents and profits. Enquiry of the vendor will not suffice.

If occupation is not visible to a purchaser then he cannot make the enquiry and thus avail himself of the provision. It could be argued that this second part of para (g) supports the contention that para (g) as it relates to occupation is based on notice. If there is no occupation, a purchaser is not bound. If there is, he is bound but with the provision of an escape route which assumes he is aware of the occupier. If occupation under parag (g) is not based on notice then a purchaser is in a very invidious position if occupation is not apparent. He gets the worst of both worlds, which is what happened in *Chhokar* v *Chhokar* (1984).

On the other hand the escape route is also available to a purchaser as regards the rights of a person who is in receipt of rents and profits who is not necessarily in occupation which perhaps undermines that argument.

Section 70(1)(k): leases not exceeding 21 years
This only applies to legal leases: *City Permanent Building Society* v *Miller* (1952). In that case the Court of Appeal based its decision on the use of the word 'granted' which in its view indicated that the legislature intended para (k) to be confined to legal leases. This is almost certainly correct despite s3(x) LRA 1925 which defines 'lease' as 'including an under-lease and any tenancy or agreement for a lease'. In unregistered land a legal lease automatically binds a purchaser and this paragraph is in line with that position.

The paragraph embraces fixed-term leases and periodic legal leases, eg weekly, monthly and yearly. The reason for the latter's inclusion is clear: it would be impracticable for lessees to protect them by entries on the register of title as minor interests. Few would realise the necessity to do so if they were classified as minor interests and the land registry would be overwhelmed by applications.

The emphasis placed by the court on the word 'granted' in *Miller*'s case (above) prompts speculation as to whether a lease created by implication of common law falls within the paragraph. When a man goes into possession of another's land with his consent and pays rent on a periodic basis common law will presume a periodic tenancy. For example, if he pays monthly a monthly tenancy will be presumed, although strictly speaking the lease has not been granted, at least not expressly granted. It could be argued that it has arisen by operation of law as opposed to an act of the parties. The more likely position is that the common law presumes from these two factors – rent and possession – the intention of the landlord to grant a lease which the tenant accepts. See the observations of Nicholls LJ in *Javad* v *Mohammed Aquil* (1991). It is possible to create a legal periodic lease without any formalities if the requirements of s54 LPA 1925 are complied with.

Reversionary leases come within the paragraph. The fact of non-possession would be of no consequence because para (k), unlike para (g), does not require occupation.

From the above examination of overriding interests it is clear that the register of title does not operate as a mirror reflecting all the facts relevant to a given title. Their existence represents a considerable crack in that mirror because they do not appear on the title. A person entitled to an overriding interest is certainly protected and need take no positive steps to protect his interest. The purchaser's case is entirely different. They represent a considerable threat and he should make diligent enquiries of the vendor, and persons in occupation, as well as making a careful visual inspection of the land in order to discover them. Visual inspection on its own will not always reveal para (a) easements, although it appears equitable easements only qualify for inclusion in that paragraph if they are openly enjoyed. In the cases of paras (f) and (k) there will generally be occupation which will put the purchaser on enquiry.

It is para (g) which can cause serious problems to a purchaser, particularly if the views of Lords Wilberforce and Scarman prevail.

In a report (Law Com No 254 (1988)) the Law Commission acknowledges that overriding interests must be retained but they should be reduced in number because of their dangers to a purchaser. Although the Commission says that the doctrine of notice should be excluded from registered land, it does conclude that as far as s70(1)(g) is concerned persons should only be regarded as being in occupation if they are physically present on the land and that presence is discoverable by reasonable inspection.

SUGGESTED ANSWER TO QUESTION TWO

General Comment

In compiling an answer to this essay title it is essential for students to demonstrate an awareness of the pre-1926 conveyancing problems in order to show how the registered land system simplifies conveyancing and to make clear that overriding interests *can* affect substantive rights.

Key Points

- Aims of the land registration system
- Pre-1926 conveyancing position
- Outline of the land registration system: three registers; registrable interests; overriding interests; minor interests and three principles
- Overriding interests: 'crack in the mirror' – s70(1)(g) – *Abbey National Building Society* v *Cann*
- Rationale of overriding interests
- The effect of overriding interest on substantive rights in certain areas

Suggested Answer

Registration of title was first introduced into England on a limited basis in the nineteenth century. However, the real impetus for the 'new system' of conveyancing came when registration of title was extended by the Land Registration Act (LRA) 1925, which came into force on 1 January 1926. The purpose of the LRA 1925 was to simplify conveyancing by providing a safe, simple and economic system of land transfer.

The unregistered system of conveyancing was cumbersome, expensive and time-consuming. It is a basic tenet of conveyancing that a vendor must be able to prove that he is entitled to the land before he can pass good title to a purchaser. Under the unregistered system of conveyancing, such proof was provided by the production of the title documents to the land (ie the conveyances or leases). The vendor had to be able to show the chain of ownership for the preceding 30 (now 15) years. A prospective purchaser then had to check those documents to confirm that the vendor was entitled to sell the property. Further, each time the land was sold all those documents had to be examined. The system involved repetitive work, and was time-consuming and expensive. Finally, since proof of title was through documents held in private custody the system was susceptible to fraud.

The system of registration of title was designed to deal with the problems posed by unregistered conveyancing so that the conveyancing process could be simplified.

How does the registered land system simplify conveyancing? It does so by replacing the title deeds with a registered title (ie one registered at the Land Registry), embodied in one document, guaranteed by the State.

Each register of the title is made up of three registers. First, there is the property register. This gives the county or place where the land is situated and describes the property by reference to a filed plan. It also contains details of any rights over other land of which the registered land has the benefit, eg legal easement. Second, there is the proprietorship register. This states who owns the land and what title (absolute, good leasehold, etc) applies to the land. Third, there is the charges register. It contains encumbrances or charges affecting land, eg a restrictive covenant.

All interests in land were recategorised by the LRA 1925 as 'registrable', 'overriding' or 'minor'. Registrable interests include a fee simple absolute in possession and leases over 21 years. Overriding interests include leases of 21 years or less and all other interests listed in s70(1)(a) to (l) LRA 1925. Finally, minor interests include anything which is neither a registrable nor an overriding interest (ie all interests come within one category or another). The system of registration of title comprises three main principles:

1   The 'mirror principle' – the register is designed to act as a mirror accurately reflecting the totality of estates and interests affecting the registered land in question. However, overriding interests (which are not usually entered on the register but bind the registered proprietor even though he may have no knowledge of them) constitute a major qualification to this principle.

2   The curtain principle – only the legal title is shown on the register. By virtue of the curtain principle all trusts are kept off the title as the beneficial interests behind the trust are overreached on sale.

3   The insurance principle – the State guarantees the accuracy of a registered title. An indemnity is paid out of public funds if a registered proprietor is deprived of his title or is otherwise prejudiced by the operation of the scheme.

Upon registration, the registered proprietor is given a land certificate which contains copies of the three parts of the register and a copy of the filed plan. However, the register, not the land certificate, is the document of title. The registered land system is much more secure than the unregistered system of conveyancing (if a land certificate is lost a replacement can be obtained upon payment of a small fee). Registration must take effect within two months of the transaction (ie the sale or granting of a long lease), failing which the grant will be void as to the legal estate unless an authorised extension has been granted by the Registrar: s123 LRA 1925. A purchaser of land subject to the registration scheme takes the land subject only to:

1   all entries on the register; and

2   any overriding interests existing at the time (overriding interests can appear on the register and if this happens they cease to be overriding interests and take their protection from the register).

The registered land system has unquestionably simplified conveyancing. It has established a safe, simple and economic system of land transfer. The quotation suggests it should not affect substantive rights. The reality is that it does in at least one important respect. As noted above, the register is intended to operate as a mirror accurately reflecting the totality of estates and interests affecting the registered land. However, overriding interests are a 'crack in the mirror' because, although they are not usually entered on the register, they still bind the registered proprietor even though he has no knowledge of them. They are supposed to be readily discoverable by anyone who takes the trouble to go and look at the property. Further, the vendor/transferor is usually bound to disclose any overriding interests he knows about under the open contract rule and the standard conditions of sale.

Overriding interests are set out in s70(1)(a)–(l) LRA 1925. The subsection includes a multitude of rights. However, the most important overriding interests are terms of years of 21 years or less, legal and equitable easements and rights of persons in actual occupation of land under para (g).

Why does the land registration system have this 'crack in the mirror'? The answer is a mixture of economic, policy and practical reasons, as demonstrated by considering two of the aforementioned overriding interests – short leases and rights of persons in actual occupation of land.

It is submitted that the exclusion of short leases from the system was for economic and practical reasons. It would have been impracticable to require all short leases to be noted on the register. A very considerable increase in the registry's resources would have been needed to facilitate their entry onto the register – resources which successive governments would not have been prepared to make available. Further, many leases which are not required to be by deed (see ss52(1) and 54(2) LPA 1925) are entered into comparatively informally, and it would have been unrealistic and unreasonable to expect a tenant to have protected his interest on the register.

Policy and practical considerations are the rationale for s70(1)(g) overriding interests – interests of persons in actual occupation of land. Paragraph (g) is drafted widely in order to protect people who from the standpoint of basic justice merit protection but whose interests (leaving aside the separate issue of whether their interests would be suitable for registration or not) are frequently created informally and are thus unlikely to be registered by lay people. More must be said about this important paragraph and its practical effect. There are three aspects to establishing an overriding interest under s70(1)(g):

1   The claimant must have a proprietary interest in the property (eg an equitable interest).
2   The claimant must be in actual occupation of the land before completion of the transaction: *Abbey National Building Society* v *Cann* (1990). Prior to this decision there was uncertainty as to when the claimant had to be in occupation for the purposes of s70(1)(g). Was it the date of registration of the purchaser or mortgagee as proprietor or was it the date of completion of the purchase? The fact that the House of Lords in the *Cann* case ruled that the claimant had to be in occupation prior to completion of the transaction has had the effect of limiting most claims under para (g) to cases of second or later mortgages, as it is unusual for purchasers to be in occupation before completion. This does not apply to the rights of persons in receipt of rents and profits.
3   If an enquiry is made by a prospective purchaser, and the right is not disclosed because of active concealment on the part of the person claiming an overriding interest under para (g), then the purchaser will take free of that right.

The ways in which s70(1)(g) may affect substantive rights is best highlighted by comparing how the unregistered and registered systems operate in relation to third party rights.

In unregistered land, the Land Charges Act 1972 provides that a number of equitable interests may be registered as land charges in the Land Charges Register. The statute does not embrace all equitable interests and, apart from those which are overreached, they remain subject to the old doctrine of notice. In registered land all interests which are neither registrable with substantive titles of their own nor overriding are minor interests: s3(xv) LRA 1925. Minor interests therefore constitute a residual class of interests, the most important of which are the equitable interests which are registrable as land charges under the LCA 1972. By contrast the LCA contains a finite list.

Minor interests should be entered on the registered proprietor's register of title by the appropriate form of entry, eg notice, restriction, caution. In the case of a notice, its entry will ensure that a purchaser is bound: s20(1) LRA 1925.

If registration is effected under the LCA 1972, this is deemed to constitute actual notice (s198 LPA 1925) and a purchaser will be bound.

Now consider the consequences of non-registration in both systems. In the case of unregistered land the effects of non-registration of the various land charges are set out in s4(5), (6) and (8) LCA 1972 and they contain no reference to either good faith or notice. *Hollington Bros Ltd* v *Rhodes* (1951) (Harman J) and *Midland Bank Trust Co Ltd* v *Green* (1981) (House of Lords) made crystal clear that a purchaser's knowledge of the 'unregistered land charge' is immaterial. In both cases the land charge in question was an estate contract (class C(iv)). In both cases it was not registered. In both cases the purchaser knew of it. In both cases the purchaser was held to be a purchaser of the legal estate in the land for money and took free.

In the case of registered land the effect of failure to protect a minor interest is set out in the LRA 1925 which is to the effect that if there is no entry on the register of title then a purchaser for valuable consideration of the legal estate in the land takes free of it. Before passing to the role of s70(1)(g) in that situation mention must be made of *Peffer* v *Rigg* (1978). In that case the equitable interest was a tenancy in common and the appropriate entry was a restriction but no such entry was made on the register of title. Section 59(6) LRA 1925 provides that 'a purchaser ... shall not be concerned with any ... matter ... (not being an overriding interest ...) which is not protected by a caution or other entry on the register, whether he has or has not notice ... express, implied or constructive.' A difficulty appears on examination of the word 'purchaser' in s3 LRA 1925 where it is defined as being 'a purchaser in good faith for valuable consideration'. (Note in s3(xxxi) valuable consideration includes marriage but excludes a nominal consideration in money. Contrast this with the position in unregistered land. In *Midland Bank Trust Co Ltd* v *Green* (1981), the House of Lords held that a purchaser for money in s4(6) LCA 1972 included a purchaser who had given only nominal consideration.) It was the reference to 'good faith' which lead Graham J in *Peffer* v *Rigg* (1978) to introduce the doctrine of notice into this area of registered land. He held that a purchaser who had knowledge of the unprotected minor interests could not take advantage of non-protection because, having notice, she could not be said to be in 'good faith' and therefore not a purchaser within the relevant statutory provisions. She therefore took subject to it. *Peffer* v *Rigg* was decided at first instance and is generally regarded as being a decision that the legislature would not have intended.

Turning now to s70(1)(g) LRA 1925, we see a major difference between the two systems. Section 70(1)(g) may be said to constitute a safety net for some unprotected minor interests, a safety net which is not enjoyed in unregistered land. Overriding interests do not appear on the register of title but they nevertheless bind a purchaser: s3 LRA 1925. They are listed in s70(1) LRA 1925. A minor interest which should have been protected, say, by the entry of a Notice on the register of title will not bind a purchaser of the legal estate for valuable consideration in its capacity as a minor interest if it has not been so protected. It may however be re-classified as overriding under s70(1)(g). Take an equitable lease. In unregistered land it is registrable as an estate contract, land charge class C(iv). If not registered it is void against a purchaser of the legal estate in the land for money or money's worth. It is then lost beyond resuscitation. In registered land it is not listed in s70(1) and is accordingly a minor interest in need of protection by the entry of a notice. If not so protected, then provided the requirements of s70(1)(g) are satisfied, it will constitute an overriding interest under that paragraph. Sometimes an examiner, having set a problem in the context of unregulated land, will ask 'would your answer be different if title to the land was registered?' Frequently the answer is in the affirmative because of s70(1)(g).

Further differences between the two systems can be observed in relation to overreaching and equitable easements. In both cases the result of the application of either system produces different results.

Overreaching arises in connection with settlements, trusts for sale and trusts of land. For overreaching to occur a purchaser must pay the purchase money to two trustees (or a trust corporation). It sometimes happens that payment is made to only one trustee because the purchaser is unaware that there is trust because it has arisen by implication, eg where two beneficiaries have made contributions to the purchase price of land but the legal title is vested in only one of them. In that case there is no overreaching. In unregistered land the purchaser will take subject to the beneficial interests of the party not on the legal title unless he can establish that he is a bona fide purchaser of the legal estate on the land, for value, without notice.

In the case of registered land the result is different. There should have been a restriction entered on the register of title to ensure that payment is made by the purchaser to two trustees. In the absence of a restriction the purchaser will in all innocence pay the sole trustee with again the same result: there will be no overreaching. However, the beneficial interest, in this case, will nevertheless bind a purchaser if it falls within the ambit of s70(1)(g).

In unregistered land, if a person is in occupation this will constitute constructive notice to a purchaser of his rights. It might be thought that since s70(1)(g) is based on occupation then it too is based on the same principle enunciated in *Hunt* v *Luck* (1902) but in *Williams & Glyn's Bank* v *Boland* (1981) Lords Wilberforce and Scarman were emphatic that that was not the case. What was necessary was the fact of occupation and notice had no application. Whether the occupation was of such a nature as to give notice to a purchaser or put him on enquiry was immaterial.

These views have not always been followed in subsequent cases. See, for example, *Lloyds Bank* v *Rosset* (1989) in the Court of Appeal, and the position is in need of clarification by the House of Lords.

It should be noted that a beneficial interest that falls under para (g) may be overreached by payment to two trustees: *City of London Building Society* v *Flegg* (1988).

The existence of overriding interests in registered land has given rise to a further difference in respect of equitable easements. In unregistered land an equitable easement is registrable as a land charge class D(iii) (s2(5) LCA 1972), provided it arose on or after 1 January 1926. Equitable easements arising before that date are subject to the old rule of Notice.

In registered land there is a reference to equitable easements in the first group of overriding interests listed in s70(1)(a) LRA 1925. This group includes 'other easements not being equitable easements required to be protected by notice on the register'. The LRA 1925 however contains no such requirement. The point arose for consideration by Scott J in *Celsteel* v *Alton House Holdings* (1985).

The wording suggests that equitable easements can fall within para (a) if they are not required to be entered on the register of title. Given that no such requirement is made by the statute, Scott J construed the words 'required to be protected' as meaning 'which need to be protected' and having surmounted the difficulty in that way went on to hold that such an equitable easement fell within the paragraph if it was openly enjoyed. His reasoning was accepted and approved in *Thatcher* v *Douglas* (1995).

Thus, although the system of registration of title may have been only to simplify conveyancing, whatever the intention of the legislature, there is no doubt that it has affected substantive rights in the ways described above. It is interesting to note the comment of the Law Commission Report No 125, *Property Law: Land Registration* (1983) at para 1.5: 'The process was previously designed to simplify the process of land transfer rather than alter the substantive law relating to land, though some aspects of the substantive law are affected by the system.'

3

Co-ownership

Introduction

Co-ownership is a topic covering a wide area as the selection of questions clearly indicates. Students should note the importance of the Trusts of Land and Appointment of Trustees Act 1996 in this topic and that an overall view of the statute is not enough. Question 2 in particular requires a detailed knowledge of the Act, while Question 3 necessitates a reference to the bankruptcy provisions contained in the third schedule. Question 4 is a reminder that the examiner can require of students attempting a co-ownership question a detailed knowledge of s70(1)(g) LRA 1925. Question 5 takes the student in some depth into the realms of resulting and constructive trusts where again s70(1)(g) LRA 1925 is relevant.

Questions

INTERROGRAMS

1   What is jus accrescendi?
2   What are the different implications of the phrase 'equal shares'?
3   What are the four unities?
4   How may a joint tenancy be severed?

QUESTION ONE

'The Trusts of Land and Appointment of Trustees Act 1996 has at last placed the law relating to settlements and trusts for sale of land on a rational and straightforward basis.'
   Discuss.

London University LLB Examination
(for external students) Land Law June 1997 Q1

QUESTION TWO

William lived on his farm with his wife, Anthea, and his daughter, Emma. As he became older, Emma took over more of the management of the farm. William died in 1997 and in his will he left his farm to Anthea for life and then to his three children, Emma, Fred and George in equal shares. He appointed his friends, Bill and Ben, as his executors. Emma wants to continue managing and living on the farm for the rest of her life, but she is worried that Anthea, or (after Anthea's death) her brothers, might want to sell or let the farm to a third party.
   Advise Emma.

London University LLB Examination
(for external students) Land Law June 1998 Q4

QUESTION THREE

Herbert and Wilma were married in 1980. They bought a house, Hersanmyne, for £20,000 of which £5,000 was contributed by Wilma's mother, Martha, who was to live with them in Hersanmyne. The house was conveyed to Herbert and Wilma on trust for themselves and Martha as joint tenants. Herbert and Wilma had a son Sam in 1983 and a daugher Dawn in 1986. In 1989 Herbert left Hersanmyne and has never returned. In 1990 Martha sent a letter to Herbert saying that she wished to have her share in the house repaid so that she could provide during her lifetime for Wilma and the grandchildren. Herbert ignored the letter. Martha died in 1991, leaving all her property to Wilma.

Herbert owned a business which failed in 1998, and he has debts of £30,000. His creditors are now pressing for payment and threatening bankruptcy proceedings. His only asset is his interest in Hersanmyne, now worth £50,000.

Wilma wishes to remain in Hersanmyne. She has no capital other than her interest in the house, but she has enough income to run the house and maintain herself and the children.

Advise Wilma.

Prepared by Holborn College

QUESTION FOUR

In 1997, Albert and Victoria decided to buy a house to live in together. They agreed to buy Blueacre (registered title) from Bertie for £60,000. Victoria paid £40,000 cash towards the price; Albert agreed to pay the other £20,000 which he intended to borrow from his business partner, pending completion of a business deal. Victoria was abroad, and left Albert to arrange the legal formalities. Completion of the purchase took place on 1 December, and the transfer was into the sole name of Albert.

Unfortunately, Albert's partnership collapsed, and Albert had hurriedly to borrow £20,000 from the Ripoff Bank. Although the bank advanced the money in time for the purchase, the mortgage deed was only executed on 3 December. Bertie, moreover, had problems in moving out and, with Albert's consent, remained in the house until 7 December. However, Victoria's valuable collection of books and Albert's cases of vintage claret were stored in the spare bedroom on 2 December, and, on the same day, Charles, Albert's builder, started renovating the cellar. On 8 December Albert and Victoria occupy Blueacre, and on 10 December Albert's title and the mortgage to Ripoff Bank were both registered.

After six months, Albert left Victoria and refuses to pay the mortgage. Ripoff Bank wish to sell Blueacre, but Victoria claims they are bound by her interest.

Discuss.

London University LLB Examination
(for external students) Land Law September 1998 Q7

QUESTION FIVE

In 1990 Mr and Mrs Jones purchased a house as their matrimonial home. For tax reasons it was conveyed into Mrs Jones' sole name and she was registered as the sole proprietor. The purchase price of the house was £200,000, of which Mr Jones contributed £120,000 and Mrs Jones £60,000; the remaining £20,000 was provided by Martha, Mr Jones' mother, as a wedding present. In 1994 Mr and Mrs Jones invited Martha (who was becoming old and infirm) to go and live with them and she agreed to pay for the construction of an extension to the house for her occupation. Martha spent £30,000 on the extension and moved into occupation in 1995. In 1996 Mr Jones took Martha on a world cruise and, while they were away, Mrs Jones mortgaged the house to the Oxter Bank. She has recently fallen into arrears on her mortgage instalments and the bank is seeking possession of the house with a view to selling it.

Advise Martha and Mr Jones.

London University LLB Examination
(for external students) Land Law November 1998 Q4

Answers

ANSWERS TO INTERROGRAMS

1   It means right of survivorship. When a joint tenant dies his share will automatically accrue to his surviving joint tenants who will share it between them. Contrast this with the position when a tenant in common dies. His share will not go to his surviving tenants in common but to his estate which will be distributed according to the terms of his will, or, if there is no will, according to the rules of devolution on intestacy.

2   Care must be taken with this phrase as it can appear in two different contexts and carry different meanings. If the words appear as words of severance in a conveyance, will or trust deed, eg to A, B and C in equal shares, they denote a tenancy in common. If they appear as describing the contribution purchasing co-owners of land are making towards its purchase price they will denote a joint tenancy unless the conveyance states otherwise.

Equity leans against joint tenancies and if the contributions are unequal, presumes a tenancy in common. However, if the conveyance in those circumstances describes them as joint tenants, then joint tenants they are because the declaration in the conveyance is conclusive: *Goodman* v *Gallant* (1986).

If the purchasers have contributed equally, and there is no declaration in the conveyance that they are joint tenants then another equitable presumption that they are tenants in common may apply. If the purpose of the acquisition is for a business venture equity will presume a tenancy in common: *Malayan Credit Ltd* v *Jack Chia MPH Ltd* (1986).

3   These are unity of time, title, interest and possession and if all are present there will be a joint tenancy. If one is missing there can only be a tenancy in common. Only one unity is necessary for a tenancy in common: unity of possession.

Unity of time means all of the joint tenants must have acquired their interests at the same time; unity of title means their interests must derive from the same instrument of creation; unity of interest means their interests are of equal value; and unity of possession means they are all entitled to possession of all of the property.

4   The effect of severance is to convert a joint tenancy into a tenancy in common. Only equitable joint tenancies may be severed: s36 LPA 1925 forbids severance of legal joint tenancies. *Williams* v *Hensman* (1861) decided that there were three methods of severance in relation to personalty:

a   an act of any one person operating on his share;
b   mutual agreement;
c   any course of dealing sufficient to intimate that the interests of all were mutually treated as constituting a tenancy in common.

Section 36 LPA 1925 made these applicable to realty and introduced a fourth method: service of a written notice of intention to sever a joint tenancy.

Answers

SUGGESTED ANSWER TO QUESTION ONE

General Comment

A very topical question given that the Act came into force on 1 January 1997. A good answer should succinctly summarise the shortcomings of the pre-Act law and outline and evaluate the key provisions of the new legislation. Given the remit of the question the answer should focus on Part I of the Act.

Key Points

*   Pre-1997 methods of holding land in trust – strict settlement and trust for sale
*   Shortcomings of pre-Act law
*   Law Commission Report
*   Scope of the Act
*   Main provisions of the Act: the new trust of land; no new strict settlements after 1996; trusts for sale automatically trusts of land; doctrine of conversion abolished; trustees of land have a power to sell and a power to retain land; and wider powers for the court
*   Evaluation

Suggested Answer

The Trusts of Land and Appointment of Trustees Act 1996 received the Royal Assent on 24 July 1996 and came into force on 1 January 1997. It effects some of the most important reforms to real property law since the 1925 legislation and it forms part of a clear programme to review and revise the trust system which has remained substantially unaltered since the 1925 legislation.

Prior to 1 January 1997 there were two distinct ways of holding land in trust – either by a strict settlement (related to successive interests in land) or a trust for sale (related principally to concurrent interests in land, although it could also relate to successive interests as well). Each had a different rationale. The strict settlement was traditionally used to keep ownership of land within a given family while under a trust for sale land was held as an investment asset. The effectiveness of a strict settlement in keeping land within a family was broken by the Settled Land Acts 1882 and 1925 which as a general rule vested the legal estate to settled land in the tenant for life (s16(1) SLA 1925); gave the tenant for life the power to sell the land (ss38 and 39 SLA 1925); and stipulated that this and other powers of the tenant for life could not be expressly excluded by a trust instrument (s106 SLA 1925). In view of these provisions, you would not have created a strict settlement if your aim was to keep land within the family because you could not prevent a tenant for life possessed of the legal estate from selling it if he wanted to. However, strict settlements still arose, usually unintentionally, eg where a will was drawn up without professional advice which left a house to a testator's wife for life and then to the testator's children absolutely. In contrast, a trust for sale was used to convert property into cash which in turn could easily be distributed amongst the beneficiaries. Under a trust for sale, the beneficiaries were deemed to have an interest in the proceeds of sale into which the estate was to be converted rather than in the property itself (the doctrine of conversion). This was the position even before the land had been sold. Accordingly, in the case of a trust for sale land was held as an *investment* asset rather than for long-term occupation (this explained why the trustees were under a *duty* to sell).

In addition to the fact that the strict settlement and the trust for sale each had a different rationale, there were also significant differences between the two systems as to how the legal estate was held and who had powers of management. For example, in the case of a strict settlement the legal estate was usually vested in the tenant for life (with the settlement trustees in a more peripheral role), whereas in the case of a trust for sale the legal estate was vested in the trustees.

A primary catalyst for the new legislation was the 1989 Law Commission Report *Transfer of Land: Trusts of Land*. The Law Commission concluded that there was a need for 'an entirely new system' in order to clarify and rationalise the law, and that any new system should be based upon a new type of trust. They identified a number of weaknesses with the pre-Act law, four of which are particularly noteworthy. First, the existence of a dual system gave rise to a number of difficulties. Second, the settled land regime was unnecessarily complicated. Third, it was possible to create a strict settlement unintentionally, eg a will drawn up without professional advice in the terms set out above. Fourth, the trust for sale mechanism was not appropriate to the conditions of modern home ownership. In particular, the duty to sell was artificial and inconsistent with the wishes of the majority of co-owners.

The Act is in three parts. Part I deals with Trusts of Land and derives substantially from the Law Commission Report. Some of the key provisions of Part I of the Act are outlined in the following paragraphs.

A new concept, the trust of land, is created. The 'trust of land' is defined widely and includes any trust of property which consists of or includes land: s1(1). The new regime applies as follows: (i) to all trusts of land whether the trust is created expressly or implied by statute; (ii) to both concurrent and successive interests in land; and (iii) whenever equitable interests in land arise by way of resulting or constructive trusts. No new strict settlement can be created after 31 December 1996: s2(1). However, pre-Act settlements and resettlements of settlements in existence at the latter date are still governed by the SLA regime. In the case of such resettlements, the conclusion that they are to continue to be subject to the SLA regime can be avoided by an express statement in the creating instrument to the effect that this result is not intended (ie they can be converted to trusts of land).

The doctrine of conversion referred to above was based on the equitable maxim: 'Equity looks on that as done which ought to be done'. Treating the beneficiaries' interests as interests in money made sense if the property subject to the trust for sale was regarded primarily as an investment. As domestic property ownership increased the emphasis on this intention diminished, to be replaced by an intention to purchase property for the purpose of providing a home. In such cases the intention was to retain the property and not to sell it. To regard the interests of beneficiaries who were co-owners under a trust for sale as interests in the proceeds of sale was therefore entirely inappropriate and the courts increasingly gave expression to that view: see *Bull* v *Bull* (1955) where the court held that two tenants in common had interests in land. See also *Williams and Glyn's Bank* v *Boland* (1981). Section 3 of the 1996 Act abolished the doctrine as far as it applied to trusts for sale and s3(3) made its abolition retrospective. In abolishing the doctrine the Act gave effect to developing judicial thinking and removed an irrationality from this area of law.

Before the Act, trustees for sale were under a duty to sell the land, but s25 LPA 1925 implied into every trust for sale a power to postpone sale unless a contrary intention appeared. The concept of the trust for sale still remains, although its definition in s205(1)(xxix) LPA has been altered by the deletion of the word 'binding' and the phrase 'and with or without a power at discretion to postpone the sale'.

Before the 1996 Act where there was co-ownership there was always a trust for sale. If there was no express trust for sale then a statutory trust for sale as defined by s35 LPA 1925 would be implied under s34 LPA 1925 (where the co-owners were tenants in common) or s36 (where they were joint tenants). Situations relating to tenants in common arose which did not fit into the wording of s34 and the courts would then construe s36(4) SLA 1925 to create a trust for sale. For example, see *Bull* v *Bull* (1955).

These three sections have now been amended to produce a trust of land instead of a trust for sale under which the trustees will have a power of sale and not a duty to sell. Sections 34 and 36 have been amended to this effect by s5 and paras 3 and 4 of Sch 2. Section 36(4) SLA 1925 has been amended by para 2(11)(b) of Sch 3. Oddly enough there is no provision in Sch 3 to make the amendment retrospective.

Thus, no longer can there be implied trusts for sale but express trusts for sale may still be created. In such cases, although the trustees' duty to sell remains, the position relating to postponement of sale has been changed. Section 25 LPA 1925 has been repealed and s4 of the 1996 Act now governs the position. Section 4 provides:

'In the case of every trust for sale of land created by a disposition there is to be implied, despite any provision to the contrary made by the disposition, a power for the trustees to postpone sale of the land, and the trustees are not liable in any way for postponing the sale of the land, in the exercise of their discretion, for an indefinite period.'

Thus, the power to postpone the sale can no longer be excluded as it could have been under s25 LPA.

Section 30 LPA 1925 has been replaced by ss14 and 15 of the 1996 Act. A trustee or any person with an interest in property subject to a trust of land can apply to the court for an order under s14. On such an application, the court can make any order it thinks fit: (i) relating to the exercise by the trustees of any of their powers (s14(2)(a)); or (ii) declaring the nature or extent of any person's beneficial interest in the property subject to the trust: s14(2)(b). Under s14 the court can make orders for sale, preventing sale, etc. In two respects, the powers of the court under s14 are wider than those it enjoyed under s30 LPA 1925. First, it can declare the nature or extent of a person's interest in the property subject to the trust. Second, the wording of s14(2)(a) is sufficiently wide to allow it to sanction a transaction which would otherwise be a breach of trust.

In exercising its powers under s14 the court must have regard to the matters set out in s15 which reflects a good deal of the earlier judicial decisions made under s30 LPA 1925. However, s15 has no application where a trustee in bankruptcy of a co-owner's equitable share is making an application under s14. In such a case the court must have regard to the matters set out in s335A of the Insolvency Act 1986 which has been inserted by para 23, Sch 3 to the 1996 Act.

The Act is a modernising one. It unquestionably improves and rationalises the law as to the holding of land in trust. One of its main attributes is that it removes the complications associated with the old system of two distinct ways of holding land in trust. Not only is it advantageous that no new strict settlements can be created after 31 December 1996 (not least because of the complexities of the SLA regime), but the clear expectation is that pre-Act strict settlements will be phased out. The new system now in place has many similarities to the trust for sale. However, the Act has removed those aspects of the trust for sale which were inappropriate to the conditions of modern home ownership, eg the doctrine of conversion. It was clearly entirely artificial to have maintained under the old law that equitable joint tenants or equitable tenants in common had no interest in a house or flat held on trust for sale, but had only an interest in the sale proceeds when no sale was actually contemplated.

Like the Law of Property (Miscellaneous Provisions) Act 1994, the 1996 Act aims to make the law more comprehensible to lay people. However, time alone will tell whether that goal will be achieved.

SUGGESTED ANSWER TO QUESTION TWO

General Comment

A question which requires of the candidate a detailed knowledge of the Trusts of Land and Appointment of Trustees Act 1996, and which serves as a reminder that a general overall knowledge of it is not enough. Efforts to master the Act's details will bring their own rewards and enable a candidate who has done so to achieve high marks.

Key Points

- Effect of will – trust of land – tenants in common
- Anthea's position – beneficiary under a trust of land
- Bill and Ben executors – necessity for written assent establishing them as trustees
- Trustees decide whether to sell or not
- Anthea has no power of sale
- Powers of trustees: s6
- Delegation of powers by trustees to Emma not possible
- Nor does Emma have rights of occupation
- Trustees' duty to consult beneficiaries entitled to possession – s11
- Is the duty to consult embodied in the will?
- If Anthea applies to the court for an order for sale can Emma oppose it?
- When Anthea dies, Emma's position becomes stronger
- Trustees may be obliged to consult other beneficiaries under s11
- Relevance of s13 to Emma's application to occupy
- Emma's rights to apply to court under ss14 and 15
- Emma can be given no guarantee that she will achieve what she wishes

Suggested Answer

William's will, which came into force when he died in 1997, conferred upon Anthea a life interest which is necessarily equitable under s1(1) LPA 1925 and therefore it must take effect behind a trust. This trust will be a trust of land under the Trusts of Land and Appointment of Trustees Act 1996.

The will also left the farm to Emma, Fred and George to take effect on Anthea's death. These three therefore will become co-owners of the farm and because the will stipulates that they are to hold in equal shares they will be tenants in common because the phrase 'equal shares' are words of severance. Formerly this devise would have had to take effect as a statutory trust for sale under s34 LPA 1925. This has now been amended by s5 and para 3(1) and (2), Sch 2 of the 1996 Act to produce a trust of land without a duty to sell the land.

If the will had taken effect before 1 January 1997 it would have created a settlement under the Settled Land Act (SLA) 1925 as regards Anthea's life interest with a trust for sale arising at her death under which Emma, Fred and George would have been equitable tenants in common. The legal estate would have vested in Anthea as tenant for life and she would have enjoyed a considerable number of powers under the SLA including a power of sale: s38. In exercising these powers she would not have needed the consent of the other beneficiaries under the will.

However since 1 January 1997 because of s2 of the 1996 Act no new settlements can be created under the SLA and instead a trust of land with the same beneficial interests arises but with the major difference that Anthea does not enjoy the pre-1997 position she would have enjoyed under the SLA. The legal estate is vested in the trustees of the land instead.

William has appointed Bill and Ben as his executors; he did not appoint them as trustees. Consideration must be given to the question as to whether, when they have completed the administration of William's estate, they automatically change their capacities from executors to trustees of the land. The authorities on the point are not clear and, for the avoidance of doubt, Bill and Ben would be well advised to make a written assent vesting the legal estate, which they held as executors, into their names as trustees to hold on a trust of land.

It is essential that there can be no doubt that they are trustees since the statute confers powers and imposes duties on trustees. Section 6 of the 1996 Act sets out the general powers of the trustees. The overreaching powers referred to in Sch 3, para 4 are only exercisable by trustees. Thus, Emma need not be concerned that Anthea might sell the land. She no longer has that power. It is the trustees who now have the power of sale but it must be emphasised that they have no duty of sale either during Anthea's lifetime nor after her death when the co-ownership of the three children takes effect. Before 1 January 1997, at that point, an implied trust for sale would have arisen under which the trustees would have been under a duty to sell, although they would have enjoyed a statutory power of postponement under s25 LPA 1925. Express trusts for sale can still be created but no express trust for sale was created by the will and it is no longer possible to have implied trusts for sale: s5 of the 1996 Act.

What happens to the land is a decision for the trustees and their powers must now be examined. These are contained in s6. Section 6(1) must be read with care because, although it appears to confer on them the powers of an absolute owner, the wording of the subsection makes clear that these powers are limited to the exercise of their functions as trustees. Moreover, a further restriction is placed on the exercise of their powers by s6(5): 'In exercising the powers conferred by this section trustees shall [must] have regard to the rights of the beneficiaries.'

Does the statute confer specific powers that would enable them to satisfy Emma's wishes? She wishes to continue living on the farm and managing it. Of particular importance to Emma in this respect are the powers of the trustees to delegate their functions under s9 which reads as follows:

> 'The trustees of land may, by power of attorney, delegate to any beneficiary or beneficiaries of full age and beneficially entitled to an interest in possession of land subject to the trust any of their functions which relate to the land.'

Delegation may be for any period or indefinitely. The immediate difficulty for Emma is that she is not as yet beneficially entitled to an interest in possession of the land. Any such interest cannot arise until Anthea's death, and in the meantime only Anthea has an interest in possession. Thus, the trustees cannot exercise their powers of delegation in Emma's favour until Anthea dies.

The further immediate difficulty for Emma is that she does not even have the right to occupy the land because of Anthea's life interest, and without occupation she cannot continue to manage the farm. Section 12 of the 1996 Act confers upon beneficiaries the right to occupy the trust land but, again, only if they are entitled to an interest in possession which is not currently Emma's case.

She cannot therefore at present seek either delegation or occupation. Her immediate problem is Anthea. If she is to continue living on the farm and managing it, it has to be with Anthea's consent which may or may not be forthcoming. She has the consolation that the power of sale is now vested in the trustees and no longer in Anthea as tenant for life. However although Anthea cannot decide to sell the land herself she can request the trustees to sell it, or they may of their own initiative contemplate selling it. In the latter event the provisions of s11 must be considered. Section 11(1) provides:

'(1) The trustees of land shall in the exercise of any function relating to land subject to the trust –
(a) so far as is practicable, consult the beneficiaries of full age and beneficially entitled to an interest in possession in the land, and,
(b) so far as consistent with the general interest of the trust, give effect to the wishes of those beneficiaries, or (in case of dispute) of the majority (according to the value of their combined interests).'

The will could have excluded this duty (s11(2)(a)) but there is no indication that it has done so. Section 11(2)(b) enacts that the duty of consultation in s11(1) does not apply to a trust arising under a will made before the commencement of the Act. The Act came into force on 1 January 1997.

We do not know the precise date in 1997 when William died and he would have made the will at any time before that date. He may have made it before 1 January 1997 or afterwards. If before, the duty of consultation in s11 does not apply. It cannot be said for certain therefore whether the duty to consult exists or not. If the duty is applicable it only applies in relation to Anthea because the trustees are only under an obligation to consult the beneficiaries beneficially entitled to an interest in possession. Emma cannot therefore benefit from s11 because, as yet, she has no beneficial interest in possession. If Anthea, when consulted, expressed the wish that the land should be sold then, under s11, the trustees would be bound to give effect to those wishes so far as they are consistent with the general interest of the trust.

It is not necessary for an applicant to the court under s14 to have an interest in possession in the land, so technically Emma could apply to the court asking that the land be retained, but s15(3) could prove to be an obstacle. It states that 'the matters to which the court is to have regard also include the circumstances and wishes of any beneficiaries of full age and entitled to an interest in possession in property subject to the trust'. The court would be obliged to give considerable weight to Anthea's wishes under this provision.

Emma then is dependent on Anthea's not wanting to sell the land and her allowing Emma to continue living there and managing the farm as before. However, when Anthea dies Emma's position becomes stronger. Emma will then have an interest in possession as an equitable tenant in common and can apply to the trustees for delegated functions and occupation. She can apply to the trustees for delegated functions under s9 of the 1996 Act. If the trustees agree to delegate their functions, or some of them, Emma will, in relation to those functions, be in the same position as a trustee with the same duties and liabilities. She will not, however, enjoy the powers of overreaching.

In considering Emma's request the trustees will be under a duty of consultation imposed by s11 to which reference has already been made, if the section is applicable. It may not be applicable because of s11(2)(b).

Emma could experience difficulties at that point, because when consulted by the trustees, Fred and George may object. In that case the trustees must give effect to the wishes of the majority according to the value of their combined interests. Emma is entitled to one-third of the farm's value; Fred and George between them are entitled to two-thirds.

Before considering whether Emma can invoke s14, attention should next be given to Emma's wishes to occupy the farm which she will need to do if she is to manage the farm. Section 12 deals with the right of beneficiaries to occupy trust land. Under s12:

'(1) A beneficiary who is beneficially entitled to an interest in possession of land subject to a trust of land is entitled by reason of his interest to occupy the land at any time if at that time –

(a) the purposes of the trust include making the land available for his occupation (or for the occupation of beneficiaries of a class of which he is a member or of beneficiaries in general);

(b) the land is to be held by the trustees so as to be available.'

Section 13 deals with the situation where two or more beneficiaries are entitled to occupy the land. The trustees may exclude or restrict the entitlement of any one or more of them but not all of them. In so doing the trustees must not act unreasonably. The trustees may impose reasonable restrictions on an occupying beneficiary. Section 13(4) imposes on the trustees the obligation to take into account certain matters, eg the settlor's intentions and the circumstances and wishes of each beneficiary entitled to occupy the land under s12. Section 13(6) entitles the trustees to impose on the occupant a condition that he pays compensation to a non-occupying beneficiary.

Fred and George are also entitled to be consulted under s11 if applicable, which again could give rise to difficulties for Emma since she is in a minority.

If Emma's applications to the trustees were rejected by them she could make an application to the court under s14 which confers upon that court wider powers than those contained in s30 LPA 1925 which it replaces. The court may make an order 'relating to the exercise by the trustees of any of their functions … as the court thinks fit': s14(2)(a).

Section 15 lists a number of matters to which the court must have regard in determining an application under s14. No such provision was contained in the repealed s30. The cases decided under that section will continue to be of use in applications made under its successor. It should be remembered, however, that when an application for sale was made under that section the court had to bear in mind that, since there was a trust for sale, the trustees were under a duty to sell (although they had a statutory power to postpone sale under it) and this tended to incline the court towards making an order for sale. With a trust of land there is no such duty which may incline the court to be more sympathetic to an applicant opposing sale. Subject to the matters in s15 each case will be decided on its merits because the court may make such order as it thinks fit. If Fred and George oppose Emma, she could be in difficulties because of s15(3) (referred to above).

All one can do for Emma is to set out her rights under the Act. Whether her wishes are fulfilled depends on the trustees, her co-beneficiaries and the court. While Anthea is alive, her position is very insecure, although better than it would be had Anthea been a tenant for life under the Settled Land Act. After Anthea's death her position becomes stronger but with no guarantee that she will obtain what she wants.

Supplementary

In this problem mention has been made of certain obligations imposed on the trustees when exercising their powers (s6(5)), in that the trustees shall have regard to the rights of the beneficiaries when exercising their powers under s6, and the duty of consultation under s11. Although the issue does not arise in this problem students should be aware of a purchaser's position where the trustees have sold the land to him without observing the requirements of those sections. Section 16 is a purchasers' protection provision. A purchaser of trust land need not be concerned to see that any requirement imposed on the trustees by s6(5), 7(3) or 11(1) has been complied with: s16(1).

The section does not applied to registered land: s16(7).

SUGGESTED ANSWER TO QUESTION THREE

General Comment

In answering this question candidates must remember the impact of the Trusts of Land and Appointment of Trustees Act 1996 and its retrospective effect on the statutory trust for sale which was created in 1980. The possibility of severance must be examined and, since it is not certain whether severance was effected or not, candidates must be prepared to argue in the alternative. Section 15 must be discussed but since there is a prospect of Herbert going bankrupt, candidates should be aware that, in that eventuality, s15 has no application and be prepared to discuss the provisions of s335A of the Insolvency Act 1986 which was inserted by the Trusts of Land and Appointment of Trustees Act Sch 3, para 23. This could produce a different and adverse result for Wilma than if s15 had applied.

This question is a reminder that all aspects of Part I of the 1996 Act should be known and candidates are strongly recommended to a thorough knowledge of its details, including the schedules.

Key Points

- Co-ownership joint tenancy
- Implied trust for sale in 1980 – Trusts of Land and Appointment of Trustees Act 1996 operates retrospectively to create a trust of land
- Martha is a joint tenant: *Goodman* v *Gallant*
- Has Martha severed from Herbert? – rules of severance: *Williams* v *Hensman* – s36 LPA 1925
- Consequences of effective severance by Martha – position if no severance
- Wilma need do nothing if she wishes to stay but Herbert may desire sale: ss14 and 15
- Position different if Herbert actually made bankrupt – s335A Insolvency Act 1986

Suggested Answer

This is a case of co-ownership in the context of unregistered land.

When Herbert and Wilma purchased the house in 1980 it was conveyed to them on trust for themselves and Martha as joint tenants. Although co-ownership was created there was no express trust for sale in consequence of which a statutory trust for sale, as defined by s35 LPA 1925, was created by s36 LPA 1925. The effect of s36 was to vest the legal estate in Herbert and Wilma as joint tenants to hold on trust for sale for themselves and Martha as equitable joint tenants. Section 36 expressly forbids severance of a legal joint tenancy while s1(6) LPA 1925 declares that a tenancy in common cannot subsist at law.

However, that position created in 1980 has been altered by the Trusts of Land and Appointment of Trustees Act 1996 which took effect from 1 January 1997. Section 5(1) provides:

> 'Schedule 2 has effect in relation to statutory provisions which impose a trust for sale of land in certain circumstances so that in those circumstances there is instead a trust of land (without a duty to sell).'

Schedule 2 amends ss34 and 36 LPA 1925 so that their application now produces a trust of land without a duty to sell. Further, the amendments operate retrospectively: Sch 2, paras 3 and 4. As from 1 January 1996 the trust for sale created in 1980 was converted into a trust of land with Herbert and Wilma being joint trustees of the legal estate as before, but holding it as a trust of land, without a duty to sell, for themselves and Martha as joint tenants in equity.

It will be noted that Martha contributed £5,000 to the purchase price while Herbert and Wilma contributed between them the larger sum of £20,000. Nevertheless, they are all joint tenants in equity because the conveyance declares them to be so: *Goodman* v *Gallant* (1986). A declaration to that effect in the conveyance is regarded as conclusive and displaces any presumption of a tenancy in common arising from unequal contributions to the purchase price.

The next question for consideration is whether Martha's letter to Herbert in 1990 amounted to an act of severance and it will now be necessary to examine how the equitable joint tenancy may be severed so as to produce a tenancy in common. The distinction is a vital practical one. Joint tenants enjoy the right of survivorship; tenants in common do not. If a joint tenant dies his share automatically accrues to the surviving joint tenants. When a tenant in common dies his share goes to his estate which will devolve either according to the terms of his will or the rules of intestacy. It should be noticed that severance cannot be effected by will because a will does not take effect until the testator's death and it is at that point that the right of survivorship operates.

A joint tenancy may be severed in various ways so as to produce a tenancy in common but it must always be remembered that this only applies to an *equitable* joint tenancy. Section 326(2) LPA 1925 expressly forbids severance of a legal joint tenancy. Moreover, s1(6) LPA enacts that a legal estate is not capable of subsisting as an undivided share (tenancy in common of land). Thus if A, B, C and D hold a legal estate on trust of land for A, B, C and D as joint tenants in equity, if any severance of the equitable joint tenancy occurs the legal joint tenancy which A, B, C and D hold as trustees remains completely unaffected. Also, for example, if A disposes of his equitable share to P this will sever A's equitable joint tenancy from those of B, C and D. P will become an equitable tenant in common in place of A but A will remain a trustee and joint tenant of the legal estate. B, C and D continue as joint tenants in equity.

There are four methods of severance of an equitable joint tenancy in land. Three of them are contained in *Williams* v *Hensman* (1861). Although that was a case of personalty, the three methods were made applicable to land by s36(2) LPA 1925. The three methods are as follows:

1   an act of any one of the persons interested operating on his own share;
2   mutual agreement;
3   any course of dealing sufficient to intimate that the interests of all were to be mutually treated as constituting a tenancy in common.

A fourth method was added by s36(2) LPA 1925 where 'any tenant desires to sever the joint tenancy in equity, he shall give to the other joint tenants a notice in writing of such desire'. The words following 'or do such other acts or things as would, in the case of personal estate, have been effectual to sever the tenancy in equity' apply the methods of *Williams* v *Hensman* to land.

The four methods must be examined in turn:

1   *An act of one party operating on his share, eg sale or mortgage of that share*. Supposing that A, B, C and D are equitable joint tenants and A sells his share to P. This will effect severance in the way described above, but as between themselves B, C and D will remain joint tenants.

In *Hawksley* v *May* (1956) Havers J said that this first method 'obviously includes a declaration of intention to sever' but did not indicate whether this had to be in writing or whether an oral declaration of intention would be sufficient. If an oral declaration would have been sufficient this would have rendered s36(2) (notice in writing) superfluous. In *Burgess* v *Rawnsley* (1975), Pennycuick J clarified the position: 'a mere verbal notice by one party to another clearly cannot operate as a severance'.

Although the wording of this method contemplates a voluntarily disposition of the share it also covers the position where that party is declared bankrupt because his equitable share will then vest in his trustee in bankruptcy. The date when severance occurs in this situation is probably the date of the bankruptcy order.

2   *Mutual agreement*. The leading case here is *Burgess* v *Rawnsley* (1975) (CA) and the student should study it in detail, particularly the judgment of Pennycuick J. In 1967 Mr Honick (H) and Mrs Rawnsley (R) decided to buy a house. They contributed equally to the purchase price and the house was conveyed to them as legal joint tenants to hold on trust for sale for themselves as equitable joint tenants. Thereafter R and H made an oral agreement that R would sell her share to H for £750. Shortly afterwards she changed her mind and told H she was not prepared to sell at that price. H then died and his son claimed his share in the house. His argument was that there had been a severance of the equitable joint tenancy which made H a tenant in

common. In consequence, on his death, his share did not go to R by right of survivorship which is the characteristic of a joint tenancy, but to H's estate to which he, the plaintiff son, was entitled.

The trial judge found that there had been an oral agreement for sale and purchase for £750, and this finding was accepted by the Court of Appeal although not without some reservations.

Did the oral agreement constitute an act of severance? The difficulty was that under s40 LPA 1925 (since repealed) it was unenforceable for want of writing and either party could have withdrawn from it. R contended that because of this it could not constitute severance, citing in support Walton J in *Nielson-Jones* v *Fedden* (1975) who said that conduct cannot amount to severance unless it is irrevocable.

The Court of Appeal *Burgess* v *Rawnsley* held that even though the oral argument was not specifically enforceable, it nevertheless constituted an act of severance because it evinced an intention to sever. To quote Lord Denning, 'it clearly evinced an intention by both parties that the property should henceforth be held in common and not jointly'. Pennycuick J agreed, stating 'the significance of an agreement is not that it binds the parties, but that it serves as an indication of a common intention to sever'.

In the result, therefore, the court held that the plaintiff was entitled to succeed to H's share on the latter's death.

Pennycuick J took the opportunity to clarify the relationship between methods (2) and (3) of *Williams* v *Hensman*. There had always been a doubt as to whether method (3) was a subheading of (2) or whether the two were independent of each other. He expressed the view that 'I do not think that rule 3 [in *Williams* v *Hensman*] is a mere subheading of rule 2. It covers acts of the parties including … negotiations which although not resulting in agreement, indicate a common intention that the joint tenancy should be regarded as severed.'

In *Burgess* v *Rawnsley* the failure to comply with s40 did not render the agreement void but merely unenforceable by action. Section 40 was repealed by the Law of Property (Miscellaneous Provisions) Act 1989 which substituted more stringent requirements that contracts for the sale of land must be made in writing, contain all the contractual terms and be signed by all parties with the consequence that if those requirements were not satisfied the contract was void. Thus, if *Burgess* v *Rawnsley* had been decided today the contract would have been void, not merely unenforceable. Would the result have then been different? It is thought not. The common intention would still have been there, albeit finding expression in a void contract and there would still have been severance. It must be remembered that *Burgess* v *Rawnsley* was not a case where enforcement of the contract was sought.

3   *Course of dealing.* This is the more difficult of the three methods, particularly in relation to its applicability to any given set of facts. Pennycuick J referred to negotiations falling short of agreement but which had reached a point from which it is possible to infer a common intention to sever. It is not always easy to see if that point has been reached and an illustrative case is to be found in *Gore and Snell* v *Carpenter* (1990). Blackett-Ord J found that there had been negotiations but pointed

out that 'negotiations are not the same thing as a course of dealing'. He felt unable to find a common intention to sever.

Each case must be decided on its own facts.

Greenfield v *Greenfield* (1979) is perhaps a surprising case where there was held to have been no course of dealing to amount to severance, although in that case it was stressed that the onus of proof lay on the party asserting severance. Two brothers were joint tenants of a house. They converted it into two flats and lived in them with their families. One brother died and his widow claimed that there had been severance (the conversion amounting to a course of dealing) and that he therefore died as a tenant in common with the consequence that she was entitled to his share. Her claim failed because the court held that had been no severance.

4   *Section 36: notice in writing.* This method was introduced by LPA s36(2). The section does not specify any particular form which the notice must take, nor is there any requirement that it should be signed. The notice, which must be served on all of the other joint tenants by the party wishing to sever, may take a variety of forms and may come into being without it being realised that it could be construed as a notice of severance, particularly in matrimonial disputes: *Re Draper's Conveyance* (1969) and *Harris* v *Goddard* (1983).

In *Re Draper's Conveyance* a husband and wife were joint tenants of the matrimonial home. They divorced and after the decree nisi the wife issued a summons under s17 of the Married Women's Property Act 1882 seeking an order for sale and distribution of the proceeds. The summons was supported by an affidavit by the wife embodying the application. Both were served on the husband. The husband died and the question arose as to whether the wife had severed. If she had then she was a tenant in common at his death and not entitled to his share. Plowman J held that service of the summons and affidavit constituted an act of severance either under method (1) of *Williams* v *Hensman* or under s36(2) LPA 1925. As regards method (1) it amounted to a written declaration of intention to sever which had been communicated to the other party. It should be noticed that this was so even though the wife could have changed her mind and withdrawn the proceedings.

Harris v *Goddard* (1983) was another matrimonial case and one which was argued in the Court of Appeal. Again husband and wife were joint tenants of the matrimonial home. The wife petitioned for a divorce and in her petition prayed that an order be made 'by way of transfer of property and/or settlement of property and/or variation of settlement as may be just'. The husband later died and again the question was: Had there been severance by the wife so as to convert her joint tenancy into a tenancy in common in which case she was not entitled to the husband's share by right of survivorship? The Court of Appeal decided that there had been no severance. Lawton LJ, in discussing s36(2), pointed out that a notice served under s36(2) must take effect forthwith and that it followed that the desire to sever contained in the notice 'must evince an intention to bring about that wanted result immediately. A notice in writing, which expresses a desire to bring about the wanted result at some time in the future … is not a notice in writing s36(2) … paragraph 3 of the prayer in the petition does not more than invite the court to consider at some future time whether to exercise jurisdiction under s24 [MCA 1973] and, if it does so, in one or more of three different ways.' Accordingly, he held, that the prayer and the petition did not amount to a valid s36(2) notice.

He referred also to the consequences set out in s36(2): the notice to be valid must show an intention to bring about the consequences, namely that the net proceeds of the statutory trust for sale 'shall be held upon the trusts which would have been requisite for giving effect to the beneficial interests if there had been actual severance'. A notice which shows no more than a desire to bring the existing interest to an end is not a good notice.

Has Martha severed the joint tenancy between her and Herbert? It is not entirely clear what exactly was in Martha's mind when she wrote to Herbert. Was she writing to him in his capacity as a trustee or was she writing to him in his capacity as a fellow joint tenant in equity? As a trustee he could not respond on his own without the agreement of his fellow trustee, Wilma. If Martha had mind that the property should be mortgaged to raise sufficient money to buy out her share, the mortgage could only be effected by both trustees. The alternative is that she was writing to Herbert in his capacity as an equitable co-owner asking him to buy her share. That would not have been a wise course as it would have the effect of increasing the value of Herbert's share so that it was greater than Wilma's share, as well as destroying the unity of interest between them and making them tenants in common. Martha, not being a lawyer, did not have a clear conception of the implications of her letter, but we must deal with the matter on such facts as we have.

We must consider whether her letter can amount to an act of severance from Herbert. Section 36 requires service of the written notice on all of the joint tenants and she has only written to Herbert. Thus, her letter cannot amount to a s36 notice. There is no mutual agreement between Martha and Herbert; Herbert did not reply. Nor can there be said to have been a course of dealing between them. There only remains method (1) of *Williams* v *Hensman*. This will include a declaration of intention to sever (*Hawksley* v *May*) but it must be in writing: *Burgess* v *Rawnsley*. There is writing here but that writing must evince a clear intention to sever and be intended to take effect immediately. *Harris* v *Goddard* stressed the latter point and although that case was concerned with a s36 written notice it would be an inconsistency if the same did not apply to a written declaration of intention to sever under method (1). It is arguable whether these requirements have been satisfied by Martha's letter. There may or may not have been severance and one must consider the consequences of both alternatives. If there was no severance, then when Martha died her one-third share automatically accrued to both Herbert and Wilma, each taking half of that share. Since their shares remained equal, Wilma and Herbert would continue to remain as joint tenants in equity. However, if Martha's letter to Herbert, sent to him in 1990, amounted to severance of her share from Herbert's then, when she died in 1991, as regards him she died as a tenant in common, but as a joint tenant with Wilma. Her share would therefore go to Wilma by right of survivorship between joint tenants. This would have the effect of doubling Wilma's share in the house and destroying the unity of interest between Wilma and Herbert, thus converting them from joint tenants into tenants in common. Martha's will that Wilma would inherit her property would not in any way operate on Martha's share. Her share would pass to Wilma by virtue of the right of survivorship and not her will.

Neither severance nor the conversion of Wilma's share into a tenancy in common would affect the trusteeship of Herbert and Wilma and the joint tenancy of the legal estate (under s36 LPA 1925 a legal joint tenancy is non-severable).

Wilma wishes to remain in Hersanmyne and she need take no action in order to do so. However, Herbert may well wish for the property to be sold in order to release his share to stave off his creditors. It is open to him to apply to the court under s14 of the 1996 Act for an order for sale. Section 14 replaces s30 LPA 1925, the latter being repealed by the Act. Section 15 sets out the matters which the court is obliged to consider when making an order. Section 15(1)(d) refers to the interests of any secured creditors of any beneficiary but this will not apply here because none of Herbert's creditors appear to be secured. However, other matters in s15 will be relevant: '(a) the intentions of the person or persons … who created the trust, (b) the purposes for which the property subject to the trust is held, and (c) the welfare of any minor who occupies … the land … as his home'.

The purpose of the trust was certainly to provide Herbert, Wilma and Martha with a home. Herbert has gone; Martha has died; Wilma and the children remain. It is highly probably that Herbert and Wilma intended that the house would provide a home for any children they might have. The welfare of Sam, now 16, and Dawn now 13, would need the court's consideration under s15(1)(c).

Under s30 LPA 1925 when the courts had to consider whether land held subject to a trust for sale should be sold there was some inclination towards ordering a sale because of the trustees' duty of sale, but it is thought that this inclination may have been diminished because under a trust of land the trustees are no longer under a duty to sell. Nevertheless, s15 embodies a good deal of the principles developed in the cases decided under s30 and those cases will still be relevant to decisions made by the court under s14.

Although it is not possible to be certain about the outcome of any application by Herbert for an order for sale, Wilma appears to have reasonably strong grounds for resisting the application in view of the s15 matters. It is possible for the court to make an order for sale suspended until both children have attained the age of 18 years and that is a possible outcome in this case.

Although Herbert has not actually been declared bankrupt, the possibility of this occurrence must be considered. If that occurs the position alters. His equitable share would be severed if a joint tenancy and vest in his trustee in bankruptcy who could then make an application under s14 for an order for sale. He would be a person who 'has an interest in property subject to a trust of land'. If such an application is made then s15 has no application (s15(4)) and the court, instead, is obliged to consider the matters set out in s335A of the Insolvency Act 1986 which has been inserted into that act by Sch 3, para 23 of the 1996 Act. The court to whom application must be made is 'the court having jurisdiction in relation to bankruptcy': s335A(1). That court must make an order which it thinks just and reasonable: s335A(2). The subsection then lists a number of matters to which it must have regard in reaching its decision:

'(a) the interests of the bankrupt's creditors;

(b) where the application is made in respect of land which includes a dwelling-house which is or has been the home of the bankrupt or the bankrupt's spouse or former spouse –

(i) the conduct of the spouse or former spouse so far as contributing to the bankruptcy;

(ii) the needs and financial resources of the spouse or former spouse; and

(iii) the needs of the children; and

(c) all the circumstances of the case other than the needs of the bankrupt.'

Section 335A(3) represents the most serious threat to Wilma. If the application by the trustee in bankruptcy is made after the end of the period of one year since Herbert's share became vested in his trustee then 'the court shall assume, unless the circumstances of the case are exceptional, that the interests of the bankrupt's creditors outweigh all other considerations'. In order to escape the impact of this provision Wilma would have to prove exceptional circumstances. Some guidance as to what these can be derived from *Re Citro (A Bankrupt)* (1991). Wilma must hope, therefore, that Herbert manages to avoid bankruptcy because if he does not, then in all probability an order for sale will be made.

In the meantime she need do nothing to preserve the status quo. Any initiative will come from either Herbert seeking a sale or his trustee in bankruptcy. If the house is sold she will be entitled to two-thirds of its value if Martha's letter of 1990 amounted to severance. If it did not then she will be entitled to half of its value.

SUGGESTED ANSWER TO QUESTION FOUR

General Comment

Candidates should notice that this question is another example of how an examiner can combine co-ownership (in this case a resulting trust) with s70(1)(g) Land Registration Act 1925. There is a heavy emphasis on the latter in this question and a detailed knowledge of its practical application is required. The question serves as a reminder that despite the apparent simplicity of the wording of s70(1)(g) it is a good deal more complex than the words suggest. In view of its potential application to a variety of situations in land law, candidates are strongly recommended to pay particular attention to it.

Key Points

- Has Victoria a beneficial interest in the house? – resulting trust?
- Trust of land – Albert sole trustee: Albert and Victoria tenants in common in equity – Albert cannot overreach
- Can Victoria claim an overriding interest under LRA s70(i)(g)? – meaning of actual occupation – is s70(1)(g) based on the doctrine of notice? – conflicting dicta
- Occupation must exist at the time when mortgage was executed (*Abbey National Building Society* v *Cann*) – part occupation under s70(1)(g): *Ferrishurst Ltd* v *Wallcite Ltd*

- Did Victoria know that Albert was going to mortgage to the bank? – *Paddington Building Society* v *Mendelsohn*; *Bristol and West Building Society* v *Henning*; *Abbey National Building Society* v *Cann*

Suggested Answer

Although Victoria provided two-thirds of the purchase monies the transfer was into Albert's sole name. The first question to be answered is: Has she acquired a beneficial interest in the house despite not being on the title?

There appears to be no written declaration of trust by Albert that she should have a beneficial interest in the house. Even if there had been an oral declaration this would be to no effect because s53 LPA 1925 requires such a declaration to be in writing. Since she has made a direct contribution this could give rise to a resulting trust in her favour: *Bull* v *Bull* (1955). Such a trust is based on the presumed intention of the parties. It is a rebuttable presumption but there is no evidence here of rebuttal. The presumption arises when a party not on the title to a purchased property makes a direct financial contribution to the purchase monies. That is the case here with the result that Albert, as a registered proprietor, holds the legal estate on trust for himself and Victoria to the extent of their respective contributions. Since the contributions are unequal they will be equitable tenants in common. The trust is a trust of land under the Trusts of Land and Appointment of Trustees Act 1996. Victoria's equitable interest is overreachable but this did not occur when Albert mortgaged the property to the bank since the mortgage monies were advanced to him as sole trustee. Payment to two trustees (or a trust corporation) is required for overreaching to be effected.

On the assumption that Victoria has a beneficial interest under a resulting trust with Albert being the sole trustee, the question now is: Can she claim that interest to be an overriding interest under s70(1)(g) LRA 1925 binding on the bank? Section 70(1)(g) defines the overriding interest as being:

> '… rights of every person in actual occupation of land … save where enquiry is made of such person and the rights are not disclosed.'

The equitable interest falls within this paragraph: *Williams and Glyn's Bank* v *Boland* (1981). However, can she be said to be a person in actual occupation of the land? The meaning of this phrase requires detailed analysis, particularly here as she did not live on the premises until 8 December. Does her storage of books in one room amount to actual occupation for the purposes of s70(1)(g)?

Lord Denning observed in *Williams and Glyn's Bank* v *Boland* that occupation is a matter of fact, not of law. Whether actual occupation is present or not depends on the nature and condition of the property. 'The paragraph applies to all types, and the acts which constitute actual occupation of a dwelling-house, a garage or woodland cannot all be the same': per Mustill LJ in *Lloyds Bank* v *Rosset* (1989). According to the same judge, it must 'involve some notion of continuity'. He also said 'for want of a better synonym, the person in occupation should be identified as the person who is "there" on the property, although what that entails will be dependent on the nature of the property and the circumstances of the individual case.'

In that case the Court of Appeal considered whether Mrs Rosset was in occupation when she was supervising building works on a semi-derelict farm, the vendor having given permission for such works to be done before completion. She was not living there but attending the site on a day-to-day basis. Nichols and Purchas LJJ decided she was in actual occupation. Mustill LJ said she was not because her presence was not continuous enough.

In *Abbey National Building Society* v *Cann* (1991) it was said that occupation does not necessarily involve the personal presence of the person claiming actual occupation.

Chhokar v *Chhokar* (1984) was a case where the wife claimed that her equitable interest under a trust for sale came within s70(1)(g) although she was temporarily away at the relevant time, having a baby in hospital. Ewbank J held she was in actual occupation because her furniture remained in the house and she intended to return home on her discharge from hospital.

Victoria could argue that her books were an indication of her occupation and that she intended to move in. On the other hand, in *Cann* the claimant argued that she was in occupation at completion because 35 minutes beforehand carpet laying had commenced and furniture and personal belongings had been moved into the house, but the House of Lords decided that this did not amount to occupation. On the whole, Victoria's claim to be in occupation, although arguable, does not look very strong.

The meaning of 'actual occupation' despite its apparent simplicity, has not obtained judicial agreement as to its rationale. In *Strand Securities* v *Caswell* (1965) Lord Denning MR expressed the view that para (g) is simply the doctrine of *Hunt* v *Luck* (1901) brought forward into registered land, ie it is based on the old doctrine of notice. *Hunt* v *Luck* said that a tenant in occupation was constructive notice of his rights. In *Williams and Glyn's Bank* v *Boland* this view was unambiguously rejected by Lords Wilberforce and Scarman. 'It is the fact of occupation that matters,' said Lord Wilberforce, 'no further element is material.' Lord Scarman was even more explicit, stating that 'the statute [the LRA 1925] has substituted a plain factual situation [occupation] for the uncertainties of notice, actual or constructive, as the determinant of an overriding interest.'

One might have thought that would have been the final word but it was not to be. In the Court of Appeal in *Lloyds Bank* v *Rosset*, their Lordships expressed other views: 'The provisions of s70(1)(g) were clearly intended to import into the law relating to registered land, the equitable doctrine of constructive notice': per Purchas LJ. Mustill LJ expressed the view that the legislature must 'have intended to produce a result which did reasonable justice to the bona fide purchaser'.

In *Cann*'s case, Lord Oliver in the Lords stated that 'paragraph 70(1)(g) clearly intended to reflect the rule discussed in *Hunt* v *Luck* with regard to unregistered conveyancing.'

It has to be said, therefore, that the question as to whether occupation has to be of such a nature as to put a purchaser on notice or not remains open, and one which will have to be settled by the House of Lords at some future date. It should be noted that the Law Commission has expressed the view that notice should have no part to play in registered land, but has recommended that the existence of actual occupation should be confined to situations where the person claiming actual occupation is physically present on the land and such presence is reasonably discoverable by a purchaser: *Land Registration for the Twenty-first Century* (1998) (Law Com No 254).

Since Victoria might just be able to argue that her books represented actual occupation (ignoring for the moment the second limb of s70(1)(g) regarding enquiries) the time for occupation must be considered. When must a claimant be in occupation in order to claim the overriding interest? This has now been resolved by *Abbey National Building Society* v *Cann*. Lord Oliver stated that 'The relevant date for determining the *existence* of overriding interests is ... the date of registration', but he went on to ask if that date is also the relevant date for determining whether a claimant to a right (under s70(1)(g)) is in actual occupation, and concluded that the relevant date for *occupation* is the 'date of completion of the transaction by transfer and payment of the purchase money'.

In this case, unusually, the bank advanced the mortgage money in time for the purchase on 1 December, despite the fact that the mortgage had not then been executed and was not executed until 3 December. The mortgage would be of no effect until executed and it must be assumed that completion as regards the mortgage was on 3 December. If Victoria is to claim the benefit of para (g) she must establish that she was in actual occupation, if at all, on that date.

Assuming that the storage of books can constitute actual occupation, does the fact that only one room of the premises was being used for that purpose affect Victoria's claim? It appears from *Ferrishurst Ltd* v *Wallcite Ltd* (1999) that an occupier need not be in occupation of the whole of the land for the purposes of s70(1)(g). Thus, the fact that only one room was being used is not necessarily fatal to Victoria's claim.

The second limb to para (g) must now be examined, ie 'save where enquiry is made of such person [ie the person in actual occupation or in receipt of rents and profits] and the rights are not disclosed.' Whereas the first limb of para (g) protects the rights of a person in actual occupation or in receipt of rents and profits against a purchaser, the second limb provides the purchaser with an escape route. A major difficulty with this second limb is that it pre-supposes that the person in occupation is apparent to a purchaser, otherwise he cannot make the enquiry.

The second limb cannot be treated in isolation from the first limb, and only makes sense if the occupation in the first limb is discoverable by a purchaser which leads to the conclusion that the views of Lords Wilberforce and Scarman are to be rejected in favour of the judicial views expressed in *Lloyds Bank* v *Rosset* and *Abbey National Building Society* v *Cann*. In the latter case Lord Oliver observed 'Conveyancing sense requires that relevant occupation must take a form and must subsist at a time which enables a purchaser to make a purposeful and fruitful enquiry before completion'.

The law is certainly in need of clarification and the views of Lords Wilberforce and Scarman do raise problems as to how the second limb of s70(1)(g) operates. This is particularly obvious in Victoria's case. The mere presence of books would give a purchaser no indication as to whom a purchaser should direct his enquiry. How is he to make enquiry of 'such a person'? This difficulty would perhaps incline the court to conclude that Victoria was not in occupation under the paragraph since if it concluded to the contrary, the second limb would be unworkable. You cannot make enquiry of books.

There is yet a possible further obstacle in Victoria's path. She may have known that Albert needed to borrow £20,000, although we are not expressly told that. Nor is there any suggestion of Albert granting a mortgage of the property to his partner to secure the loan.

We know that Albert was obliged to take a mortgage from the Ripoff bank but it appears unlikely that Victoria knew of this since she was abroad. We must deal with the possibility that she might have been informed by Albert of the necessity for a mortgage. If she did know then the court will impute to her an intention that she intended that any equitable interest she had would be postponed to the interest of the mortgagee: *Paddington Building Society* v *Mendelsohn* (1985); *Bristol and West Building Society* v *Henning* (1985). This issue was further explored by Lord Oliver in *Abbey National Building Society* v *Cann* (1991). Mrs Cann was claiming that her equitable interest was binding on the mortgagee by virtue of s70(1)(g). She had argued that she did not know that her son was going to raise a mortgage to fund the purchase of the property. She knew, however, that there was a shortfall of about £4,000 which would have to be raised somehow and, even if she had no knowledge of the specific mortgage, she nevertheless had given implied consent for the property to be mortgaged. She left it to her son to raise the balance and placed no restriction on the means. She had impliedly consented to postpone her interest to that of the mortgagee. In 1992 the issue was further discussed by the Court of Appeal in *Equity and Law Home Loans Ltd* v *Prestridge* (1992).

The applicability of the principles to Victoria's case is uncertain because we do not know the state of her knowledge about the mortgage to the Ripoff bank.

In response to the question as to whether Victoria's equitable interest will bind the Ripoff bank, although Victoria has an arguable case it does not appear to be a strong one, and her chances of resisting a claim by the bank that it took free of any equitable interest she might have are slim. She therefore faces successful possession proceedings by the bank prior to it selling the property in order to recover its £20,000.

SUGGESTED ANSWER TO QUESTION FIVE

General Comment

A knowledge of resulting and constructive trusts is required to answer this question together with a grasp of the application of the s70(1)(g) Land Registration Act (LRA) 1925. Candidates should note that the topics of co-ownership and s70(1)(g) LRA 1925 can be combined to provide useful material for an examiner.

Key Points

- Co-ownership – beneficial rights in equity of Mr Jones and Martha
- Did the bank take subject to the rights of Mr Jones and Martha? – Mr Jones' rights – resulting trust in his favour? – *Midland Bank plc* v *Cooke*; *Drake* v *Whipp*
- Martha's rights – constructive trust in her favour? – common intention and detriment – *Lloyds Bank* v *Rosset*
- LPA 1925 s70(1)(g) – were they in actual occupation? – *Williams and Glyn's Bank* v *Boland*; *Lloyds Bank* v *Rosset*

• Time of occupation: *Abbey National Building Society* v *Cann*

Suggested Answer

This is a co-ownership question in the context of registered land and Mrs Jones is the sole registered proprietor.

The basic question to be answered is: When the property was mortgaged by Mrs Jones, did Oxter Bank take subject to the rights, if any, of Mr Jones and Martha, or free of them? The first step is to examine their possible rights.

Mr Jones

Has Mr Jones acquired any beneficial interest in the house even though he was not on the title? He has made a direct contribution in money towards the purchase price, amounting to £120,000 (ie 60 per cent). Given this, we must ask if there is any written declaration of trust which complies with s53(1)(b) LPA 1925. This provides that a declaration of trust in respect of land must be manifested and proved by some writing and signed by the declarer of the trust. A good example is to be found in *Goodman* v *Gallant* (1986).

However, there is no evidence here of any written declaration of trust. Since s53 does not apply to resulting or constructive trusts we must now consider if Mr Jones may establish a claim under either of these types of trust.

A resulting trust is based on the presumed intention of the parties. It is a presumption that is rebuttable. The presumption will arise when a party who is not on the title makes a direct contribution to the purchase price, which is the case here. This contribution can be made in various ways, eg payment of, or towards, the deposit, legal costs of the purchase, substantial contributions to the mortgage instalments, etc.

There is nothing to suggest that the presumption of a resulting trust in Mr Jones' favour is rebutted and we may proceed on the basis that he will be successful in establishing a resulting trust. A constructive trust need not therefore be considered.

The next step is to assess the value of his beneficial interest and until relatively recently this was done by a straightforward arithmetical calculation. What was the proportion of the contribution to the purchase? See the Court of Appeal decision in *Springette* v *Defoe* (1992). Applying that case Mr Jones' share should be 60 per cent of the house's value. However, in *Midland Bank plc* v *Cooke* (1995), the Court of Appeal departed from this orthodox approach and adopted a more flexible one. In that case the house was conveyed into the husband's sole name. The purchase price was £8,500 and was funded by a mortgage of £6,450, the shortfall being made up by a wedding gift to the couple of £1,100 by the husband's parents. In the county court the judge found there was a resulting trust and decided that the wife's contribution consisting of half of the wedding gift, ie £550, entitled her to 6.74 per cent of the house's value.

The Court of Appeal, however, decided the wife was entitled to half of the value of the house. It acknowledged that the couple had never discussed what each other's share should be and that there was no evidence available about their intentions on the issue. The Court decided that the proper way to approach the matter was to make an assessment of their prospective proportions on the basis of what the parties were assumed to have intended by looking at the whole course of dealing between them. This was to be preferred to the arithmetical approach of *Springette* v *Defoe*.

Thus, in *Midland* the Court took into account factors which in the past had not been considered: see *Burns* v *Burns* (1984). The wife had provided a home for the family and made improvements to the house and garden. She had brought up three children of the marriage and had paid household bills and helped out with a second mortgage. These factors gave rise to the conclusion, in the view of Waite LJ, that 'one could hardly have a clearer example of a couple who had agreed to share everything equally'. Accordingly, the wife was entitled to half the value of the house.

Whether this departure from established principles relating to quantum will be sustained remains to be seen.

Mention may also be made of another decision of the Court of Appeal, in the same year: *Drake* v *Whipp* (1995). At first instance the county court judge found there was a resulting trust and assessed Drake's share on the orthodox principles of *Springette* v *Defoe* as being 19.4 per cent of the value of the premises (a renovated barn). The Court of Appeal held he was wrong to find that the facts gave rise to a resulting trust and that the appropriate form of trust was a constructive one which enabled the Court to adopt 'a broad breach' approach and take into account factors other than her financial contribution. She had done work on the barn's renovations and conversion as well as contributed to the household expenses. She was, therefore, the Court concluded, entitled to one-third of the barn's value.

The Court emphasised the importance of maintaining the distinction between resulting and constructive trusts. The distinction was relevant to quantum since different results could be arrived at depending on which was applicable. This judicial reminder was timely since some confusion had been developing in the area for some time with, on occasions, the difference between the two becoming blurred.

The domestic factors that were considered relevant in *Cooke* do not apply here and in the event of litigation the most likely outcome is that Mr Jones' share will be assessed according to the orthodox principles of *Springette* v *Defoe*. However, he was a joint recipient of Martha's wedding gift of £20,000 which in effect increases his £120,000 contribution by half that sum (£10,000) to £130,000. Thus, his equitable share will be 65 per cent.

Martha

The gift of £20,000 was an outright gift without any intention that she should acquire thereby a beneficial interest in the house and it may therefore be discounted.

The payment of £30,000 for the extension is, however, an entirely different matter and should be approached as follows. Was there any express written agreement that she should have an interest in the house, or any written declaration of trust which complied with s53 LPA 1925? There is no such evidence on those issues and the possibility of a constructive trust must now be considered.

The next step to consider is whether there was any oral expression of common intention by Mrs Jones and Martha that she should have a beneficial interest in the house. Again there is no evidence about this. If there had been such an expression of common intention, this of itself would not have been sufficient because of s53. Martha would then have had to establish that she had acted to her detriment in reliance on it, thereby giving rise to a constructive trust to which s53 does not apply. *Grant* v *Edwards* (1986) and *Eves* v *Eves* (1975) provide good examples of this type of situation.

In *Grant*, which was a co-habitation case, the house was in the defendant's sole name, and he told the plaintiff that the reason for this was that if he put her name on the title her matrimonial proceedings might be prejudiced. The Court of Appeal held that the defendant's explanation as to why the plaintiff was being excluded from the title was evidence of the common intention that her substantial indirect payments towards the mortgage payments were sufficient to constitute conduct upon which she could not have been reasonably expected to embark unless she expected to have a beneficial interest in the house. The Court held that she was entitled to a half share in the house.

In *Eves*, the facts were similar. The excuse that the defendant gave for not putting the plaintiff's name on the title was that she was not yet 21 years of age. Again this was regarded by the court as evidence of common intention. The conduct of the plaintiff in relying on that common intention consisted of considerable manual work on the house. The two factors combined to give rise to a constructive trust, with the plaintiff being entitled to a quarter share in the value of the house.

In Martha's case, we are told that Mr and Mrs Jones invited Martha to go and live with them 'and she agreed to pay for the construction of an extension to the house for her occupation'. There is nothing in those facts to indicate a common intention that Martha should have a share in the house.

In *Grant* Nourse LJ indicated that in the absence of an express oral common intention, such an intention may nevertheless be inferred from conduct. Such conduct he said, is almost invariably constituted by expenditure of money referable to the acquisition of the house. This would be applicable to an extension of the house. In this type of case the conduct performs two roles: it provides evidence of common intention and constitutes the plaintiff's detrimental reliance on that common intention.

Further guidance in this situation may be derived from Lord Bridge's judgment in *Lloyds Bank* v *Rosset* (1991). He pointed out that the conduct of the plaintiffs in *Grant* and *Eves*, while being sufficient to constitute detrimental reliance, would not have been sufficient to prove a common intention. Fortunately for the plaintiffs in those cases there was, in each case, oral expression of common intention and it was not necessary to infer intention from their conduct. Referring to the type of conduct from which common intention could be inferred in the absence of express common intention he said:

'Direct contributions to the purchase price whether mutually or by payment of mortgage instalments will readily justify the inference … but it is extremely doubtful if anything less will do.'

Martha has made a direct contribution in money and this would enable her to claim a share in the house's value based on either a resulting trust or a constructive trust. In the latter case the common intention between her and Mrs Jones can be inferred from the direct payment of money and it would also constitute conduct amounting to detrimental reliance.

As regards quantum this seems straightforward in this case. Martha will probably be entitled to a share on the proceeds of sale in the same ratio that £30,000 bore to the value of the house at the time that the contribution was made in 1994/95.

Having discussed the respective rights of Mr Jones and Martha it remains to consider whether the bank took subject to them and this necessitates an examination of the applicability of s70(1)(g) LRA 1925.

That equitable rights are embraced by s70(1)(g) is clear from *Williams and Glyn's Bank* v *Boland* (1981). The next step is to consider the question of 'actual occupation' since 70(1)(g) states the 'rights of every person in actual occupation'.

It is therefore necessary to define what is meant by 'actual occupation', particularly as Mr Jones and Martha were not physically present when the house was mortgaged in 1996, and also the time when claimants under 70(1)(g) need to be in actual occupation if they are to claim its protection. 'Actual occupation' was discussed in *Williams and Glyn's Bank* v *Boland* and *Lloyds Bank* v *Rosset*. In the latter case it only received attention in the Court of Appeal since the point was not discussed in the Lords.

In the former case, Lord Wilberforce said the words meant that physical presence was required and he was emphatic that such physical presence did not need to be of a nature which would put a purchaser on enquiry. Lord Scarman echoed this view and both declared that s70(1)(g) was not based on notice. All that was needed for the application of s70(1)(g) was the plain fact of occupation, and this was a matter of fact and not of law.

However this is not as simple as it seems. In *Lloyds Bank* v *Rosset* it was pointed out in the Court of Appeal that whether there was occupation depended on the nature and condition of the land. In that case the wife claimed to be in occupation of land which was in a derelict condition and which she attended on a daily basis to supervise building works. She did not sleep on the premises and could not be described as living there. Nevertheless Nichols and Purchas LJJ thought she was in occupation. Mustill LJ disagreed; he thought her presence was intermittent. In *Stockholm Finance Ltd* v *Garden Holdings Inc* (1995) Walker J admitted the difficulties. Absence from the premises, eg a holiday, does not mean a person has ceased to be in occupation. The reason for, and length of, absence must be considered.

In *Chhokar* v *Chhokar* (1984) the wife was in hospital having a baby. The furniture was still in the house and she fully intended to return. Ewbank J held that she was in actual occupation and so absence of physical presence at the relevant time is not fatal. There must, it appears, be an element of stability as well as continuity of presence, although continuous presence is not required. It is a matter of degree and each case must be decided on its merits.

It is probable that Mr Jones and Martha would be regarded as still in occupation despite their embarkation on a cruise. There is no suggestion that their belongings have been cleared away and they certainly had the intention to return.

The final issue to be considered relates to the time of occupation. In registered land there are two stages in a purchase or mortgage transaction – completion and registration in the land registry of the transaction which must occur within two months of completion. In *Abbey National Building Society* v *Cann* (1991) Lord Oliver said that 'the relevant date for determining the existence of overriding interests ... is the date of registration'. He went on to hold that 'actual occupation' in para (g) refers to the date of completion and that actual occupation must exist at that date.

Thus, for Mr Jones and Martha to claim that their interests are binding on the bank under s70(1)(g) they must establish that they were in occupation at the date of completion of the mortgage and given that in all probability they were, the bank will take subject to their rights.

4

Leases

Introduction

The first two questions deal with basic material. The differences between legal and equitable leases must be understood, as must be the different treatment of them in unregistered and registered land.

The lease/licence debate continues despite *Street* v *Mountford* and can still be the subject of an examination question.

The running of benefits and burdens of leasehold covenants forms a very important part of leasehold law and the position both before and after the Landlord and Tenant (Covenants) Act 1995 must be known. Further, although the 1995 Act only applies in general to leases created on or after 1 January 1996, the two important retrospective provisions discussed in Question 3 must not be overlooked. Students are also reminded that it is not enough to discuss whether an assignee of a lease is in breach of covenant, the landlord's remedies must also be described. Candidates should be aware that the remedies for breach of covenants to pay rent are different from the remedies for breaches of other covenants and in particular that s146 LPA 1925 has no application to the former.

Questions

INTERROGRAMS

1 What is meant by the phrase 'term of years absolute'?
2 What is a perpetually renewable lease?
3 In 1997 L leased Blackacre to T for seven years 'if he shall so long live'. What is the effect of this disposition?
4 Define the term 'demise'.
5 What is a fine?
6 Define the term 'reversion'.
7 What is a reversionary lease?
8 Can legal estates subsist concurrently?
9 Define the phrase 'in possession'.

QUESTION ONE

'An agreement for a lease is as good as a lease.'
   Discuss

Prepared by the author

QUESTION TWO

'Since *Street* v *Mountford* the lease/licence distinction has ceased to cause problems for the courts.'

Discuss.

University of London LLB Examination
(for external students) Land Law June 1998 Q8

QUESTION THREE

In 1994 John granted Tim a lease of Blackacre House for a term of ten years, Tim covenanting (1) to pay a quarterly rent of £5,000, (2) to use the house for residential purposes only, and (3) to maintain the house in a good state of repair. Late in 1996 Tim assigned his lease to Alf who then, in February 1997, granted a three-year sublease to Stan. Since Tim assigned his lease John has received no rent and the house has been allowed to fall into disrepair. Stan is proposing to open a travel agency in the house.

Advise John. Would your advice be the same if John had granted Tim the lease in January 1996?

London University LLB Examination
(for external students) Land Law June 1997 Q3 (as amended by the author)

QUESTION FOUR

In 1987 L, the freeholder of a small shopping arcade, granted a lease of one of the shops to T for 30 years. In the lease T covenanted:

a   not to assign or underlet without L's consent;
b   not to compete with the greengrocery business which L carried on in another of his shops; and
c   to keep the premises in good repair.

L reserved a right of re-entry for breach of covenant. In 1995 T sought permission to sub-let to ST for seven years but L refused giving no reason. T nevertheless granted the sub-lease to ST; the sub-lease contained the above three covenants and reserved a right of re-entry to T. L has now sold and conveyed the freehold to NL who has discovered the existence of the sub-lease and also that ST is selling greengrocery and that the premises are in need of repair.

Advise NL.

London University LLB Examination
(for external students) Land Law June 1986 Q5

Answers

ANSWERS TO INTERROGRAMS

1   This phrase denotes a legal lease and is defined in s205(1)(xxvii) LPA 1925 as:

> '... a term of years (taking effect in possession or in reversion whether or not at a rent) ... subject or not to another legal estate, and either certain or liable to determination by notice, re-entry, operation of law ... and in this definition the expression "term of years" includes a term for less than a year, or for a year or years or a fraction of a year or from year to year.'

Note: a term of years absolute is one of the two estates capable of subsisting at law: s1(1)(b) LPA 1925.

It might be thought that the word 'absolute' has the same meaning as 'absolute' in the term 'fee simple absolute in possession'. There it means that a fee simple estate has been granted without any conditions or provisos. Compare it with modified fee simples: determinable fee simple and a fee simple defeasible by condition subsequent. In these cases the fee simple may determine on the occurrence of an event specified in the grant and they are known as modified fee simples. A fee simple which is absolute contains no provision which may bring it to an end. Therefore it continues in perpetuity.

The word 'absolute' in the phrase 'term of years absolute' cannot mean this because the definition itself provides that it is 'liable to determination by notice, re-entry, operation of law'.

The fact is that the word has no meaning at all and is superfluous. It neither adds to nor subtracts from the definition.

2   A perpetually renewable lease is one which contains a clause giving the tenant the option to renew the lease on identical terms or 'on the same terms and conditions'. Thus, if the tenant chose to exercise the option the new lease would contain the same terms including the option to renew. The tenant therefore could renew the lease indefinitely so that the landlord might never regain possession of the premises. Section 145 LPA 1922 and Schedule 15 converted such leases into leases for 2,000 years. Such leases can only be terminated by the tenant and he must do so by giving not less than ten days' notice to the landlord, expiring on any of the dates on which the converted lease could have been renewed.

A good example of the wording which creates perpetually renewable leases is to be found in *Parkus* v *Greenwood* (1950). Here, a lease for three years included a clause that 'the lessor will, on the request of the tenant, grant him a tenancy at the same rent containing the like provisions as are herein contained including the present covenant for renewal.'

The court leans against finding a perpetually renewable lease: *Marjorie Burnett Ltd* v *Barclay* (1980).

3   No mention is made as to whether the lease is granted for either a rent or a fine (premium). If there is a provision for rent or a fine then s149(6) LPA 1925 is applicable:

'Any lease ... at a rent, or ... a fine, for life or lives or for any term of years determinable with life or lives, or on the marriage of the lessee ... shall take effect as a lease ... for a term of ninety years determinable after the death or marriage (as the case may be) of the original lessee, or of the survivor of the original lessees, by at least one month's notice in writing ...'.

The lease to T takes effect as a lease for ninety years not seven years, a result which L doubtless did not contemplate. He or his successors can only terminate the lease when T or his successor dies, which may not occur until a date much later than seven years from the date when the lease was created.

Section 149(6) is a serious trap for unwary landlords.

4   This is a term of some antiquity and is referred to by Coke in 2 Inst 483. In *Greenaway* v *Adams* (1806) it was said that 'the strict technical import of "demise" from the verb "dimitto" is any transfer or conveyance; although by habit it is generally used to denote a partial transfer by way of lease.'

Today it is used as an alternative word to 'lease'. The premises subject to the lease are sometimes described as the demised premises.

5   This is a capital sum payable on the grant of a lease. The word appears in the 1925 legislation. Nowadays the word 'premium' is used in place of the rather old-fashioned word 'fine'.

6   When a landlord grants a lease he is said to retain the reversion. It is indicative of his right to recover possession of the premises at the termination of the lease. The word comes from the Latin verb 'revertere' which means to go back to. Possession goes back to the landlord at the lease's termination.

The landlord, if he is a head landlord, holds the fee simple absolute in possession, ie he is the freeholder. When he sells the fee simple (freehold), he is often described as assigning the reversion. This is not strictly speaking a correct description because he is assigning more than the reversion as defined in the first paragraph above. Nevertheless it is a description in common usage.

7   A lease may be granted either in possession or in reversion: s205(1)(xxvii) LPA 1925. A lease taking effect in possession commences immediately it is executed and the tenant is entitled to enter in possession at once. A reversionary lease, by contrast, is one limited to commence at some future date, although this date cannot be postponed for more than 21 years from the date of the instrument purporting to create it if the lease is for a rent or in consideration of a fine: s149(3) LPA 1925. If it does, it is void.

8   One of the great advantages of the English doctrine of estates is that it enables different persons to hold different estates in the same piece of land at the same time. A good example of this is provided by a legal lease. The landlord holds the fee simple absolute in possession (for 'in possession' see Interrogram 9), while at the same time the tenant holds, in the same piece of land, the estate known as the term of years absolute.

The fee simple absolute in possession and the term of years absolute are the only two estates capable of subsisting at law: s1(1) LPA 1925. 'All other estates, interests, and charges in or over land take effect as equitable interests': s1(3) LPA 1925.

9   This has a more extended meaning than is to be found in everyday usage. It is defined in s205(1)(xix) LPA 1925 as including 'receipt of rents and profits or the right to receive the same'. This definition explains why a landlord who has granted a lease with exclusive possession to a tenant can be described as having a fee simple absolute in possession even though he is not in physical possession. His right to receive rent from the tenant brings him within this definition of 'in possession'. Were he not in possession he could not be described as having a fee simple absolute in possession in consequence of which he could not have a legal estate but only an equitable interest: s1(3) LPA 1925.

SUGGESTED ANSWER TO QUESTION ONE

General Comment

This is a basic question requiring an appreciation of the difference between a legal and an equitable lease, which is an important distinction in land law, particularly for purchasers. The position of equitable leases in unregistered and registered land must be carefully noted.

Key Points

- Creation of legal leases – necessity for a deed (s52 LPA) – exception: s54 LPA 1925
- Creation of an equitable lease – necessity of writing (Law of Property (Miscellaneous Provisions) Act 1989) – equity may regard a lease in writing as an agreement (or contract) to create a legal lease – ingredients of a valid contract must be present – must be one which equity will enforce by specific performance – 'equity looks on that as done which ought to be done'
- Source of the quotation in the question – misunderstanding of *Walsh* v *Lonsdale*
- The disadvantages of an equitable lease: does not always bind third parties (purchasers) – unregistered/registered land – specific performance – an equitable remedy which is discretionary – an equitable lease is not a 'conveyance' for purposes of s62 LPA 1925 – the passing of benefits and burdens of leasehold covenants – there must be privity of estate for the rules to operate – they do not apply to equitable leases because there is no privity of estate between parties to an equitable lease

Suggested Answer

A legal lease, or term of years absolute as defined by s205(1)(xxvii) LPA 1925, is one of the two estates capable of subsisting at law: s1(1) LPA 1925. A legal lease binds the whole world.

A legal lease must be created by deed. Section 52(1) LPA 1925 provides that 'All conveyances of land or of any interest therein are void for the purpose of conveying or creating a legal estate unless made by deed.'

Section 54(2) provides a dispensation from this general requirement in the cases of leases not exceeding three years. If it takes effect in possession at the best rent reasonably obtainable without taking a fine (premium) then it will be legal even if created by parol (orally); neither a deed nor writing is necessary.

A lease made for longer than three years without a deed cannot be legal. It does not comply with s52 and nor does it come within s54(2). In such a case equity may intervene and treat the parties' arrangement as a contract to create a legal lease (*Parker v Taswell* (1858)), enforceable by the equitable remedy of specific performance. Obviously all the essential ingredients of a valid contract must be present before equity can intervene. Further, the provisions of Law of Property (Miscellaneous Provisions) Act 1989 must be satisfied. That statute, repealing s40 LPA 1925, provides that contracts for the sale or other disposition of an interest in land must be made in writing, contain all the terms of the contract and be signed by all of the parties. The contract is void and of no effect in the event of non-compliance with these provisions. Thus, unless there is a written lease complying with the requirements of the statute, equity can do nothing.

In determining, therefore, whether a lease is legal or equitable, consideration must be given to the following matters:

1   How has the lease been created? By deed, writing or parol? Candidates must distinguish between the first two. The 1989 Act abolished the need for deeds to be sealed. It is enough if they are signed and delivered. With the abolition of the seal, a deed must declare itself as such. Deeds generally open with the words: 'This deed is made between ...'. Alternatively, it may contain a clause declaring that it is a deed. All deeds are in writing but not all written documents are deeds. The distinction between deeds and mere writing is a fundamental factor in deciding whether a lease is legal or equitable.
2   If there is no deed, consider next the length of the lease, because if it does not exceed three years it may be eligible to be legal under s54(2).
3   If there is no deed but the lease exceeds three years, are the ingredients of a valid contract present and is there writing to comply with the 1989 Act? If so equity will treat the parties as having entered into a contract for the granting of a legal lease, providing the agreement is one which it will enforce by specific performance. It must be remembered that specific performance, being an equitable remedy, is in the discretion of the court which is exercised on well recognised principles. If the agreement is one for which the court would not decree specific performance, then it is of no effect in equity.

Equity will then go one stage further. Applying the maxim 'Equity looks on that as done which ought to be done', it will treat the parties as being in the relationship of landlord and tenant and they may be said, therefore, to have an equitable lease.

Thus, equity may acknowledge the existence of a lease which common law does not, and it may be asked if it matters whether a lease has been granted at law if equity will step in and recognise it in default of the common law so doing. Speculation along these lines arose after the decision of *Walsh* v *Lonsdale* in 1882. In his *Lectures on Equity* (1909), F W Maitland remarks on p161, 'I have heard remarks upon *Walsh* v *Lonsdale* which seemed to imply that since the Judicature Act an agreement for a lease is in all respects as good as a lease.' He goes on to say 'Now Jessel [MR] certainly did not say this, and to say it would certainly be untrue. An agreement for a lease is not equal to a [legal] lease.' Maitland was referring to a passage from Jessel's judgment which could be misunderstood, giving rise to an interpretation that an agreement for a lease is as good as a legal lease, and he says of the words in the passage: 'Now I am not sure that these words are not a little misleading'.

Thus, although *Walsh* v *Lonsdale* gave rise to speculation on this point, such speculation must be rejected as false since there are four respects in which an agreement for a lease (or an equitable lease) is inferior to a legal lease. Before coming to those, *Walsh* v *Lonsdale* must be examined. In that case L agreed in writing to let a mill to W for seven years. It was not a legal lease for want of a deed but it was equitable. One of the terms of the lease was that one year's rent was payable in advance if so demanded by the landlord. W entered into possession with L's consent and paid rent quarterly in arrears. L then demanded a year's rent in advance. W refused to pay and L then levied distress. W sued L for unlawful distress.

W's argument was that he was holding under a legal yearly tenancy by reason of his going into possession and paying rent on a quarterly (quarter of a year) basis and that the term in the written lease entitling L to demand a year's rent in advance was not incorporated into his yearly lease since it was inconsistent with the common law rule that a yearly lease is determinable by six months' notice.

The issue for the Court of Appeal was: which lease ought to prevail? The equitable lease on which L relied or the yearly tenancy for which W argued?

Section 25 of the Judicature Act 1873 provided that where law and equity were a conflict, equity prevailed and, applying that provision, the Court of Appeal held that W's equitable lease prevailed over the yearly legal lease and in consequence L was entitled to levy distress for a year's rent in advance.

The four disadvantages of an equitable lease will now be considered:

1   A legal lease automatically binds the whole world. If a purchaser buys land subject to a legal lease he takes subject to it, regardless of whether he knows of it or not. Under the Land Registration Act 1925 a legal lease granted for a term not exceeding 21 years is an overriding interest: s70(1)(k).

There is no such guarantee of inviolability in the case of an equitable lease. In unregistered land, an equitable lease is a land charge, class C(iv): s2(4) LCA 1972. If registered in the Land Charges Register registration is notice to the whole world (s198 LPA 1925) and a purchaser takes subject to it regardless of his lack of knowledge of it or his failure to search the register. If there is a failure to register, then the equitable lease is void against a purchaser of the legal estate in the land for money or money's worth (s4(6) LCA 1972), and this, despite his actual knowledge of it: *Hollington Bros* v *Rhodes* (1951); *Midland Bank Trust Co Ltd* v *Green* (1981).

In the case of registered land, an equitable lease does not appear in the list of overriding interests in s70(1) LRA 1925, and accordingly it is a minor interest and should be protected by entry of a notice on the landlord's register of title. Failing this protection, it will be void against a purchaser of the legal estate and land for valuable consideration: s20(1) LRA 1925.

However, in contrast to the position in unregistered land, there is a safety net if for some reason a notice is not entered on the register. The equitable lease may be re-classified as an overriding interest under s70(1)(g) LRA 1925 providing the requirements of that paragraph are satisfied, eg the tenant is in occupation.

Thus, as can be seen, there are occasions when an equitable lease will not bind a purchaser and it will then be lost beyond possibility of revival.

2   Equity will treat the written lease as an agreement or contract to create a legal lease, assuming all the ingredients of a valid contract are present, and providing it is one which the court will enforce by a decree of specific performance. Specific performance will not be granted if damages would be an adequate remedy but this will not normally apply in cases of contracts for the transfer of land. The decree is almost invariably granted in such cases but it remains, nevertheless, a discretionary remedy, ie it cannot be claimed as of right. If the court considers that the tenant has not come to equity 'with clean hands' as a result of some form of unconscionable behaviour on his part (*Coatworth* v *Johnson* (1886)), or he is in breach of his covenants, his application may well be refused. If the granting of the decree would operate to the prejudice of three parties, it could also be refused.

Thus, an equitable tenant's position is not as secure as one holding under a legal lease.

3   An equitable lease is not a conveyance for the purposes of s62 LPA 1925. Section 62(1) LPA 1925 provides that:

> 'A conveyance of land shall be deemed to include and … operate to convey with the land all buildings, erections, fixtures … liberties, privileges, easements, rights and advantage whatsoever, appertaining or reputed to appertain, to the land or any part thereof'.

And s62(4) states: 'This section applies only if, and as far as, a contrary intention is not expressed in the conveyance'.

The section is only applicable to a 'conveyance of land' as defined by s205(1)(ii) LPA 1925 which means that a conveyance is constituted by any writing which transfers or creates a legal estate in land. Normally this means the writing must take the form of a deed: s52(1) LPA 1925.

There are exceptions to the requirement for a deed in s52(2), eg assents made by a personal representative. Note also s54(2), under which a legal lease may be created, by parol, providing it takes effect in possession, does not exceed three years and is for the best rent reasonably obtainable without taking a fine (premium). An oral lease made under this provision would be legal but it would not come within the definition of a 'conveyance' because of the absence of writing. If the lease was in writing it would come within the definition of a 'conveyance of land'.

An equitable lease cannot be a 'conveyance' because it does not confer upon the tenant a legal estate in land: *Borman* v *Griffith* (1930).

If there is no 'conveyance' then recourse may be had to *Wheeldon* v *Burrows* (1879).

Section 62 LPA 1925 is considered in more detail in Chapter 5.

4   In leasehold law the benefit and burdens of leasehold covenants may pass on assignments of the reversion and the lease if certain conditions are satisfied. However, the present discussion will be limited to the leases created before 1 January

1996 when the Landlord and Tenant (Covenants) Act 1995 came into force. The conditions referred to are:

a   the covenant must touch and concern the land; and
b   between the respective assignees, ie the assignee of the reversion and the assignee of the lease, there must be 'privity of estate'. This can only apply to parties to a legal lease since only the tenant of a legal lease can have an estate in land. The tenant of an equitable lease has no legal estate in the land, only an equitable interest. Thus, the provisions indicated above have no applicability to an equitable lease.

In *Boyer* v *Warbey* (1953) Denning LJ argued that because of the Judicature Act 1873 'since the fusion of law and equity, the position is different', and he went on to say that because the distinction between agreements under hand and covenants under seal has been largely obliterated, there was no reason why the rules governing the passing of benefits and burdens of a legal lease should not apply to equitable leases.

This does not represent the orthodox position and it is not accurate to describe the Judicature Act as fusing law and equity. The Act fused the administration of law and equity, not the rules themselves.

Thus, as has been demonstrated, an agreement for a lease cannot be considered as good as a lease.

SUGGESTED ANSWER TO QUESTION TWO

General Comment

This question is about developments after *Street* v *Mountford* but it does require some knowledge of the previous law in order to explain its significance. Candidates need to be familiar with Lord Templeman's judgment, but the emphasis of the answer must be on subsequent cases as these reveal the limits of the decision and the problems it left unresolved.

Key Points

- Reasons for the importance of the distinction between leases and licences – statutory provisions and third parties
- The development of the law regarding the distinction
- *Lynes* v *Snaith*
- *Errington* v *Errington*
- *Street* v *Mountford*
- Although *Street* v *Mountford* clarified the law, it left unanswered questions – it did not deal with shared occupancies (*Hadjiloucas* v *Crean*)
- *AG Securities* v *Vaughan* showed that Lord Templeman's test (a tenant or a lodger?) to be inadequate
- *Antoniades* v *Villiers*
- Conclusion – the statement in the question is not accurate

Suggested Answer

The distinction between a lease and a licence has been of fundamental importance for a number of years for basically two reasons:

1 legislative provisions conferring on tenants various important rights not enjoyed by licensees; and
2 the different effects of leases and licences on third parties.

Taking the legislative provisions first, the Rent Acts conferred on domestic tenants considerable security of tenure and the benefits of controlled rents: see the Rent Act 1977. These measures were, of course, unpopular with landlords who sought to evade them by granting licences to occupants instead, which did not come within the ambit of the Acts. The Housing Acts of 1988 and 1996 went a long way to alleviating landlords' problems in this respect by allowing them to grant assured tenancies which did not give the tenants anywhere near the same degree of security of tenure. Moreover, the control of rents was considerably reduced. Under these statutes, therefore, landlords were enabled to grant tenancies (as opposed to licences) without the considerable disadvantages which attached to tenancies created under the earlier Rent Acts.

As far as domestic tenancies are concerned then, the importance of the distinction between leases and licences has considerably diminished and landlords need no longer fear the consequences of granting tenancies under the Housing Acts referred to.

Legislation also conferred rights on business and agricultural tenants which landlords considered detrimental to their interests (see the Landlord and Tenant Act 1954 and the Agricultural Holdings Act 1986), although the Agricultural Tenancies Act of 1995 has reduced the degree of security of tenure conferred upon business tenancies.

In 1967 the Leasehold Reform Act gave tenants holding a long lease of a house the right to purchase the freehold. The Leasehold Reform, Housing and Urban Development Act 1993 extended this right to tenants of flats.

The efforts of landlords to create licences instead of tenancies so as to avoid the effects of the legislative provisions embracing the latter, has led to much litigation between landlords and occupants in which the landlords have sought to argue that the occupant was a contractual licensee while the occupant argued that he was a tenant. This litigation will be examined later.

The distinction between a lease and a licence is also important as regards third parties. If a lease is legal it will automatically bind a third party (a purchaser of the reversion). In the case of registered land, it will either be an overriding interest under s70(1)(k) LRA 1925 or registered with its own substantive title. If equitable, in the case of unregistered land, it will bind a purchaser if registered under the LCA 1972 as a land charge, class C(iv). In the case of registered land, it should be protected as a minor interest by entry of a notice on the landlord's register of title. Failing that protection it may bind a purchaser if it falls within s70(1)(g) LRA 1925.

If, on the other hand, the occupant only enjoys a contractual licence, none of the foregoing applies. The traditional view is that licences, being personal, do not bind purchasers: *King* v *David Allen & Sons Billposting Ltd* (1916). In rare instances contractual licences have been held to bind third parties through the medium of a constructive trust (see *Binions* v *Evans* (1972)), although there are limits to this as pointed out in *Ashburn Anstalt* v *Arnold* (1988).

The evolution of the law dealing with the distinction between leases and licenses will now be examined in stages.

In 1899 the distinction was clear: if the occupant enjoyed exclusive possession he was a tenant; if not, he was a licensee: *Lynes* v *Snaith* (1899). However, the straightforward distinction became blurred in *Errington* v *Errington* (1952) when Denning LJ held that a licensee could also enjoy exclusive possession and as a result the volume of litigation on the issue increased. Attention then focused on the question: What did the parties intend: a lease or a licence? If the intention was not clear it had to be deduced from the surrounding circumstances of the case. The description applied to the arrangement was a factor to be taken into account but it was not conclusive.

In the 1970s life became more difficult for landlords, with the further extension of protection to tenants. Furnished tenancies came within the ambit of protection and even occupants enjoying exclusive occupation under a contractual licence. Lawyers advising landlords began to develop agreements which did not confer inclusive possession on occupants. It will be appreciated than an essential characteristic of a lease is exclusive possession. Without it there can be no lease.

If an arrangement could be established where there were two occupants, neither of whom had exclusive possession, then such an arrangement could not be a lease and this idea was ingeniously developed in *Somma* v *Hazelhurst* in 1978, which was upheld by the Court of Appeal, despite the artificiality of the arrangement.

The next stage was reached by the House of Lords in *Street* v *Mountford* (1985) which was a case of a domestic tenancy. This case clarified the law considerably and went a long way to clear up the confusion which had developed since *Errington* v *Errington*.

It is clear that the parties in *Street* v *Mountford* intended to create a licence. The document they signed leaves no doubt about it, but Lord Templeman was not impressed. Acknowledging the parties' freedom to contract, he went on to point out that:

> '... the consequences in law of the agreement ... can only be determined by consideration of the effect of the agreement. If the agreement satisfied all the requirements of a tenancy, then the agreement produced a tenancy and the parties cannot alter the effect of the agreement by insisting that they only created a licence.'

He summarised the position in these words: 'the only intention which is relevant is the intention demonstrated by the agreement to grant exclusive possession for a term at a rent.' That intention was obviously present and accordingly there was a lease, not a licence.

He agreed that it is not always easy to find whether exclusive possession had been conferred or not, and that if there had been it was possible that it might be that the right to exclusive possession was referable to a legal relationship other than a tenancy, eg where exclusive possession was given to a purchaser under a contract of sale of land, or where it was enjoyed pursuant to a contract of employment. It may be, he noted, that the parties did not intend to enter into a legal relationship. In that case there would be no lease.

Thus, exclusive possession, although necessary for the existence of a tenancy, does not inevitably result in one. He refers to rent but strictly speaking this is not a necessary ingredient for a tenancy because of the wording of the definition of a term of years absolute in s205(1)(xxvii) LPA 1925, ie 'a term of years (taking effect either in possession or in reversion whether or not at a rent)'. As Fox LJ pointed out in *Ashburn Anstalt* v *Arnold* (1988) Lord Templeman was not saying you cannot have a tenancy without rent. What he was saying was that where you had exclusive possession for a term at a rent, this was a tenancy unless there was no intention to create legal relations or the exclusive possession was referable to some other relationship between the parties.

The decision in *Street* v *Mountford* unquestionably meant that thereafter it would be much more difficult for landlords to assert that they had only conferred upon their occupants a licence. Of the three ingredients listed by Lord Templeman, two are inevitably present: a term and rent. If exclusive possession is also present then, in the absence of a legal relationship other than landlord and tenant, there will be a tenancy assuming there is an intention to create a legal relationship.

However, although *Street and Mountford* provided much needed clarification of this area of law, it did not provide for every situation. Three points should be noted:

1   exclusive occupation was not disputed in that case;
2   there was only one occupant (Mrs Mountford); and
3   it did not deal with commercial occupancies. It was a case concerned with a residential occupancy.

Also, it did not deal with cases of shared occupancy. Those cases are much more complex than cases of sole occupation as Mustill LJ pointed out in the later case of *Hadjiloucas* v *Crean* in 1988. In such cases:

'The choice is not simply between licence and tenancy, but rather a three-fold choice between a licence and two different kinds of tenancy. One kind will involve a pair of parallel tenancies, each between the landlord and one tenant, in relation to an identifiable separate portion of the premises; the other will consist of a single tenancy for the whole of the premises with the two occupiers as joint tenants of the whole'.

Moreover, he noted, *Street* v *Mountford* gave no indication as to the manner in which the intention to create exclusive possession should be ascertained since the landlord in that case conceded that Mrs Mountford, the occupant, enjoyed exclusive possession. He observed that:

'Sometimes the task is straightforward and sometimes it will be difficult … sometimes a meticulous perusal of the document will be required … on other occasions it will not. The surrounding circumstances will always be material on this point as well as on the questions of sham and the intention to create legal relations. *Street* v *Mountford* does not itself explain how the exercise is to be performed.'

Two important cases of 1988, both concerned with shared occupation must now be examined: *AG Securities* v *Vaughan* and *Antoniades* v *Villiers*. Both were decided by the House of Lords.

In *AG Securities* v *Vaughan* the appellants owned a block of flats, one of which contained six rooms in addition to a kitchen and bathroom. They furnished four rooms as bedrooms, a fifth as a lounge and the sixth as a sitting-room and entered into short-term agreements with four individuals, each referred to in the relevant agreement as a 'licensee'.

The agreements were made at different times and on different terms and were normally for six months' duration. Each agreement provided that the licensee had 'the right to use [the flat] in common with others who have or may from time to time be granted the like right … but without the right to exclusive possession of any part of the … flat'. When a licensee left, a new occupant was mutually agreed by the appellants and the remaining licensees.

In *Vaughan* there was no question that the agreements were in any way sham agreements. They reflected the true bargains between the parties. The question was: were the occupants licensees or did the agreements collectively create a joint tenancy between the occupants with joint exclusive possession? Lord Templeman had said in *Street* v *Mountford* that 'An occupier of residential accommodation for rent is either a lodger or a tenant.' He went on to say that 'the courts which deal with these problems will, save in exceptional circumstances, only be concerned to enquire whether as a result of the agreement relating to residential accommodation, the occupier is a lodger or a tenant.'

AG Securities v *Vaughan* shows that this is not an exhaustive test. The occupants were not lodgers and if Lord Templeman's test was to be applied they were, therefore, joint tenants with exclusive possession. That could not be the case here. A joint tenancy requires the four unities of time, title, interest and possession. The agreements were made at different times and on different terms. Lord Oliver found that none of these factors were present and it was 'impossible to say that the argreements entered into … created either individually or collectively, a single tenancy either of the entire flat or of any part of it'. In the result, despite Lord Templeman's dicta, the occupants were held to be licensees.

In *Antoniades* v *Villiers* the attic of the respondent's house was converted into furnished residential accommodation. Wishing to live together there, the applicants signed identical agreements called 'licences' which were executed at the same time and each stressed that they were not to have exclusive possession. In particular, the agreements provided that 'the licensor shall be entitled at any time to use the rooms together with the licensee and permit other persons to use all of the rooms together with the licensee.' No attempt was made by the respondent to use the rooms or to have them used by others. Stressing, too, that the real intention of the parties was to create a licence not coming under the Rent Acts, the agreements provided for a monthly payment of £87 and that they were determinable by one month's notice by either party.

The landlords argued that the occupants were licensees while the occupants maintained they were joint tenants with joint exclusive possession.

The premises were clearly not suitable for occupation by more than one couple. Lord Oliver said that there was an air of total unreality about the two licence documents signed by the occupants because the occupants were seeking a flat as a quasi matrimonial home. Nor, he opined, could the clauses entitling the landlord to occupy the premises personally, or introduce a third party into them, have been seriously intended to have any practical operation.

Looking at the substance of the transaction, rather than its face value, the occupants were joint tenants of the premises with joint exclusive possession and not licensees.

It is clear that although *Street* v *Mountford* brought the law into sharper focus, making it much more difficult for landlords to create licences as opposed to tenancies, the decision was limited by the facts of the case. It did not deal with shared occupancies, although Lord Templeman did say that the shared occupancy case of *Somma* v *Hazelhurst* (1977) was wrongly decided because the agreement was a sham, and warned courts in the future to be aware of sham devices. Nor did it offer guidance as to how exclusive possession was to be ascertained. Serious problems remain in cases of shared occupancies which did not arise in *Street* v *Mountford*.

The simple test of whether the occupant a lodger or a tenant is not sufficient for all cases as *AG Securities* v *Vaughan* demonstrated. And this test is clearly inapplicable to commercial occupancies. The extent to which *Street* v *Mountford* will apply to them needs further clarification.

Thus, the statement that since *Street* v *Mountford* the lease/licence distinction has ceased to cause problems for the courts cannot be considered to be accurate.

SUGGESTED ANSWER TO QUESTION THREE

General Comment

A question that requires a knowledge of the rules relating to the passing of the burden of leasehold covenants both before and after 1 January 1996. The landlord, John, will not only want to know against whom he can enforce the covenants but also the remedies available to him.

Key Points

* Passing of benefits and burdens of leasehold covenants
* Two conditions must be satisfied:
  - covenants must 'touch and concern the land'
  - privity of estate
* Stan: no privity of estate between a head-landlord and sub-tenant
* Alf:
  - breach of rent covenant – remedies
  - breach of covenant to use the house for residential purposes – remedies
  - breach of repairing covenant – remedies – damages
  - continuing liability of Tim as original tenant: Landlord and Tenant (Covenants) Act 1995 contains two retrospective provisions which could assist Tim (s17 and overriding lease)
* The rule in *Moule* v *Garrett*
* The position if the lease had been created in January 1996: Landlord and Tenant (Covenants) Act 1995 applies
* Abolition of the necessity for covenants to 'touch and concern the land'

- Alleviation of original tenant's position by s5
- Authorised guarantee agreements under s16
- Amendment by s22 to s19 Landlord and Tenant Act 1927
- No scope here for s16 agreement
- The remedies against Alf are the same as described before

Suggested Answer

The lease was granted in 1994 and therefore the Landlord and Tenant (Covenants) Act 1995 does not apply. The Act only covers leases created on or after 1 January 1996.

Therefore the old rules concerning the passing of benefits and burdens of leasehold covenants apply. Under s141 LPA 1925 the benefits of the lessee's covenants pass with the reversion when it is assigned. Under s142 the burden of the lessor's covenants pass with the reversion on assignment. However, this does not apply to all covenants but only those which 'have reference to' the subject-matter of the lease. The meaning of this statutory phrase is the same as that of the older common law phrase 'touching and concerning the land'.

As regards benefit and burdens relating to the lease as opposed to the reversion, the position is governed by *Spencer's Case* (1583) which decided that these will pass to an assignee of the lease if they touch and concern the land.

The meaning and extent of the phrase must be therefore understood. In *Congleton Corporation* v *Pattison* (1808) Bailey J described a covenant which touches and concerns the land in these terms, ie 'the covenant must either affect the land itself during the term, such as those with regard the mode of occupation, or it must be such as per se, and not merely from collateral circumstances, affect the value of the land at the end of the term'.

In *Breams Property Investment Co Ltd* v *Stroulger* (1948) another definition received judicial approval: a covenant will touch and concern the land if it affects the landlord qua landlord and the tenant qua tenant. It seems generally accepted that it is not possible to frame a definition that comprehensively embraces every case but some of the main examples should be noted:

- covenants: to repair; to pay rent; prohibiting assignment or subletting;
- re-entry or forfeiture clauses touch and concern the land as do all implied covenants;
- other examples are covenants not to carry out a specific trade on the demised premises (*Congleton*) and a covenant by a third party to guarantee the performance of the tenant's covenants: *P & A Swift Investments* v *Combined English Stores Group plc* (1988).

One important covenant that does not touch and concern the land is one that gives the tenant the option to purchase the landlord's reversion: *Woodall* v *Clifton* (1905). However, the effect of such a covenant is to confer upon the tenant an equitable interest in the land (*London and SW Railway* v *Gomm* (1882)), so that when the lease is assigned that interest (the benefit) will automatically pass to the assignee. In unregistered land an option to purchase the reversion is an estate contract (land charge class C(iv) under the Land Charges Act 1972) and registrable in the land charges register. If so registered, registration will constitute notice to the whole world (s198 LPA 1925) and an assignee of the reversion, providing registration is made before the assignment, will take subject to it (the burden).

In registered land the option will be a minor interest and should be the subject of an entry on the register of title. If it is not so protected then it may be protected as an overriding interest under s70(1)(g) LPA 1925: *Webb* v *Pollmount* (1966).

In addition to the requirement that a covenant must touch and concern the land if its benefits and burdens are to pass, the party seeking to enforce the benefit must show that the relationship of privity of estate exists between him and the person against whom enforcement is being sought. Another way of expressing this relationship is by the phrase 'the relationship of landlord and tenant'. If the reversion has been assigned by the landlord (L) to L_1 then clearly L_1 has stepped into the shoes of L, and is the new landlord.

If the tenant (T) has assigned the lease to T_1 then T_1 has replaced T as the tenant. In those circumstances the relationship of privity of estate will exist between L_1 and T_1. If, instead of assigning the lease T granted a sub-lease in favour of ST then the relationship of privity of estate would not exist between L and ST. They will not be landlord and tenant. T will remain as L's tenant and the fact that he has sub-let will in no way release him from his obligations to L.

The position may be summarised as follows: if both reversion and lease have been assigned to L_1 and T_1 respectively, and L_1 wishes to enforce, say the tenant's repairing covenant against T_1, he must show:

1   that the benefit of the covenant has passed to him;
2   that the burden of the covenant has passed to T_1.

In order to establish that this has occurred he must show that:

1   the covenant 'touches and concerns the land'; and
2   that privity of estate exists between him and T_1.

In this example both conditions are satisfied.

It must be emphasised that these rules only apply to legal leases because privity of estate cannot exist between parties to an equitable lease since an equitable tenant does not have estate on the land, only an equitable interest.

The application of these principles to the problem may now be considered.

The lease is a legal lease, there being no indication that it is equitable. All three covenants impose a burden (or obligation) on the tenant (Tim) and the benefits of them are enjoyed by the landlord (John). Since John continues as landlord and has not assigned the reversion it is unnecessary to consider the transmission of those benefits.

John's initial target will be Stan since he is a possession under his sub-lease and the house has fallen into disrepair. Further, Stan is proposing to open a travel agency in the house. If John wishes to enforce the covenants regarding repair and residential use against Stan, he must show that Stan is subject to the burdens of those covenants. Both covenants touch and concern the land but because Stan is a sub-tenant there is no privity of estate between John and Stan which means that under the principles explained above John cannot proceed against Stan.

Tim has assigned the lease to Alf who is now the new tenant. All three covenants in the lease touch and concern the land and there is privity of estate between John and Alf. John may therefore proceed against Alf. The remedies available to John are as follows:

1   In relation to the arrears of rent there are a number of options:

    a   John may sue Alf for these, although under the Limitation Act 1980 he cannot recover more than six years' worth of arrears.

    b   Distress – this is a levying execution on Alf's chattels and would involve selling them to recover the arrears and costs of execution. This is not a particularly effective remedy.

    c   Forfeiture or re-entry – this is only available if there is a clause to that effect in the lease. Relief from forfeiture is available to the tenant under the Common Law Procedure Act 1852. The necessity of making a final demand for the rent is dispensed with by the Act. The tenant can only take advantage of the Act if one half of a year's rent is in arrears.

If the tenant pays all the arrears and costs before judgment the forfeiture proceedings instituted by the landlord are automatically stayed. If he pays the arrears and costs after judgment and within six months from that date then he may apply to the court for relief, ie ask the court to re-instate him as tenant. This is at the court's discretion and of course will not be possible if the property has been re-let.

Note: Section 146 LPA has no application to rent covenants: s146(11).

2   Concerning the use the house for residential purposes, there is an impending breach of this covenant for which Alf will be responsible, despite the fact that it is Stan who is proposing to open a travel agency.

The obvious remedy is for John to seek an injunction against Alf but the difficulty here lies in the fact that Alf may not be able to observe it since he has sub-let the premises. If there is a similar covenant in the sub-lease then an injunction would be effective because Alf would be able to secure an injunction himself against Stan. If there is no such covenant then it is unlikely that the court would grant an injunction against Alf. In the circumstances, John would be best advised to contemplate forfeiture proceedings against Alf, although he could only do this if there was a forfeiture clause in the lease and we are not told if there is. Forfeiture would not only terminate Alf's tenancy but also Stan's sub-lease which has been carved out of it.

Forfeiture would take the form of an action for possession but before commencing proceedings John would be obliged to serve upon Alf, and Stan as the sub-tenant, a notice in accordance with s146(1) LPA 1925. The section specifies the contents of the notice which must:

    a   identify the breach; and

    b   require it to be remedied, if it is capable of being remedied; and

    c   demand compensation.

Having served the notice the landlord must then allow the tenant a reasonable time in which to remedy the breach. How long will depend on its nature.

If the tenant does not comply with the notice, the landlord may then commence proceedings.

In this case John cannot serve a s146 notice as yet since the breach has not actually occurred. Stan is only proposing to open the travel agency. However, if he goes ahead and Alf's lease is forfeited, then he will lose his sub-tenancy because of the forfeiture and doubtless this possibility will cause him to reconsider his position.

John will have to be alert to the possibility that if he does bring forfeiture proceedings both Alf and Stan may apply to the court for relief from forfeiture.

3   The remedies of a damages injunction and forfeiture are available for breach of the covenant to repair, although again it must be emphasised that the latter is only available if there is a forfeiture clause in the lease.

A special procedural provision must be noted if John is minded to sue Alf for damages. He must comply with the requirements of the Leasehold (Property Repairs) Act 1938. Before commencing proceedings he must serve upon Alf a s146 notice which must contain a clause advising the tenant of his right to serve a counter notice within 28 days. If the tenant does serve a counter notice the landlord cannot commence proceedings for damages without leave of the court. The grounds on which the court may grant leave are set out in the 1938 Act.

The 1938 Act only applies to leases granted for at least seven years with at least three years still to run.

Further, the Landlord and Tenant Act 1927 imposed a limit to the amount of damages a landlord can obtain against a tenant for breach of a repairing covenant. Section 18(1) provides that the damages must not exceed the damage to the reversion and that if at the end of the tenancy the premises are to be substantially structurally altered or demolished the landlord cannot obtain damages at all.

If Alf is unable to pay the rent arrears then John could have recourse to Tim, the original tenant. John and Tim remain contractually bound to each other for the duration of the lease even after they have disposed of their respective interests. The unfairness of this, which weighed heavily on an original tenant, has been substantially remedied by the Land and Tenant (Covenants) Act 1995 but it does not apply in this case since the Act applies to leases commencing on or after 1 January 1996.

However there are two provisions in the Act which are retrospective and apply to a lease created before 1 January 1996. Because the Act does not apply to leases created before that date, the original tenant remains in an exposed position but the two provisions go some way to easing his plight. The first provision is contained in s17 which imposes on a landlord (in this case, John) an obligation to serve on the original tenant (Tim) a notice informing him that what the Act describes as a 'fixed charge' is due and that the landlord intends to recover it, plus interest, from him. This notice must be served within six months of the money becoming due. If the landlord fails to serve the notice within the six-month period, then the tenant's obligation lapses and his liability is extinguished.

A 'fixed charge' is defined in s17(6) as to include rent, service charges and any other liquidated sum, for which the tenant has become liable due to a breach of covenant.

If John sued Alf for breach of the repairing covenant and obtained damages then these too could be obtained from Tim, providing the notice requirements were satisfied.

Before the Act, once the original landlord had obtained money from the tenant, there was no redress for the tenant except under the rule in *Moule* v *Garrett* (1872) which was of little practical use. The rule is based on quasi contract and only applies to covenants which touch and concern the land. The liability of the original tenant and defaulting assignee must be the same. In those circumstances the original tenant and assignee are joint debtors to the original landlord and if the former pays the creditor (the original landlord) then he is entitled to recover half of the money paid from his joint debtor (the assignee). In most cases the assignee is in financial difficulties which renders the tenant's entitlement worthless.

The second provision referred to improves the original tenant's position considerably. It is contained in s19. It provides that when the original tenant has satisfied his obligations to the original landlord he has the right to compel the landlord to grant him an 'overriding lease'. Such a lease is in effect a lease of the landlord's reversion with the result that the tenant then becomes the defaulting assignee's landlord. He is interposed between the head landlord and the assignee. The usual landlord's remedies are available to him, including the right to forfeiture. Thus, whereas before the original tenant received nothing in return for discharging his liabilities to the original landlord, now he has some compensation in the form of an overriding lease.

If John had granted the lease in January 1996 the position would be governed by the Landlord and Tenant (Covenants) Act 1995 which took effect on 1 January 1996. Formerly, the transmission of leasehold covenants was limited to those which 'touched and concerned the land' or as far as those attached to the reversion were concerned 'had reference to the subject matter': ss141 and 142 LPA 1925. The statutory phrase had the same meaning as 'touch and concern the land'. These sections have now been repealed.

The new position is set out in s3 of the 1995 Act. Section 3 provides:

'(1) The benefit and burden of all landlord and tenant covenants of a tenancy –
(a) shall be annexed and incident to the whole, and to each and every part of the premises demised by the tenancy and of the reversion in them, and
(b) shall … pass on an assignment of the whole or any part of these premises or of the reversion in them.'

Personal covenants are excepted from this provision by s3(6)(a).

Thus, the benefits and burdens of all of the covenants in the lease will automatically pass to the assignees of the reversion and the lease unless they are of a personal nature.

Section 5 of the 1995 Act contains the most important and fundamental provision in the statute in that it changes the law by which the original tenant (and landlord) remained liable to each other on the respective covenants, even when both reversion and lease had been assigned. The reason for this liability was because there was privity of contract between them which endured for the duration of the lease. It was of particular concern to a tenant where he had assigned his lease but the original landlord had not assigned his reversion. If a subsequent assignee of the lease fell into arrears with his rent, then the landlord could attempt to recover them from the original tenant even if he had long ago assigned his lease because of his continuing liability to the original landlord for the performance of his covenants.

Now under s5 when the original tenant assigns his lease he is released from this continuing liability to the original landlord. At the same time he will lose his right to enforce the covenants against the landlord. It must be stressed, however, that does not release the tenant from any accrued liability he has incurred from breaches of covenants committed before the date of assignment: s24 of the 1995 Act. It should also be noted that the tenant only obtains release where he assigns the lease. The provision does not apply if he sub-lets.

If the landlord had committed breaches of covenant before the assignment date then the tenant retains his right of action against the landlord even though the tenant has assigned his lease.

There are two situations where the tenant does not obtain automatic release under s5 and they contained s11 under the heading of 'excluded assignments'. These are where the tenant has assigned the lease in breach of covenant and where it has occurred by operation of law

On the face of it, these new provisions look very favourable from a tenant's point of view and far less favourable from that of the landlord, but the statute has effected a compromise between the two by means of 'authorised guarantee agreements' under s16. If the lease contains a covenant that the tenant will not assign without the landlord's consent (a qualified covenant), then the landlord may make it a condition of his consent that the tenant enters into a guarantee agreement by which he guarantees the performance of the covenants by his assignee. This guarantee only applies to the tenant's immediate assignee. It does not apply to the assignee's successors. It is difficult to imagine that landlords will not take advantage of s16 but at least the tenant will only be liable for breaches of his immediate successor.

This is a convenient place to mention changes made by the statute in respect of commercial leases. Under s19 Landlord and Tenant 1927, where a lease contains a qualified covenant, ie when the tenant covenants not to assign or sub-let without the landlord's consent, then the statute stipulates that such consent will not be unreasonably withheld. There is a substantial amount of case law on what constitutes the unreasonable withholding of consent. Section 22 of the 1995 Act amends the 1927 Act so as to give more control to the landlord over the tenant's assignments. It permits the landlord and tenant, at any time before the tenant applies to the landlord for consent to assign, to enter into an agreement setting out the circumstances in which the landlord may withhold consent to assign and any conditions he may impose in giving assent to assign. In practice this agreement will normally be included in the lease itself but this is not necessary. Thus, if the landlord refuses consent or imposes a condition in accordance with the agreement, he will not be regarded as having unreasonably withheld his consent. The landlord could take advantage of this amendment to s19 by imposing a condition that the tenant enters into a s16 authorised guarantee agreement.

These provisions do not apply to residential tenancies or to sub-leases.

If John had granted the lease to Tim after 1 January 1996 the statute would apply. There is no tenant's covenant against assigning or sub-letting and therefore Tim is free to assign to Alf without obtaining Tim's consent. Thus, there is no scope here for John to impose on Alf a s16 authorised guarantee agreement under which he guaranteed Alf's performance of the covenants in the lease. On assignment to Alf, Tim would be automatically released from performing his covenants, so John could not sue Tim for Alf's liability.

The breaches of covenant have occurred since Tim assigned the lease to Alf.

The fact that Alf has sub-let to Stan in no way releases Alf from his obligation to John to perform his covenants. The burden of those covenants automatically passed to Alf under s3 when he took the assignment.

SUGGESTED ANSWER TO QUESTION FOUR

General Comment

This is a good leasehold question since it provides the candidate with an opportunity to demonstrate an overall knowledge of leasehold cases: the running of the benefits and burden of covenants; the important covenant against assigning and sub-letting; and repairing covenants. Candidates are reminded of the importance of knowing about remedies for breach of covenants since no advice to persons in NL's position is complete without them.

Key Points

The law relating to the running of benefits and burdens of leasehold covenants: ss141 and 142 LPA 1925; *Spencer's Case*

a • Covenant against assigning and sub-letting
   • Two general observations
   • Landlord and Tenant Act 1927, s19(1)
   • Landlord and Tenant Act 1988
   • Difficulties for NL in considering forfeiture because L's reasons for refusing consent are not known
   • The question as to what is a reasonable or unreasonable withholding of consent by a landlord – cases on the issue
   • LPA 1925, s146 – irremediable breaches

b Does this covenant touch and concern the land? If not, the benefit will not pass to NL

c • Repairing covenants – remedies
   • Landlord and Tenant Act 1927
   • Leasehold Property (Repairs) Act 1938

Suggested Answer

The candidate is asked in this question to advise NL who is the assignee of the reversion from the original landlord L. There are three covenants in the head-lease, all of which appear to have been broken. The person currently in possession of the premises is ST.

The position regarding the covenant (a) will be considered later. The immediate problem for NL is: Can he enforce the covenants (b) and (c) against ST? In order for NL to do this he must establish that the benefits of these covenants (the right to enforce them) has passed to him and that the burdens (the obligation to perform them) have passed to ST.

Benefits and burdens of covenants will run with the reversion providing they 'have reference to the subject matter' ss141 and 142 LPA 1925. Benefits and burdens of covenants will run with the lease if 'they touch and concern the land': *Spencer's Case* (1583). The phrase 'touch and concern the land' has the same meaning as the phrase 'having reference to the subject matter in ss141 and 142'. Further, between the contending parties, in this case NL and ST, there must be 'privity of estate' and that is not the case here. The expression refers to the relationship of landlord and tenant and it exists where transferees of the reversion and the lease enjoy the same estates as were enjoyed by their respective transferors. The freehold was sold to NL by L (ie L assigned the reversion to NL) and NL now has the estate originally enjoyed by L. However, T did not convey his lease to ST. He retained it and carved out of it a sub-lease in favour of ST. Thus, ST does not enjoy T's estate and the relationship of landlord and tenant (privity of estate) does not exist between NL and ST with the result NL cannot enforce the burdens against ST.

NL's alternative must now be to seek enforcement of the covenants against T. There is a relationship of privity of estate between NL and T, and it must be emphasised that in granting the sub-lease to ST T's liability to perform his covenants is is no way affected. That liability remains. NL must show that the benefits of the covenants have passed to him under s141 LPA 1925 and they will do so if the covenants have reference to the subject-matter or in the older common law phrase they 'touch and concern the land'. In *Congleton Corporation* v *Pattison* (1808) it was held that such a covenant was one which affected the mode of occupation of the land or its value. Another definition was formulated by Dr Cheshire: a covenant touches and concerns the land if it affects the landlord qua landlord and the tenant qua tenant.

The individual covenants will now be considered.

Covenant (a)

Two general observations must be made about this type of covenant:

1   It may be absolute or qualified. A qualified covenant is one which does not absolutely forbid assigning or sub-letting but stipulates that it cannot be done without the landlord's consent.

2   They are strictly construed. For example, a covenant forbidding assignment of a lease does not prevent the tenant sub-letting: *Sweet & Maxwell Ltd* v *Universal News Services Ltd* (1964). A covenant against sub-letting the premises is not broken by sub-letting part of them: *Cook* v *Shoesmith* (1951).

This covenant is a qualified one and is subject to s19(1) of the Landlord and Tenant Act 1927 which provides that in the case of a qualified covenant a landlord shall not unreasonably withhold his consent.

It is essential that the tenant first seeks the landlord's consent. If he fails to do so and goes ahead then he is in breach of covenant: *Lewis and Allenby (1909)* v *Pegge* (1914).

We are told that in 1996 'T sought permission to sub-let to ST for seven years but L refused, giving no reason'. At this point the provisions of the Landlord and Tenant Act 1988 must be considered. Before the statute, if a tenant sought permission to assign or sub-let under a qualified covenant the landlord was under no obligation to respond. He could ignore the tenant's request which left the tenant in a very difficult situation. He could seek a declaration from the court authorising the assignment or sub-letting and it would be for the landlord to appear and raise his objections. The court would then decide whether the landlord was being reasonable or not. Alternatively, the tenant could go ahead with the risk that the landlord might in the case of a sub-letting, then attempt to forfeit the lease from the tenant or, in the case of an assignment, forfeit the lease from the assignee. In practice few assignees would be prepared to expose themselves to such a risk. They would not normally take an assignment without a sight of the landlord's written consent.

If the landlord did respond and refuse consent but gave no reason the tenant was little better off since, not knowing the landlord's reasons, he would be unable to decide whether they were reasonable or not.

The 1988 Act was devised to remove these difficulties for the tenant but it cannot be stressed too strongly that a tenant only enjoys its advantages if he makes a *written* application to the landlord. If he does not, the Act does not apply. In this question we are not told if T sought consent in writing or not, and accordingly the case must be argued in the alternative.

If application was made in writing by T, then the Act obliges the landlord (L) to respond within a reasonable time and (i) give consent (except in a case where it is not reasonable to give consent); and (ii) serve upon the tenant a written notice of his decision; and (iii) if refusing consent, give reasons for so doing.

Section 1(6) revises the burden of proof. Before the Act it was for the tenant to prove that the landlord was being unreasonable in withholding his consent: *Shanly* v *Ward* (1913). Now it is for the landlord to prove he was acting reasonably if he withholds consent.

Section 4 provides that if the landlord is in breach of the duties imposed upon him by the Act the tenant may sue him for breach of statutory duty.

If the tenant did not seek consent in writing, then the Act does not apply and he has no redress against L for refusing consent without giving reasons. In sub-letting to ST in those circumstances, T exposed himself to the various remedies available to a landlord for breach of covenant, including forfeiture, as there is a forfeiture clause in the lease. These remedies are now vested in the current landlord NL. In his defence to any proceedings for damages or forfeiture T could argue that under the Landlord and Tenant Act 1927 the landlord must have reasonable grounds for withholding consent.

If T did apply in writing, then L was in breach of his obligation under the Act to provide his reasons for refusing consent, bringing into play s4 referred to above, but T could only recover damages for any financial loss he has sustained and he does not appear to have done so here. If he had delayed the proposed sub-letting, with the consequence that ST changed his mind and refused to go ahead, then T would have sustained a loss which could have provided the basis of a claim against L.

NL should consider forfeiture proceedings against T but he must bear in mind that T could raise as a defence that L had unreasonably withheld his consent in breach of the 1927 Act.

Since L's reasons for withholding consent are unknown, both NL and T are in a difficult position. The question of L's reasonableness or otherwise would have to be adjudicated upon at the hearing of the forfeiture proceedings. Since the demised premises consist of a shop NL could re-enter peaceably, ie without taking proceedings in the county court for possession, but both T and ST could still apply to the Court for relief from forfeiture: s146 LPA 1925; *Billson* v *Residential Apartments* (1990). Again the question of L's reasonableness could be raised by T at that point.

The fact that L gave no reasons would tend towards the court concluding that L was in breach of s19(1) of the 1927 Act.

What is a reasonable or unreasonable refusal of consent by landlords has been the subject of litigation and there is a substantial volume of case law on the subject. In *Bickel* v *Duke of Westminster* (1977), Lord Denning MR observed that it was impossible to formulate strict rules as to how a landlord should exercise his power of refusal. The cases, he said, can only provide guidelines; no decision should be treated as a binding precedent.

Examples in plenty can be found on either side of the line, but each case must be decided on its merits. In *International Drilling Fluids Ltd* v *Louisville Investments (Uxbridge) Ltd* (1986) Balcombe LJ summarised the position in a number of propositions which is of great assistance in applying s19(1) of the 1927 Act.

In proposition 3 he pointed out that the onus of proof is on the tenant to prove unreasonableness by the landlord. It must be noted that this was said in 1986. In 1988, the Landlord and Tenant Act reversed this in cases to which the Act applied.

The most important proposition is the first where he emphasised the importance of finding the *purpose* behind the inclusion of the covenant in the lease. Generally, the purpose is to protect the landlord from having his premises used or occupied in an undesirable way or occupied by an undesirable tenant or assignee.

An illustrative case is to be found in *Bromley Park Garden Estates Ltd* v *Moss* (1982). The tenant sought consent to assign to Moss but the landlords refused. The reason for refusal was that they hoped that the tenant would then surrender the lease which would enable them to gain possession. Having acquired possession they then intended to grant a tenancy of the whole premises to the current tenant of the ground floor so that they would have only one tenant of the premises instead of two, which in their view constituted good estate management.

The Court of Appeal held that although their plans made good commercial sense they were not entitled to refuse consent for that purpose. The Court summarised the matter this way:

'If the landlord's refusal of consent was designed to achieve the purpose of the covenant, the refusal was reasonable, but if the refusal was designed to achieve a collateral purpose or benefit wholly unconnected with the terms of the lease ... it was unreasonable even if made for the purposes of good estate management.'

As indicated before, it is not possible to give firm advice to NL because it is not known what L's reasons were for refusing T consent to sub-let.

If NL does decide to forfeit T's lease under the re-entry clause in the lease he must first serve upon him and ST a notice under 146 LPA 1925 specifying the breach. The section provides that he must also require the breach to be remedied if it is capable of remedy. In this case the requirement may be omitted because a breach of covenant against sub-letting is not capable of being remedied: *Scala House and District Property Co Ltd* v *Forbes* (1974).

The section also requires a third ingredient, namely that the tenant be required to make compensation. However, if this requirement is omitted it does not invalidate the notice: *Rugby School Governors* v *Tannahill* (1935).

Having served the notice the landlord must wait a reasonable time before proceeding to forfeiture. This is to enable the tenant time to remedy the breach, but where the breach is irremediable, as is the case here, then this does not have to be taken literally and proceedings may be commenced almost immediately: *Scala House and District Property Co Ltd* v *Forbes*.

If the court, having heard arguments from the parties as to the reasonableness or unreasonableness of L's refusal, decided to order forfeiture without granting relief, then the sub-lease would also be lost since it was granted out of the lease.

Covenant (b)

Does the covenant touch and concern the land? It is not always easy to decide whether a covenant comes within the definition or not. There are examples of cases which come within the definition and those which do not. Had the prohibition in this covenant been simply not to sell greengrocery on the premises almost certainly it would have come within the definition: *Congleton Corporation* v *Pattison*. However, the covenant is worded so as to forbid the tenant not to compete with the greengrocery business which the landlord carried on from another of his shops situated elsewhere. It would appear from *Congleton* that this particular covenant as worded would not touch and concern the land. In that case there was a covenant by the tenant not to employ people in the demised mill if they lived in other parishes. The purpose of this covenant was to benefit other property which the landlord owned in the parish. It was held the covenant did not touch and concern the land. Since the purpose of this covenant was to benefit an activity carried on by L at another of his shops, it is highly unlikely that it comes within the definition.

That being the case, its benefit will not pass to NL under s141 LPA 1925 and he will be unable to enforce it against T.

Covenant (c)

It is clear that the repairing covenant has been broken and that T is liable to NL for its breach. There are three remedies available to NL: damages; injunction; and forfeiture.

If he wishes to sue for damages, two statutory provisions must be observed: Section 18 Landlord and Tenant Act 1927 stipulates that the damages for breach of a repairing covenant must not exceed the damage to the reversion and, further, that if premises are to be demolished or substantially altered at the termination of the lease, then no damages are recoverable at all. The Leasehold (Property Repairs) Act 1938 provides that, before issuing proceedings for damages, the landlord must first serve upon the tenant a notice in the form provided by s146 LPA 1925, with the addition of a term advising the tenant of his right to serve a counter notice within 28 days. If the tenant does so the landlord cannot proceed further without obtaining the court's leave. The Act sets out the matters which the landlord is required to prove before the court can give leave. The Act only applies to leases granted for at least seven years and there must be at least three years still to run.

An injunction would also be an appropriate remedy because although T is not in possession he will be able to comply with it by enforcing the covenants in the sub-lease, if necessary by threatening ST with forfeiture since there is a forfeiture clause in the sub-lease. It will be remembered that forfeiture of any lease is only available if the lease contains a forfeiture clause.

Finally, NL may forfeit the lease although he must first serve upon T and ST a s146 notice which in the case of this covenant must include the requirement to remedy the breach since it is capable of remedy. L must give T a reasonable time to effect the necessary repairs and how long this will be will depend on the extent of the repairs. T is not in possession but he may enforce the repairing covenant in the sub-lease against ST by again threatening ST with forfeiture.

It should be noted that where there is a tenant and sub-tenant, and the landlord is proposing to forfeit the lease he must serve the s146 on both. Section 146(1) requires a landlord to serve the notice 'on the lessee' and s146(5) defines lessee as including an under-lessee.

5

Easements and Profits à Prendre

Introduction

There are two main parts to the topic of easements: the nature of easements and acquisition, both of which can appear in the same question. The first part is examined in Question 1, while acquisition is discussed in Questions 2, 3 and 4. In dealing with acquisition by implied grant students should first ask who it is who is claiming the easement and then proceed to identify the claimant as the grantor or grantee. It is important to do this because the grounds on which a grantor can claim an easement are narrower than those on which a grantee can make a claim. It must be remembered too that the words grantor and grantee do not refer to the grantor and grantee of an easement. They refer to someone who has granted land, eg a vendor or a lessor. Similarly, a grantee is someone who has been granted land, eg a purchaser or a lessee.

In the case of presumed grants, the questions can always be identified by evidence of long user, ie at least 20 years. There are three methods of acquisition and students must apply them to a problem in the following order: the Prescription Act 1832, common law prescription and lost modern grant.

Although the questions tend mainly to centre on easements, the possibility that an examiner might ask a question on profits à prendre should not be overlooked. Students should therefore look carefully at the right being claimed to identify it as an easement or a profit. This is particularly important when the Prescription Act is being considered since the prescriptive periods are different.

Questions

INTERROGRAMS

1   Define and distinguish:

    a   an easement;
    b   profit à prendre;
    c   a licence.

2   Distinguish between a positive and negative easement.
3   What is meant by:

    a   a profit appurtenant; and
    b   a profit in gross?

4   What are easements of necessity?
5   What are easements of common intention?
6   What is a 'quasi-easement'?

7   Explain the doctrine of the lost modern grant.
8   How may easements and profits be extinguished?
9   What is the extent of an easement?
10 What is the meaning of 'interruption' as defined by the Prescription Act 1832?
11 How is an easement of light dealt with under the Prescription Act 1832?
12 Explain what is meant by the requirement that user must be on behalf of a fee simple estate in the dominant land and against the fee simple estate in the servient land.

QUESTION ONE

'The categories of servitudes and easements must alter and expand with the changes that take place in the circumstances of mankind': per Lord St Leonards in *Dyce* v *Hay*.
  Discuss

London University LLB Examination
(for external students) Land Law June 1988 Q2

QUESTION TWO

'Section 62 of the Law of Property Act has significantly reduced the importance of the rule in *Wheeldon* v *Burrows* as a method of acquiring easements.'
  Discuss.

London University LLB Examination
(for external students) Land Law June 1999 Q7

QUESTION THREE

Rita, Sara and Tina occupy three adjacent large workshops. Sara owned the middle workshop and also Tina's workshop, which had been let to Tina, and her father before her, for a total of thirty years, under a series of leases. Rita owns her own workshop.

  Ever since the first lease was granted, Tina's father and then Tina herself, walked through the yard of the middle workshop to reach their end workshop, as this is quicker than going along the road. Sara never said anything about this and Tina doesn't know if she was aware of the fact or not. In 1988 Sara agreed to Tina's request to use a lean-to shed at the rear of Sara's workshop, and Tina had used it, on and off, ever since, for storage.

  Rita and her staff have also walked over the yard to Sara's workshop to reach Rita's workshop 'for as long as anyone can remember'.

  In 1998 Tina bought the freehold of her workshop from Sara. The conveyance made no mention of the use of the shed, but Tina still uses it.

  Sara has now sold her workshop to VAX Developments Ltd, who have a proposal to redevelop the site. They have told Rita and Tina to keep off the land and have demanded that Tina clear out the shed and hand over the key.

  Advise Rita and Tina.

London University LLB Examination
(for external students) Land Law June 1990 Q5

QUESTION FOUR

For nineteen-and-a-half years Alf has used a path across Bert's land as a short-cut to the railway station. Last December Bert put up a fence to stop Alf and has told Alf that he is hoping to sell his land to Jerry, a builder, who wishes to build a block of flats.

   Advise Alf.

Prepared by the author

Answers

ANSWERS TO INTERROGRAMS

1   a   An easement is a right 'in alieno solo' – a right in the soil of another. It is not easy to define an easement accurately but a working definition may be given: a right in the land of another which enables the holder of that right to either do something on that land or restrict its use for the benefit of his own land. It will be noted that the latter part of the definition overlaps with the definition of a restrictive covenant relating to freehold land, and illustrates the difficulty of formulating a precise and comprehensive definition of an easement.

   Because of this difficulty, when seeking to establish whether a given right is an easement or not, enquiry should be made as to whether the right has the four characteristics examined in the leading case of *Re Ellenborough Park* (1956).

   b   A profit à prendre is a right to take something from the land of another. Contrast this with an easement which confers no such right. It may be enjoyed as a several profit, ie by one person only, or in common, ie the enjoyment is shared between several persons. Examples of profits are:

   •   profits of pasture, ie grazing of cattle on the servient land;
   •   profits of turbary – the right to dig and remove from the servient land, peat or turf to use as fuel on the dominant tenement;
   •   profits in soil – the right to take from the servient land, sand, minerals, coal, gravel;
   •   profits of piscary – the right to catch and remove fish from lakes or rivers on the servient land.

   Other examples are the right to hunt or shoot on the servient land.

   What is taken must form part of the land and this includes wild animals living on the land. It might be thought that taking water from the land should be classified as a profit but this is not the case because the water is not part of the land nor when it was extracted was it owned by anybody. Such a right is therefore not a profit: see *Polden* v *Bastard* (1865).

   c   The word 'licence' means permission and a landowner may grant to his neighbour a licence to come on to his land for a particular purpose, but such a licence will not confer on the grantee an interest in the land. It will not therefore be binding on third parties.

   However, there are several different types of licences. The one described is a bare licence and is revocable at will by the landowner. No formalities are required for its formation. The other types of licence are a contractual licence and a licence by estoppel. A contractual licence is one arising from a contract between the parties. Again, it confers no interest in land, although it may bind third parties through the vehicle of the constructive trust: see the judgment of Lord Denning MR in *Binions* v *Evans* (1972) and that of Fox LJ in *Ashburn Anstalt* v *Arnold* (1989).

A licence by estoppel creates an equitable interest in land and is capable of binding third parties: *Ives (ER) Investments Ltd* v *High* (1967).

Benefits and burdens of easements and profits are interests in land and may be enjoyed by, and bind, third parties. Bare licences and contractual licences in themselves do not.

A licencee may enjoy exclusive possession: *Errington* v *Errington* (1952). An easement cannot confer exclusive possession on a dominant owner: *Copeland* v *Greenhalf* (1952); *Grigsby* v *Melville* (1973).

The four characteristics discussed in *Re Ellenborough Park* (1956) have no applicability to licences and in particular there is no necessity for a dominant tenement.

2   A positive easement is one which entitles the dominant owner to perform some activity on the servient land, eg to exercise a right of way over it. A negative easement does not entitle the dominant owner to go onto the servient land but instead entitles him to restrict the servient owner's use of his land for the benefit of the dominant land. The best example is an easement of light over servient land. The law is reluctant to recognise new negative easements: *Phipps* v *Pears* (1965).

3   a   A profit appurtenant is limited in its exercise to the needs of the dominant land. In the case of a right of turbary which is appurtenant, the turf or peat cannot be used other than for the needs of the dominant tenement, it cannot be sold: *Russell & Broker's Case* (1582).

    b   A profit may exist in gross. It is not necessary for there to be a dominant tenement. If the profit is attached to dominant land it is said to be a profit appurtenant. An easement cannot exist in gross; there must be a dominant tenement.

4   *Wheeldon* v *Burrows* (1879) made it clear that the courts are reluctant to imply easements in favour of land retained by a grantor (vendor or lessor) over land which he has conveyed to a grantee (purchaser or lessee). This reluctance is based on the maxim that 'a man may not derogate from his grant'.

However, as Thesiger LJ said in *Wheeldon* v *Burrows*, there are exceptions to this, one of which is that an easement will be implied into the grant in favour of the grantor's land in the case of necessity. The word 'necessity' is applied strictly and the easement will only be implied if, without it, the grantor's land cannot be used at all. It is not enough to say that it is necessary for the reasonable enjoyment of the land. That phrase was used by Thesiger LJ when discussing easements implied in favour of a grantee's land. If there is an alternative access this will defeat a grantor's claim even if its use is highly inconvenient: *Titchmarsh* v *Royston Water Co Ltd* (1899). In *Pinnington* v *Galland* (1853) the grantor conveyed land to the grantee, retaining a plot in the centre which was completely surrounded by the land he had granted. In the result he had no means of access from the plot he had retained. In those circumstances an easement of necessity was implied into the conveyance over the land he had conveyed.

5   Easements of common intention are the second exception to the rule that easements will not be implied into a conveyance in favour of a grantor's land. They are implied where it is clear that both parties would have agreed to its inclusion in the conveyance had they considered the matter at the time. In such cases it is generally the position that neither party appreciated that an easement was necessary and the common intention is generally only found in cases of necessity. There can, therefore, be an overlap between easements of necessity and intended easements, although this is not always the case: *Stafford* v *Lee* (1992).

In *Wong* v *Beaumont Property Trust* (1965), the plaintiff purchased a lease of some cellars to be used as a restaurant. The landlord retained the premises upstairs. Unknown to the parties at the time, the cellars could not be used without compliance with public health regulations which required a ventilation system to discharge the cooking odours. The plaintiff had covenanted to comply with the regulations but was unaware, as was his landlord, of the need for the ventilation system. The installation of the system required access to the defendant landlord's upstairs premises and the plaintiff claimed an easement based on the common intention of the parties to enable him to do that. It should be noted that in this case it was the grantee (the plaintiff lessee) who was making the claim.

The plaintiff's application for a declaration that he was entitled to an easement was successful, but it is not clear whether the Court of Appeal decided on the basis of necessity or common intention or a combination of both. All three judges referred to necessity, but it can be argued that they concluded that the parties would have formed a common intention to include the easement had they realised its necessity.

6   In *Wheeldon* v *Burrows* (1879) Thesiger LJ spoke of quasi-easements. He was referring to the situation where a man owns two plots of land and uses one of them for the more convenient use of the other, eg crossing the plot as a short cut to the road.

This use of passage cannot be an easement because a man cannot have, and does not need, an easement over his own land, and consequently Thesiger LJ described it as a quasi-easement. The latin word 'quasi' means 'as if' and Thesiger LJ meant that the owner was enjoying the passage as if it was an easement over the land although clearly it was not. He went on to say how a quasi-easement will be included in a conveyance of land to a grantee for the benefit of land granted to him by the conveyance.

7   To acquire an easement by common law prescription it was necessary to prove continuous user as of right back to the year 1189. Clearly this has been impossible for centuries, but if the dominant owner can prove such user for at least 20 years then the courts will presume user back to 1189: *Darling* v *Clue* (1864). However, the

servient owner can rebut that presumption by proving that the user could not have been enjoyed since that date. If, for example, the claimant is trying to establish an easement of way to a church, the servient owner can defeat it by proving the church was not built until after 1189.

The defect in this type of presumed grant was to some extent surmounted by the doctrine of the lost modern grant. Initially the claim had a basis in fact: the claimant asserted that an easement had been made by deed of grant subsequent to 1189 and then lost. It was for the jury to decide the truth of the assertion from evidence. The courts began to allow a presumption to that effect if the claimant could prove user for 20 years. In doing this the courts were trying to find a legitimate origin and justification for open and continuous enjoyment over a long period: *Attorney-General* v *Simpson* (1901).

In *Simmons* v *Dobson* (1991) Fox LJ summarised the evolution of the doctrine of the lost modern grant: 'initially juries were told by the judge that from user during living memory, or even during 20 years, they could presume a lost grant. After a time the jury were recommended to make that finding and finally they were directed to do so. Nobody believed that there ever was a grant. But it was a convenient and workable fiction and was ultimately approved by the House of Lords in *Dalton* v *Angus* (1881).'

The presumed lost grant is a fiction and consequently the claimant cannot be required to adduce evidence of its content (*Palmer* v *Guadagni* (1906)), although he must plead a date. The servient owner is not permitted to rebut the presumption: *Dalton* v *Angus* and *Tehidy Minerals Ltd* v *Norman* (1971).

In the former case Luck J described the doctrine as 'a revolting fiction'.

Because of the defects in common law prescription and the fiction of the lost modern grant, the legislature enacted the Prescription Act of 1832, and in *Gardner* v *Hodgson's Kingston Brewery Co Ltd* (1903) Lord MacNaghten explained its purpose and extent:

> 'The Act was passed, as its preamble declares, for the purpose of getting rid of the inconvenience and injustice arising from the meaning which the law of England attached to the expressions "time immemorial" and "time whereof the memory of man runneth not to the contrary". The law as it stood put an intolerable strain on the consciences of judges and jurymen. The Act was an Act "for shortening the time of prescription in certain cases". And really it did nothing more.'

Despite its defects this doctrine still has its uses. The Prescription Act 1832 provides that easements and profits may be acquired if enjoyed as of a right and without interruption for specified periods (20 and 40 years for easements, except easements of light, and 30 and 60 years for profits) 'next before action'. Thus, to claim an easement, other than an easement of light, under the 20-year period, the claimant must show the enjoyment has been for the 20 years immediately preceding a court action in which the easement is being claimed or disputed. In the case of the lost modern grant it is not necessary to prove 20 years 'next before action'. Once the required 20-year user has been established then even if subsequently user discontinues or is interrupted, the easement may still be claimed: *Mills* v *Silver*

(1991). Sometimes applications cannot be made under the Prescription Act 1832 because use cannot be shown up to the date of a court action. In such a case a claim may succeed by invoking the doctrine of the lost modern grant. An example may be found in *Tehidy Minerals Ltd* v *Norman*. In that case rights of grazing (a profit à prendre) was claimed under the doctrine. Under the statute proof of user for at least 30 years would have been necessary. The Court of Appeal held that under the doctrine of lost modern grant it was only necessary to prove 20 years user.

8   Easements and profits may be extinguished in the following ways:

a   By statute.

b   By express release. The dominant owner may release the servient land from the burden of the easement but this must be done by deed to be effective (*Lovell* v *Smith* (1857)), although a written release would be recognised by equity.

c   Implied release. The most common form of implied release is where the dominant owner has abandoned the user but an actual intention to abandon must be proved: non-user of itself is not enough, although it may raise a presumption of an intention to abandon. In *Moore* v *Rawson* (1824) a wall containing windows was replaced by a blank wall. After 17 years had elapsed the court held that the right to light to the windows had been abandoned. In *Benn* v *Hardinge* (1992) a right of way had not been used for 175 years but the Court of Appeal held that that was not of itself sufficient to infer an intention to abandon the user. The explanation for the cessation of user was not an intention to abandon but that an alternative right of way became available to the dominant owner.

   This reluctance by the Courts to infer an intention to abandon was explained by Buckley LJ in *Gotobed* v *Pridmore* (1970) who observed that property owners do not normally want to abandon rights even when they have no current need of them.

d   Unity of ownership and possession. An easement is a right in alieno solo: a right in the soil of another. An owner cannot have an easement over his own land because this would be contrary to the basic characteristic of an easement. Thus, if the dominant owner acquires ownership of the servient land the easement is extinguished, and even if the two plots are later acquired by different owners it will not revive.

   If, on the other hand, the dominant owner, instead of acquiring ownership of the servient land, leases it so that he gains possession of that land, the easement is merely suspended and when the lease is determined it will revive and continue as before.

e   Change of circumstances. Unlike restrictive covenants, there is no statutory provision for the discharge or modification of easements when they have become obsolete, but in *Huckvale* v *Aegean Hotels Ltd* (1989) Slade LJ held that the court could regard an easement as extinguished where there had been such a change of circumstances since the easement was created that it would be a violation of common sense and a disregard of reality to hold that the easement still existed.

9   The assessment of an easement's extent depends on how it was created. Problems can arise in this area for the servient tenement. For example, where the development of the dominant tenement has been such that the volume of traffic using a right of way over the servient tenement has increased or where its user has been changed with a resultant alteration in the character of the traffic.

a   In the case of express grants it is a matter of construction as to whether the dominant owner can insist that the easement must accommodate the changes. Even if the grant is widely worded using the conventional phrase 'at all times and for all purposes' the servient owner may successively argue that the increased user has become so excessive as to unreasonably interfere with the use of his tenement: *Jelbert* v *Davis* (1968). In that case, at the time of the creation of the easement by grant, the dominant tenement was used as a dwelling-house, but later the new owners converted it into a garage to accommodate their hotel. The servient owners argued that the dominant owners were now attempting to use the way for trade as opposed to domestic purposes and sought an injunction to prevent it. The Court of Appeal held that the wording of the grant was such that trade access was permissible.

  In *British Railways Board* v *Glass* (1965) a general right of way was created in favour of the dominant land in a conveyance of 1847. In 1938 the tenement began to be used for siting of caravans which gradually increased in number with a consequent increase in the number of persons using the easement to cross the servient land. The Court of Appeal held that the increased volume of traffic was permitted under the terms of the grant and that the user had not become excessive.

b   The extent of the easement will be defined by the use of the dominant tenement at the time of creation. In *Corporation of London* v *Riggs* (1880) there was an easement of necessity. At the time of its creation the dominant land was used for agricultural purposes. Subsequently the dominant owners sought to use the easement for the carting of building materials but it was held that this was not permissible because the user was confined to the user enjoyed at the time the easement of necessity came into being.

c   The nature of the user by which the prescriptive easement was acquired defines its extent: *United Land Co* v *Great Eastern Railway Company* (1875). The matter was clearly put by Bovill CJ in *Williams* v *James* (1867): 'the right acquired must be measured by the extent of the enjoyment which is proved'. Thus, the easement acquired by prescription cannot be used for a substantially different purpose. In *RCP Holdings Ltd* v *Rogers* (1953) a right of way for farming purposes had been acquired by prescription and it was held that such an easement could not accommodate the change of user of the dominant tenement to a camping ground.

  An increase in volume of the user is permissible providing that the user does not become excessive. As Plowman J pointed out in *Woodhouse & Co Ltd* v *Kirkland (Derby) Ltd* (1970) a distinction has to be drawn between an increase in user and user of a different kind or for a different purpose. The former is permissible, the latter is not.

In *Mills* v *Silver* (1991) a right of way allowing vehicular traffic had been acquired by lost modern grant. The state of the track was such that it was only usable when weather conditions were favourable. The dominant land was then acquired by the defendants who brought in contractors to build a stone road to enable it to be used at all times. The servient owners objected, arguing that the construction of a stone road amounted to an alteration in the nature of the easement and was not permissible. The Court of Appeal agreed: the nature of the prescriptive right of way was limited to the nature of the user by which it had been acquired. Although the dominant owners were entitled to repair the road they could not alter its nature even if that amounted to an improvement.

10 An interruption is defined by the Prescription Act 1832 and has a more complex meaning than is found in everyday usage of the word. The statute reads that 'no act or other matter shall be deemed to be an interruption within the meaning of this statute, unless the same shall have been or shall be submitted to or acquiesced in for one year after the party interrupted shall have had or shall have notice thereof': s4.

There are therefore several factors which must exist before it can be said that the user has been interrupted. First, there must have been some overt act on the part of the servient owner which hinders or obstructs the user: *Carr* v *Foster* (1842). It must be a positive act and hostile in nature: *Davies* v *Williams* (1851).

Second, the dominant owner must be aware of it otherwise no question of submission or of acquiescence by him can arise.

Third, he must acquiesce in it for one year. To prevent time running against him therefore he must show that he does not acquiesce.

Whether he does so or not is a question of fact. In *Bennison* v *Cartwright* (1864) it was held that he must make his objection to the servient owner with sufficient force and clarity to leave the servient owner in no doubt that he does not acquiesce. The dominant owner must act with care because until the relevant period has elapsed (eg 20 years) he is not in a position to claim an easement and until he does so he has no right to be on the servient owner's land at all. If in the meantime if he were to enter the servient owner's land and remove the obstruction he would be committing a trespass and perhaps provoke the servient owner into commencing proceedings for trespass before the period had elapsed, in which case the dominant owner would be precluded from claiming the appropriate period of user 'next before action'.

At the conclusion of one year's acquiescence, if acquiescence there be, there will be an interruption as defined by the statute, but not before.

11 This is dealt with under s3 which provides that actual enjoyment of the access of light to a dwelling-house, workshop or other building for 20 years without interruption shall make the right indefeasible unless enjoyed by written consent or agreement. The result of this provision is that the rules governing the acquisition of easements of light differ from those which govern easements other than light.

The differences are as follows:

a   Section 3 uses the phrase 'actual enjoyment'. This means that the user does not have to be 'as of right'. However, there can be no claim under s3 if the user is enjoyed by written permission. Such permission will defeat a claim. It follows that oral permission will not defeat a claim. Not even payment of rent: *Plasterers Co* v *Parish Clerks Co* (1851).

b   The general rule applicable to the acquisition of easements by prescription is that the claim must be made on behalf of the fee simple estate in the dominant land against the fee simple estate in the servient land. This rule does not apply to claims to a right to light made under s3.

c   Unlike claims to other easements where there are two prescriptive periods, for easements of light there is only one period of 20 years.

d   Sections 7 and 8 which provide for disabilities do not apply. The disabilities referred to in s7 apply except 'where the right or claim is hereby declared to be absolute and indefeasible' and that is the position prescribed by s3. Section 8 is not applicable because it only relates to acquisition under the 40-year period.

e   The definition of interruption in s4 applies to easements of light but an additional form of interruption is provided by the Rights of Light Act 1959. Under this statute a nominal interruption can be registered as a local charge. It remains effective for one year.

12 A claim to an easement by prescription, except in the case of easements of light under the Prescription Act 1832, must be made on behalf of the fee simple estate in the dominant land against the fee simple estate in the servient land: *Bright* v *Walker* (1834). In the case of common law prescription, the user must extend back to 1189, although this will be presumed from 20 years' user. Only a fee simple estate can accommodate such a long period of time.

The rule also applies to claims by lost modern grant and under the Prescription Act. In common law prescription and the lost modern grant claims, the claimant needs to establish user for 20 years to raise the necessary presumptions. If at the commencement of that user, the servient tenement was either let or subject to a life interest, then acquiescence in the user by the servient tenement owner, essential to prescription claims (*Dalton* v *Angus* (1881)), is not possible. He may not know of the commencement of the user or, if he does, he will not be in a position to prohibit it. In the absence of acquiescence by the servient owner time will not run against him: *Daniel* v *North* (1809); *Robert* v *James* (1903). If, however, the servient land was only let after the commencement of the user this will not defeat the claim: *Pugh* v *Savage* (1970).

The rule was examined in *Simmons* v *Dobson* (1991). O was the owner in fee simple of two adjoining plots of land, plot A and plot B. He leased plot B to a tenant who subsequently assigned the lease to the plaintiff. O then granted a lease of plot A to the defendant. The plaintiff crossed the defendant's land, plot A, to reach the road from his plot (B). The defendant then blocked his passage and the plaintiff claimed that he was not entitled to do so because he had acquired a right of passage by modern lost grant on behalf of his lease.

The Court of Appeal held that he was not entitled to succeed. Fox LJ examined a number of authorities. In *Wheaton* v *Maple & Co* (1893) Headly LJ said 'a right claimed by prescription must be claimed as appendant or appurtenant to land and not annexed to it for a term of years'. In *Derry* v *Sanders* (1919) Scrutton LJ observed 'it is established by decisions binding on this court that one tenant cannot acquire an easement by prescription against another tenant holding of the same landlord: *Kilgour* v *Gaddes* (1904).'

In *Simmons* the two tenants held of the same landlord and the plaintiff could not therefore succeed in his efforts to claim an easement by lost modern grant. Although there was no direct authority forbidding a person holding a lesser estate than a fee simple, eg a term of years, acquiring an easement by lost modern grant in favour of that term of years, Fox LJ held that the dicta in the authorities cited were such that a claim to that effect would be inconsistent with the authorities generally and a tenant could not therefore invoke the doctrine of the lost modern grant to claim an easement on behalf of his term of years. The same would apply to a claim made by common law prescription or the Prescription Act 1832.

SUGGESTED ANSWER TO QUESTION ONE

General Comment

A conventional question which requires a knowledge of the fundamental principles of the nature of easements with which all candidates should be familiar.

Key Points

- Two aspects for consideration:
  - traditional meaning as to lists of new easements not being closed
  - do alterations take place to easements which are on the existing list?
- New easements must comply with the four characteristics of *Re Ellenborough Park* – presence not conclusive
- Other factors may preclude recognition of a new easement
- Recreational user
- The right claimed may be too wide
- An easement must not normally impose on the servient owner an obligation to perform positive acts (exception: *Crow* v *Wood*)
- Reluctance of courts to recognise new negative easement
- Examples of new easements
- Changing circumstances may raise the question of the extent of existing easements:
  - change in extent of user of dominant tenements
  - change in dominant tenement's user

Suggested Answer

There are two aspects of this question. Under the first consider the traditional meaning ascribed to the quotation that 'The category of servitudes and easements must alter and expand with the changes that take place in the circumstances of mankind.' The second aspect reduces the emphasis on 'categories' of easements but considers whether alterations or expansion can take place to easements already within the existing category. In some respects the two become inter-connected. A right of way is within the existing category of easements but the extent of that right of way may itself 'alter and expand' to reflect changes in the use of the dominant tenement or advances in methods of transportation. In any answer emphasis should be given to the first and traditional meaning but the second interpretation should not be ignored.

At its simplest the quotation indicates that the category, or list, of easements must reflect current land use requirements. This is a general comment on any legal system. It was acknowledged in the Privy Council case of *Attorney-General of Southern Nigeria* v *John Holt & Co* (1915) that: 'The law must adapt itself to the conditions of modern society and trade.' The law has to take care, however, that in meeting the demands of modern society the existing rules continue to be observed. Any new easement must continue to meet the four essentials of an easement. In *Re Ellenborough Park* (1956) the four essential qualities of an easement, first identified in Cheshire's *Modern Law of Real Property*, were given judicial approval by the Court of Appeal.

The four characteristics are:

1   There must be a dominant and a servient tenement, the land carrying the burden of the easement being the servient tenement.
2   An easement must accommodate the dominant tenement. The right must be connected with the usefulness or amenity of the dominant tenement. For this reason, dominant and servient tenements are usually contiguous, though this is not essential. In *Hill* v *Tupper* (1863) it was held that if the right was acquired in order to exploit an independent business enterprise rather than to accommodate the land it will be treated as mere licence.
3   The dominant and servient tenements must not be owned and occupied by the same person. An easement is a right in alieno solo: a right in the soil of another. A man cannot have an easement over his own land.
4   The easement must be capable of forming the subject matter of a grant, so

   • there must be a capable grantor;
   • there must be a capable grantee;
   • the nature and extent of the right must be capable of reasonably exact definition; and
   • the right must be within the general nature of rights capable of existing as easements.

If the right being claimed as an easement does not enjoy these four characteristics then the courts will not recognise it as an easement. In *Aldred's Case* (1610) it was held that there could not be an easement of viewing because it could not be defined. Likewise, there cannot be an easement entitling a landowner to a flow of air coming over his neighbour's land to operate his windmill: *Webb* v *Bird* (1862). Nor can there be an easement of privacy: *Browne* v *Flower* (1911).

However, the presence of the four characteristics is not conclusive. Other factors may preclude the court from recognising the existence of an easement. In *Aldred's Case* Wray CJ gave another reason for disallowing the claim: 'for prospect which is a matter only of delight, and not of necessity, no action lies for stopping thereof. The law does not give an action for such things of delight.' These sentiments were echoed in *Mounsey v Ismay* (1865).

In *Re Ellenborough Park* a number of houses fronted a park and the conveyances granted to the owners the right to use the park. At first sight the rights appeared to be 'mere rights of recreation without utility or benefit'. The Court of Appeal upheld the rights as easements because 'a private garden (in this case the park) is an attribute of the ordinary enjoyment of the residence to which it is attached and the right of wandering in it is but one method of enjoying it'.

The court will also examine the extent of the right being claimed. If the claim is too wide it will be disallowed as an easement. In *Copeland v Greenhalf* (1952) a landowner claimed that he had acquired by prescription a right to park vehicles on another's land. Upjohn J held that the claim amounted to a claim of joint user of the land and observed 'the right claimed goes wholly outside any normal idea of an easement'. A similar result was reached in *Grigsby v Melville* (1973) because the claim was to the exclusive use of a cellar situated on the servient land. However, a right to storage on the servient land may constitute an easement providing the amount of space claimed is within reason: *Wright v Macadam* (1949). Each case must be decided on its own facts because, as Brightman J observed in *Grigsby v Melville*, 'to some extent a problem of this sort may be one of degree', a view in which Baker J concurred in *London & Blenheim Estates Ltd v Ladbroke Retail Parks Ltd* (1992).

Analogous to rights of storage are rights of parking. There may be an easement to park a vehicle in a defined space (*Newman v Jones* (1982)), but it must not deprive the servient owner of the reasonable use of his land: *London and Blenheim Estates Ltd v Ladbroke Retail Parks Ltd*.

Another factor which may defeat a claim to an easement is that an easement must not impose on a servient owner an obligation to perform positive acts or require him to spend money: *Regis Property Co Ltd v Redman* (1956). The exception to this is *Crow v Wood* (1971) where it was held that there could be an easement requiring a landowner to keep in repair a boundary fence. Such an easement was described in *Lawrence v Jenkins* (1873) as a 'spurious easement', but since *Crow v Wood* it is now accepted that the right can exist as an easement although it is anomalous.

In *Allen v Greenwood* (1979) the court recognised that a right of light to a greenhouse was capable of existing as an easement, but Goff LJ acknowledged that solar energy could pose a problem for the future:

'On other facts, particularly where one has solar heating (although this may not arise for some years) it may be possible and right to separate the heat, or some other property of the sun, from its light, and in such a case a different result might be reached. I leave that entirely open for decision when it arises.'

As further regards right to light, the court must take account of the present use and 'other potential uses to which the dominant owner may reasonably be expected to put the premises in the future.' In *Carr-Saunders v Dick McNeil Associates Ltd* (1986) it was held that the dominant owner is entitled to such amount of light 'as will leave his premises adequately lit for all ordinary purposes for which they may reasonably be expected to be used.'

The courts are reluctant to recognise new negative easements and this is well illustrated by *Phipps* v *Pears* (1965). In that case there were two adjoining houses. The owner of one of them demolished it leaving the wall of the adjoining house exposed to the weather. Its owner claimed damages, arguing that he was entitled to an easement protecting his house from the weather. Lord Denning MR pointed out that there were two types of easements: positive and negative. The former entitled the dominant owner to do something on the servient owner's land; the latter entitled him to stop the servient owner doing something on his. Lord Denning explained why the law was reluctant to allow new negative easements: 'it would unduly restrict your neighbour's enjoyment of his own land'. If the easement claimed was allowed, it would mean the servient owner could not demolish his own house to replace it with another. 'It would hamper legitimate development'. He concluded: 'there is no such easement known to the law as an easement to be protected from the weather'. The proper way to restrict a neighbour's activities was by means of a restrictive covenant.

That new easements are from time to time created is beyond doubt but they must conform to the four characteristics referred to above, as well as being subject to the other factors described. The right to use a neighbour's lavatory was recognised as an easement in *Miller* v *Emcer Products Ltd* (1956), as was the right to use an airfield: *Dowty Boulton Paul Ltd* v *Wolverhampton Corporation (No 2)* (1976). The right to park a vehicle was recognised as an easement in 1982 in *Newman* v *Jones*.

The words of Lord St Leonards in *Dyce* v *Hay* (1852) are demonstrably true. However, the following dicta must always be borne in mind by the courts when invited to recognise a new easement:

'It must not therefore be supposed that incidents of a novel kind can be devised and attached to property at the whim or caprice of any owner': *Keppel* v *Bailey* (1834).

'A new species of incorporeal hereditament cannot be created at the will and pleasure of the owner of property': per Pollock CB in *Hill* v *Tupper* (1863).

It is for the courts to declare whether a right can be recognised as an easement not individual property owners.

That courts are now more prepared to recognise new easements was noted by Russell LJ in *Dowty Boulton Paul Ltd* v *Wolverhampton Corporation (No 2)* when he said: 'A tendency in the past to freeze the categories of easements has been overtaken by the defrosting operation in *Re Ellenborough Park*.'

Once a right has been identified and placed in the category of easements, questions may still arise in the future as to the extent of that easement. It is in this respect that alteration and expansion may also occur within the categories of easements themselves. An easement of way is within the existing category of easements, but the question may then arise as to the extent of the right that has been acquired. In *British Railways Board* v *Glass* (1965) it was held that a right of way for caravans could expand as that use of the site increased. In such cases the primary requirement is that the character of the user should not be changed. If it is changed then the right may become the subject of a new claim for an easement under the four essentials of an easement identified earlier and the quotation would then be tested to the full. This problem has not occurred with much frequency because the courts have identified the easement of way as a particularly flexible right. Even where the dominant tenement has been increased this expansion alone will not necessarily defeat the claim to a right of way. This was seen in *Graham v Philcox* (1984) when the grant of a right of way to part of a building was construed as a grant to the whole building when it became one single home. Similarly, in *White v Grand Hotel, Eastbourne Ltd* (1913) a grant of a right of way appurtenant to a house, and to be used at all times and for all purposes, was equally available for such general purposes when the house was converted into a hotel.

If the way is enlarged to the point where its original identity is lost then such excessive user may become the subject of an action where an injunction could be the suitable remedy: *Rosling v Pinnegar* (1987).

In *Jelbert v Davis* (1968) there was a grant of an easement conferring on the owner of the dominant land 'a right of way at all times and for all purposes' across a driveway owned by the servient owner. When the grant was made the dominant land was used for agricultural purposes. Five years later this use was changed to a caravan site.

This resulted in 200 caravans being parked on the site accommodating 600 persons. Unfortunately from the servient owner's point of view, although there was a dramatic change in the user of the dominant land this was permissible by the terms of the grant 'at all times and all purposes'. Nevertheless, Lord Denning MR observed that no one entitled to such a right may use it to an extent which was beyond anything contemplated by the grant when made. He decided that the increased user was outside the reasonable contemplation of the original parties and the extent of the dominant owner's current user was not permissible. It interfered too substantially with the servient owner's use of their land.

Thus, as well as the traditional meaning ascribed to the quotation being true, so also is it true as regards the second aspect of the quotation.

SUGGESTED ANSWER TO QUESTION TWO

General Comment

Candidates are required to make a detailed analysis of both *Wheeldon v Burrows* and s62 LPA 1925, and in particular to be prepared to discuss the complexities presented by the wording of Thesiger LJ's dicta in the former. They should not be deterred by the fact that the complexities remained unresolved. The question provides an excellent opportunity for candidates to demonstrate their skills in legal analysis.

Key Points

- The rationale for the rule in *Wheeldon v Burrows*
- *Sovmots Investments Ltd v Secretary of State for the Environment* – per Lord Wilberforce
- Thesiger LJ's dicta:

- – The meaning of 'continuous and apparent'
- – The relationship between the first half of the passage and the second half – differing interpretations
- – *Wheeler* v *J J Saunders Ltd*
- • Section 62 LPA 1925:
  - – the restrictions on its application
  - – 'conveyance'
  - – *Long* v *Gowlett*
- • *Wheeldon* v *Burrows* and s62 LPA 1925 – compared and contrasted

Suggested Answer

In order to assess the accuracy of the statement in the question, it is necessary firstly to examine the rule in *Wheeldon* v *Burrows* (1879).

The case actually had to decide a question of implied reservation of an easement by a grantor (vendor or lessor), but in the course of his judgment Thesiger LJ not only dealt with the circumstances in which easements could be implied into a conveyance of land in favour of land retained by the grantor but also formulated a rule by which easements could be implied into the conveyance in favour of land acquired by the grantee (purchaser or lessee), and it is for this rule that *Wheeldon* v *Burrows* is best known.

The rationale for the rule was explained by Lord Wilberforce in *Sovmots Investments Ltd* v *Secretary of State for the Environment* (1979):

'The rule is a rule of intention, based on the proposition that man may not derogate from his grant. He cannot grant or agree to grant land and at the same time deny to his grantee what is obviously necessary for its reasonable enjoyment.'

In *Birmingham, Dudley and District Banking Co* v *Ross* (1888) Bowen LJ expressed the meaning of the proposition in these words:

'A grantor having given a thing with one hand is not to take away the means of enjoying it with the other.'

Thesiger LJ formulated the rule as follows:

'On the grant by the owner of a tenement or part of that tenement as it is then used and enjoyed, there will pass to the grantee all those continuous and apparent easements (by which of course I mean quasi-easements) or, in other words, all those easements which are necessary to the reasonable enjoyment of the property granted, and which have been and which are at the time of the grant used by the owners of the entirety for the benefit of the part granted.'

It is sometimes said that a continuous easement is one enjoyed passively, ie one that requires no activity by the dominant owner (eg a right to light), but this would exclude a right of way and the courts have never refused a claim to a right of way made under *Wheeldon* v *Burrows*. The meaning of 'apparent' is clearer. It means there must be some permanent indication on the land of the existence of the easement.

In *Ward* v *Kirkland* (1967) Ungoed-Thomas J relied on Professor Cheshire's observations on the meaning of the words 'continuous' and 'apparent' in his book *The Modern Law Real Property:*

> 'The two words ... must be read together and understood as pointing to an easement which is accompanied by some obvious and permanent mark on the land itself' [ie the servient land retained by the grantor].'

'It must be neither transitory nor intermittent; for example, drains and paths as contrasted with bowsprits of ships overhanging a piece of land': per Ungoed-Thomas J. In *Ward v Kirkland* it was held that a claim to an easement to enter a neighbour's land to maintain a wall situated at the boundary of the dominant land was not continuous and apparent.

The second part of the rule as described by Thesiger LJ is not so clear. By using the phrase 'or, in other words', he appears to be saying that continuous and apparent easements are synonymous with easements that are necessary for the reasonable enjoyment of the land. He seems to be saying they are alternatives, ie the rule covers continuous and apparent easements and also those which are necessary for the reasonable enjoyment of the land granted. A third interpretation is possible: that for an easement to fall within the rule it must be continuous, apparent and, in addition, necessary for the reasonable enjoyment of the land.

The matter received the consideration of the Court of Appeal in *Wheeler v J J Saunders Ltd* (1995) when it expressed the view that 'continuous and apparent easements' were synonymous with 'easements necessary for the reasonable enjoyment of the land'.

The issue remains unresolved and continues to be the subject of academic discussion. Eventually no doubt the House of Lords will resolve it.

It is not necessary that the grant should take the form of a conveyance of a legal estate for the rule to apply. It will operate on a transfer of an equitable interest to the grantee, eg an equitable lease: *Borman v Griffith* (1930).

The parties may exclude the application of the rule, a matter which a properly advised grantor should seriously consider.

Finally, as was pointed out in *Wheeler v J J Saunders*, care should be taken not to confuse easements necessary for the reasonable enjoyment of the land with easements of necessity. An easement of necessity is one without which the land cannot be used at all. For example, where a grantor grants land to a grantee but retains a piece of land in the middle with the result that he becomes landlocked and is unable to leave the land without crossing the land conveyed. He should, of course, have reserved an easement of access over the land conveyed and in the event of his failure to do so the law will imply an easement into the conveyance of that land in favour of the land retained on the grounds of necessity. This is an exception to the principle that the law will not normally imply an easement in favour of a grantor's land. The other exception is intended easements or easements based on the common intention of the parties.

We may now turn to s62 LPA 1925 whose predecessor was s6 Conveyancing Act 1881.

It is a word saving section and very widely drafted. It will apply unless a contrary intention is expressed in the conveyance: s62(4). Its effect may be summarised as follows.

A conveyance of land shall be deemed to include all the advantages enjoyed by the land conveyed at the time of the conveyance. It operates therefore exclusively in favour of a grantee. It is clearly wider than the rule in *Wheeldon* v *Burrows* in that it embraces a much wider range of rights, including profits à prendre, which *Wheeldon* v *Burrows* does not. Moreover, it is not confiend to a limited class of easements as is *Wheeldon* v *Burrows*. Although for those reasons it reduces the significance of *Wheeldon* v *Burrows*, it is nevertheless not without its limitations which can result in its inapplicability to certain situations necessitating recourse to *Wheeldon* v *Burrows*.

There are two main restrictions. First, it only applies to a 'conveyance' defined by s205(1)(ii) LPA 1925 as including 'a mortgage, charge, lease assert, vesting declaration, vesting instrument, disclaimer release and every other assurance of property or of an interest therein by any instrument, except a will'.

To be a conveyance there must be an 'instrument', ie a document (*Rye* v *Rye* (1962)) and that document must effect 'an assurance of property or an interest therein', ie it must create or convey a legal estate in the land granted: *Borman* v *Griffith* (1930). Accordingly, an agreement for a lease (an equitable lease) will not be a 'conveyance' for the purposes of s62. In that case, although the plaintiff could not succeed under s62 he was able successfully to claim a right of way under the rule in *Wheeldon* v *Burrows* which does not require 'a conveyance'.

It is possible to create a legal lease not exceeding three years under s54 LPA 1925 without either a deed or writing. Under such a lease the tenant acquires a legal estate in the land, even if the lease was made orally. However, it would not be a conveyance for the purpose of s62 because of the absence of writing. If it was in writing it would be a conveyance as defined by s205.

The second limitation arises from *Long* v *Gowlett* (1923), in which a claim to an implied easement was made under the predecessor to s62, namely s6 of the Conveyancing Act 1881. In that case Sargant J held that for the section to apply there must have been, prior to the conveyance, diversity of ownership or occupation, ie the dominant and servient tenements must have been owned or occupied by different persons. The reasoning behind this decision is that if ownership and occupation of both plots are vested in one person then any use he enjoys over one plot for the benefit of the other plots is enjoyed by virtue of his ownership and does not fall within the wording of s6 which operates to convey with the land 'all ways … privileges, easements, rights and advantages appertaining to the land'.

The decision and reasoning was approved by the House of Lords in *Sovmots Investments Ltd* v *Secretary of State for the Environment* (1979). In that case Lord Wilberforce explained why s62 was inapplicable:

> 'The reason is that when land is under one ownership one cannot speak in any intelligible sense of rights, or privilegfes on easements being exercised over one part for the benefit of the other. Whatever the owner does, he does as owner, and, until a separation occurs, of ownership or at least occupation, the condition for the existence of rights, etc does not exist … *Long* v *Gowlett* (1923) is in my opinion a correct decision.'

In comparing the two methods of acquisition it can be seen that in some ways s62 is wider than *Wheeldon* v *Burrows* and in other ways narrower. Section 62 is only applicable if there is a 'conveyance'. If there is no 'conveyance' recourse may be had to *Wheeldon* v *Burrows* where an equitable lease will suffice. The rule in *Long* v *Gowlett* sometimes prevents the application of s62; there is no such requirement for the applicability of *Wheeldon* v *Burrows*. Thus, although s62 has significantly reduced the importance of *Wheeldon* v *Burrows*, it has not eliminated its usefulness by any means. It can act as a safety net for those claims which fail under s62. In other respects *Wheeldon* v *Burrows* is narrower than s62. It is limited to easements and then only to certain types of easements. Unlike s62, which is much wider in the range of rights it embraces, *Wheeldon* v *Burrows* does not cover profits à prendre. Both share the same rationale in that they are based on the maxim that a man shall not derogate from his grant and both operate in favour of a grantee. A grantor claiming an easement in favour of land he has retained can invoke neither.

It may be necessary to consider whether the easements acquired by either method are legal or equitable. To be legal an easement must fall within the definition of a legal easement as defined by s1(2)(a) LPA 1925. The definition may be summarised as follows: a legal easement is one created by deed (express, implied or presumed) and which is to endure either in perpetuity or for a fixed period. An easement not conforming to s1(2)(a) is necessarily equitable: s1(3) LPA 1925.

Thus, if an easement is implied into an equitable lease under the rule in *Wheeldon* v *Burrows* it will be equitable. Easements implied under s62 will generally be legal because of the necessity for a 'conveyance'. If they are without limit of time or for a fixed period because they are implied into a legal lease they will be legal.

The two methods can produce unexpected, and from the point of view of a grantor (seller) unwelcome, results, as is illustrated by the decision in *International Tea Stores* v *Hobbs* (1903), which was a case on s6 of the Conveyancing Act 1881. In that case what was before the conveyance a mere permissive right became a legal easement because of the effect of s6. A similar result was reached in *Wright* v *Macadam* (1949), where permission to store coal in a shed was converted into a legal easement by s62. Both methods may however be excluded by the grant or conveyance but both will apply if they are not.

SUGGESTED ANSWER TO QUESTION THREE

General Comment

An interesting question which requires consideration of two methods of acquisition of easements: implied grant and prescription. Candidates must also consider whether any easements that have been created are binding on third parties.

Key Points

* Tina – acquisition by prescription:
  - three methods
  - basis of prescription – acquiescence
  - common law prescription: user since 1189
  - must be continuous – as of right – for and against fee simple estate

- Prescription Act 1832 – user 20 years 'next before action'
- easements acquired by prescription attach to the fee simple estate
- the use of the shed – easement of storage – *Wright* v *Macadam*
- acquisition under LPA s62 – 'conveyance' – *Long* v *Gowlett*
- the easement acquired under s62 would be legal and binding on VAX Developments Ltd
- Rita
  - Prescription Act 1832 – 20- and 40-year periods
  - easements acquired under the Act are legal and bind VAX Developments Ltd

Suggested Answer

To avoid confusion it is advisable to make a diagram in order to give an overview of the situation:

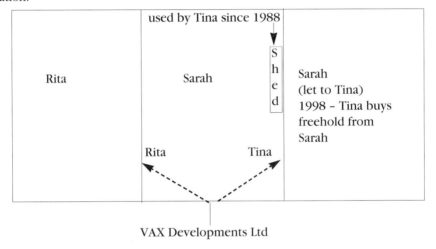

The basic question in the problem is: when VAX Developments purchased Sarah's workshop, did they purchase subject to or free from any rights, if any, that Tina and Rita had acquired over Sarah's land? It is necessary therefore to see if they had acquired any such rights and the position of both must be examined in turn.

Tina
Tina and her father before her had leased their workshop from Sarah. We do not know when the first lease was granted but we do know that ever since that date both Tina's father and Tina have been crossing Sarah's land in order to reach their workshop. It is possible that Tina has acquired an easement by long user (prescription). There are three methods of prescription: common law; lost modern grant and the Prescription Act 1832. Before considering the methods, some general observations about prescription must be made. Prescription is said to be based on acquiescence: *Dalton* v *Angus* (1881) per Fry J. In that case Fry J explained the rationale of acquisition by prescription:

'In many cases, as for instance in the case of acquiescence that creates a right of way, it will be found to involve, first the doing of an act by one man on the land of another, secondly the absence of a right to do that act, thirdly the knowledge of the person affected by it that the act is done, and fourthly the power of that person to prevent it and lastly the abstinence by him from such interference for such a length of time as renders it reasonable for the courts to say that he shall not afterwards interfere to stop the acts being done.'

As regards the third ingredient relating to knowledge of the act being done, it appears from *Sturges* v *Bridgman* (1879), per Thesiger LJ, that the knowledge can be either actual or constructive.

The period of long user required by common law to be shown is a period running from 1189. Various methods were developed to surmount the obvious difficulties imposed by this requirement, including the fiction of the lost modern grant. Parliament intervened by enacting the Prescription Act of 1832 which shortened the period of user. In Lord MacNaghten's words: 'The Act was an Act "for shortening the time of prescription in certain cases". And really it did nothing more.'

The nature of the user must be 'as of right', ie in the Roman law terminology from which the requirement is derived it must be nec vi, nec clam, nec precario. This means that user must be enjoyed without the use of force; it must not be in secret and not be as a result of permission from the servient owner. If any of these factors are present the user cannot be said to be enjoyed 'as of right'. Summarising the position, the claimant must perform the act on the servient owner's land openly and as though he were entitled to do it and without seeking the servient owner's consent. The servient owner must either know of the act or could have reasonably discovered it and have the means to stop it but failed to do so.

The user must be by or on behalf of the fee simple estate against a fee simple estate. The easement, if acquired, becomes annexed to the fee simple estate of the dominant owner and is a burden imposed on the fee simple estate of the servient owner. Thus, a tenant cannot acquire by prescription an easement which attaches to his lease. Any such easement acquired by the tenant through long user attaches to his landlord's fee simple estate: *Kilgour* v *Gaddes* (1904). As has been seen a servient owner must have actual or constructive knowledge of the user on his land and have the means of stopping it. If therefore the servient land is let when the user began then the fee simple owner may not know of it or, if he did, not have the means of stopping it because of the tenant's possession: *Diment* v *N H Foot* (1974); *Pugh* v *Savage* (1970).

In approaching the question as to whether an easement has been acquired by prescription, apply the statutory method, the Prescription Act 1832, first. If that method is not successful apply common law prescription. If that fails, then as a last resort apply lost modern grant which was the method that developed to avoid going back to 1189 as required by common law prescription.

Can Tina claim an easement by prescription to cross Sarah's land to reach her workshop? She must begin by invoking the Prescription Act 1832. The Act lays down various periods of user for easements and profits: 20 and 40 years. Take the 20-year period first. The Act provides that where user has been enjoyed, as of right, for 20 years 'next before action', 'without interruption' as defined by the Act, then the servient owner cannot defeat the claim by showing that user did not commence until after 1189. The meaning of the phrase 'next before action' must be understood. It means that there must be a court action in which the existence of the easement is being claimed or disputed. The period of 20 years is then calculated backwards from the date of commencement of the proceedings. Thus, if proceedings are commenced in 1990, the 20-year period begins in 1970. It is the last 20 years which are relevant. In Tina's case the proceedings would probably be proceedings for trespass against Tina instituted by VAX Developments Ltd. We do not know when Tina's father commenced the user but Tina can add such period as he enjoyed to the time of her enjoyment in order to show user for 20 years. There is no suggestion of any interruption in the period of user and the point need not be considered.

Since we are unable to decide if Tina can show a continuous period of 20 years user we can come to no firm conclusion on the point.

The next point Tina has to prove is that Sarah knew or should have known of the user. Such knowledge is essential if Tina is to establish her claim as is also the means of Sarah to stop it. It is most unlikely that Sarah did not know it and she certainly had the means to stop it, ie by an injunction.

Finally, any easement Tina can establish would not attach to her lease, as has been pointed out. It would attach to the fee simple estate of her landlord. However, Tina's landlord is Sarah and Sarah cannot have an easement over her own land because one of the four characteristics of an easement is that the dominant and servient tenements must not be both owned and occupied by the same person. An easement is a right 'in alieno solo' in the land of another.

Tina's claim to an easement by prescription would therefore fail on that ground even if she succeeded in establishing the other factors.

Tina's use of the shed

Has Tina acquired an easement of storage over the shed on Sarah's land which would bind the subsequent purchasers? The first question for consideration is whether it is possible to have an easement of storage. It is now well established that an easement of storage can exist: *Wright* v *Macadam* (1949). In that case the claim to an easement to store coal in a shed succeeded, although the report does not reveal how much space was claimed. Any such claim cannot succeed if it amounts to a claim to possession or joint possession of the servient land: *Copeland* v *Greenhalf* (1952); *Grigsby* v *Melville* (1972). In the latter case Brightman J concluded that it was a matter of degree, a view shared by Baker J in *London* v *Blenheim Estates* v *Ladbroke Retail Parks Ltd* (1992).

When Sarah gave Tina permission to use the shed she gave her no more than a bare licence revocable at will. In 1998 Tina purchased the freehold of her workshop from Sarah and at that point Tina may have acquired an easement of storage by implied grant under s62 LPA 1925. Under that section, which is a word saving section, a conveyance of land is deemed to include (inter alia) all liberties, privileges, easements, rights and advantages appertaining or reputed to appertain to the land at the time of the conveyance, unless a contrary intention is expressed. Two conditions must be satisfied for the section to be applicable: there must be a conveyance as defined by s205 LPA 1925 and at the time of the conveyance the dominant and servient tenements must be in separate ownership or occupation: *Long* v *Gowlett* (1923); affirmed by the House of Lords in *Sovmots Investments Ltd* b *Secretary of State for the Environment* (1979).

A 'conveyance' is defined by s205(1)(ii) LPA 1925 as including 'a mortgage, charge lease, assent ... and every other assurance of property ... by an instrument, except a will'. A conveyance must create or convey a legal estate in land and accordingly an agreement for a lease is not a conveyance for the purposes of s62: *Borman* v *Griffith* (1930). Here there was a conveyance and at the time of the conveyance there was diversity of occupation. Sarah occupied the servient tenement while the dominant tenement was in Tina's occupation. Accordingly, the section is applicable and an easement of storage was implied into the conveyance of the freehold to Tina for the benefit of the land she acquired thereby. The effect of s62 was in effect to upgrade the licence of storage into an easement of storage. In *International Tea Stores Co* v *Hobbs* (1903) a licence became a legal easement on the application of the predecessor to s62 – s6 Conveyancing Act 1881. The conveyance could have excluded the operation of s62 but there is no evidence that it did so.

The question remains as to whether VAX Developments Ltd, when it purchased Sarah's land, took subject to Tina's newly acquired easement. Since the easement was incorporated into a conveyance of a legal estate in land and was not limited in time it was a legal easement within the definition of a legal easement in s1(2)(a) LPA 1925. It will, therefore, automatically bind VAX Developments Ltd. It cannot demand that Tina vacate the shed and hand over the key.

Rita

If Rita and her staff are to continue walking over Sarah's land Rita must establish she had acquired an easement over that land which was in existence at the time of the conveyance to VAX Developments Ltd, and that it bound VAX Developments Ltd either because it was a legal easement, or if equitable, because it was registered as a land charge Class D(iii) under the Land Charges Act 1972.

The problem discloses little information about Rita's user save that it had been enjoyed 'for as long as anyone can remember'. The provisions of the Prescription Act 1832 may be applicable by applying either the 20-year or 40-year periods. The provisions relating to the 20-year period have already been discussed in Tina's case, but those relating to the 40 years should be considered in case they are applicable. There is an important difference (inter alia) between the shorter and longer periods. The requirement that user must be of right is slightly modified in the case of the 40-year period. User as of right means that the user must not be 'precario', ie with the servient owner's permission. In the case of the 40-year period, if oral consent is given at the beginning of the period this will not defeat the claim. This is the effect of the wording of s2 of the Act. See also *Healey* v *Hawkins* (1968).

If Rita can establish a claim under the Prescription Act then it will be a legal easement, since easements acquired by prescription are deemed to originate in a deed of grant to last in perpetuity which brings them within the definition of a legal easement as defined by s1(2)(a) LPA 1925.

Accordingly, if Rita can establish that she has acquired an easement then VAX Developments Ltd will take subject to it and cannot tell her to leave the land.

SUGGESTED ANSWER TO QUESTION FOUR

General Comment

A question that deals with the statutory meaning of the word 'interruption' and which demonstrates the need for care in considering its application which requires clarity of thought if confusion is to be avoided.

Key Points

- Prescription Act 1832
    - 20-year period
    - as of right
    - without interruption
- The period must be 'next before action' – s4
- Necessity for a court action
- Meaning of interruption as defined by the Act
- Effect of six months' acquiescence
- Alf as an alternative may demonstrate that he does not acquiesce: *Bennison* v *Cartwright*

Suggested Answer

There are three methods of acquiring an easement by presumed grant and they must be applied in the following order: Prescription Act 1832; common law prescription; and lost modern grant.

Alf must be advised as to whether he can claim an easement under s2 Prescription Act 1832 which provides that if there has been enjoyment of user over the servient land for:

1   20 years next before action; and
2   the user has been of right; and
3   without interruption

then the servient owner cannot defeat the claim by proving that the user commenced after 1189.

Section 4 provides that the periods of time specified in the Act for enjoyment of user must be the periods 'next before some suit or action'.

Section 2 is not applicable to easements.

Thus, the Act is not applicable until there is a court action, the subject of which is the existence of the easement. No mention is made in the question of a court action but clearly the potential for one is there. It may be that Bert will sue Alf for trespass in which case Alf will argue by way of defence that he has an easement over Bert's land or, if Bert does not institute proceedings, then Alf may sue for a declaration that he is entitled to the easement. In any event there must be a court action in order to define the time period of 20 years.

The effect of this provision is that the relevant period is 20 years culminating in a court action, or, to put the matter another way, the last 20 years before the court action. If the user commenced 30 years ago the date of commencement is irrelevant. It is the last 20 years user which matters and the relevant date of the court action is the date when proceedings are commenced.

Assuming the user has been of right, ie neither by force, secrecy or permission, Alf at first sight appears unable to invoke the Act since he has only enjoyed 19-and-a-half years user and if he waits another six months for 20 years to elapse then he will be unable to plead that his user was uninterrupted.

However, his position is much more favourable that at first appears because of the way the word 'interruption' is defined by s4 of the Act, ie 'no act ... shall be deemed to be an interruption ... unless the same shall have been or shall be submitted to or acquiesced in, for one year after the party interrupted shall have had ... notice thereof'.

It is clear that Alf can only succeed in his claim to an easement after 20 years has elapsed. If a court action was commenced by either party after only 19-and-a-half years he would lose as there would only be 19-and-a-half years 'next before some suit or action'. If no court action is commenced until the 20 years has expired then although Alf has been obliged to discontinue his user for the last six months of the period, because of the Act's definition of interruption, he can argue that the discontinuance of the user did not amount to an interruption. It is necessary, therefore, to understand what constitutes an interruption as defined by the Act.

First, there must be some hostile interruption to the user by either the servient owner or a stranger: *Davies* v *Williams* (1851). That is the case here: Bert has erected a fence. If Alf had simply stopped crossing Bert's land that would have not been enough: *Smith* v *Baxter* (1900).

A hostile interruption is not, however, enough for the purposes of the Act. That of itself does not constitute an interruption. Section 4 requires an additional element. There will only be an interruption recognised by the Act if the hostile interruption is known to the party interrupted (Alf) and acquiesced by him for one year. Thus, an interruption cannot come into existence until it is known to Alf and submitted to or acquiesced in by him for one year. Whether there has been submission or acquiescence for one year is an issue of fact to be decided upon the evidence: *Davies* v *Du Paver* (1953).

In this case Alf has two courses open to him. He may sit back and do nothing for six months. This will amount to acquiescence but in six months' time, when he will be able to sue for a declaration, there will only have been six months' acquiescence to the hostile interruption and consequently no interruption as defined by the Act. Bert will be unable to defeat Alf's claim by pleading that he does not have 20 years' interrupted user. As an alternative, although not necessary in this case, Alf could demonstrate that he does not acquiesce in Bert's conduct. He may do this by protesting to Bert about the fence: *Bennison* v *Cartwright* (1864). One thing he should not do is continue to try and cross Bert's land. If he did so he would be a trespasser, since as yet he has no easement, and cannot have one until the 20-year period has expired when he should commence proceedings. If he trespassed Bert might be provoked into instituting proceedings against him before the period had expired in which case Alf could not claim 20 years' user 'next before some suit or action'.

6

Restrictive Covenants

Introduction

The facts of restrictive covenant questions can sometimes be complicated and a systematic approach is required to avoid confusion. A person wishing to enforce a restrictive covenant has to prove he has its benefit and that the person he is suing has the burden. It is advisable to deal with the burden first. If the proposed defendant is not the original covenantor then the plaintiff must prove that the burden has been transmitted to him. The burden cannot pass at common law and so consideration must be given as to whether it has passed in equity under *Tulk* v *Moxhay* (1848). If the conditions for its passing have been met then consider whether the plaintiff has the benefit. If he is the original covenantee there is no problem. If he is not, the original covenantee must establish that the benefit has passed to him. Although the benefit of a covenant may run at common law, if it has been necessary to invoke equity to ensure the passing of the burden the common law rules cannot be used; the equitable rules for the passing of the benefit must be applied instead.

Sections 78 and 79 LPA 1925 are important provisions in this area but their phraseology should be noted with care. Because of the construction put upon s78 by *Federated Homes Ltd* v *Mill Lodge Properties Ltd* (1980) the benefit of covenants which touch and concern land will generally be annexed to the dominant land. However, a distinction must be drawn between positive and negative covenants.

Section 78 provides:

> 'A covenant relating to any land of the covenantee shall be deemed to be made with the covenantee and his successors in title and the persons deriving title under him or them. ...
> For the purposes of this subsection in connection with covenants restrictive of the user of land "successors in title" shall be deemed to include the owners and occupiers for the time being of the land of the covenantee intended to be benefited.'

The result of the wording is that the benefit of positive covenants may be enforced by the covenantee, his successors in title and those who derive title under him or them, eg lessees and mortgagees. Since a person in adverse possession is not a successor in title as defined in this wording he cannot take advantage of s78 and enforce the benefit of a positive covenant. If, however, the covenant is restrictive since, in the case of restrictive covenants the phrase 'successors in title' is more widely defined so as to include 'owners and occupiers of the land for the time being', he can enforce its benefit.

Section 79 deals with the burden in a similar fashion and it has to be remembered that in the case of freehold land the burden of restrictive covenants can pass only in equity: *Tulk* v *Moxhay*.

Questions

INTERROGRAMS

1   What was the common law rule concerning the running of the benefit of a covenant?
2   Does the burden of a covenant run with the land at common law?
3   What is the doctrine in *Tulk* v *Moxhay*?
4   Explain the significance of *Halsall* v *Brizell*.
5   Summarise the methods by which the rule that the burden of a positive covenant does not run may be avoided or mitigated.
6   Under what conditions will a restrictive covenant in a building scheme be enforced?
7   How may restrictive covenants be discharged?
8   Has the law of town and country planning made restrictive covenants less important than they were?

QUESTION ONE

Alex divided up his land (unregistered land) into four equal-sized plots (Plots A, B, C and D) and built a substantial house on each of them. He decided to live on Plot A himself and he sold Plots B, C and D to Barry, Carol and Diana in that order. When they purchased their plots, Barry, Carol and Diana entered into identical covenants 'with Alex and his successors in title', covenanting (i) to use the house as a single dwelling-house, (ii) to use the house for residential purposes only, and (iii) to maintain the house in a good state of repair. All four plots have since been sold: Plot A to Paul, Plot B to Quentin, Plot C to Rachel and Plot D to Stella. The house on Plot B has fallen into disrepair and Quentin proposes to divide the house into flats which he will sell. Rachel has started a massage business on Plot C. Paul and Stella want to enforce the covenants against Quentin and Rachel.

Advise them.

London University LLB Examination
(for external students) Land Law June 1994 Q4

QUESTION TWO

In 1988 Alice purchased a vacant piece of land, divided it into two plots and built a large detached house on each plot. She retained one plot (Plot A) for her own occupation and sold the other plot (Plot B) to Bertha. Bertha covenanted 'with Alice and her successors-in-title' to use Plot B as a private residence only and Alice covenanted 'with Bertha and her successors in title' to maintain the wall separating the two plots in a good state of repair. In 1993 Bertha sold Plot B to David expressly assigning to him the benefit of the repairing covenant and in 1994 Alice sold Plot A to Calum. The wall is badly in need of repair and David wants to convert Plot B into a guest house with a restaurant.

Advise David.

London University LLB Examination
(for external students) Land Law June 1996 Q7

QUESTION THREE

Alan owned Blackacre and the adjoining Whiteacre, and in 1960 he sold Blackacre to Douglas who covenanted with Alan and his successors in title (a) not to let the property fall into disrepair and (b) not to use the property for business purposes.

On the assumption that the land is unregistered, consider how far these covenants will be enforceable:

a   by a lessee of Whiteacre against Douglas;
b   by Alan against an adverse possessor of Blackacre; and
c   by a purchaser of Whiteacre against a purchaser of Blackacre.

London University LLB Examination
(for external students) Land Law June 1992 Q7

QUESTION FOUR

In 1985 Jack sold a plot of land which formed part of his Alban Estate to Priscilla who covenanted with Jack and his successors in title to use the land for residential purposes and to maintain the house in a good state of repair. Consider the extent to which these covenants are enforceable (i) by a lessee of the Alban Estate against Priscilla, (ii) by Jack against a lessee of Priscilla's land, and (iii) by a purchaser of the Alban Estate against a person who inherited Priscilla's land.

London University LLB Examination
(for external students) Land Law June 1997 Q8

Answers

ANSWERS TO INTERROGRAMS

1   For centuries the common law has permitted the benefit of a freehold covenant to run (*The Prior's Case* (1368)) and this applies whether the covenant is positive or negative. A number of conditions have to be satisfied before a successor in title to the original covenantee can enforce the covenant against the original covenantor.

   a   The covenant must touch and concern the covenantee's land: *Rogers* v *Hosegood* (1990).
   b   At the time the covenant was made it must have been the intention of the parties that the benefit should run with the covenantee's land (the dominant land). The wording of the covenant should be examined to see if it expresses that intention, but where it is silent on the matter s78 LPA 1925 will apply: 'A covenant relating to any land of the covenantee shall be deemed to be made with the covenantee and his successors in title'. If the covenant is restrictive, 'successors in title' is deemed to include owners and occupiers for the time being. However, the covenant must identify the dominant land: *Rogers* v *Hosegood* (1900). See *Smith and Snipes Hall Farm* v *River Douglas Catchment Board* (1949).
   c   When the covenant was made the covenantee must have owned the legal estate in the land. Before 1926 it was necessary that the covenantee's successor in title

should hold the same legal estate as the original covenantee, the reason being that the benefit was attached to that estate. However, because of the wording of s78 LPA 1925 this is no longer necessary. Thus, if the original covenantee owned the fee simple estate then his successor in title may claim the benefit if his estate is a legal lease.

2   The burden of a freehold covenant cannot run at common law: *Austerberry* v *Oldham Corporation* (1885). This principle was affirmed by the House of Lords in *Rhone* v *Stephens* (1994). Thus, if the original covenantor has disposed of the servient tenement to a successor in title, at common law, the latter will take free of the burden. It can only pass in equity. A successor in title to the covenantee seeking to enforce the burden in equity cannot then rely on the common law rules to show that the benefit has passed to him. He must use the equitable rules instead: annexation; assignment; and building scheme.

3   *Tulk* v *Moxhay* was decided in 1848 and the successor in title to the original covenantor was held to be bound by the covenant even though he was not a party to it because when he acquired the land in Leicester Square he had notice of the covenant. Since then the courts have added further requirements before the burden can pass in equity.

In addition to the necessity for the covenant to be negative in substance the following conditions must be satisfied:

a   At the time the covenant was made, the covenantee must have owned land for the benefit of which the covenant was taken: *Formby* v *Barker* (1903); *London County Council* v *Allen* (1914).

b   The original parties must have intended that the burden should run with the servient land. If that intention is not apparent from the covenant's wording then s79 LPA 1925 will apply unless a contrary intention has been expressed.

c   The covenant must touch and concern the *dominant* land, ie it must affect the land's value or its mode of occupation: *Rogers* v *Hosegood* (1900).

d   In the case of unregistered land, covenants made after 1925 should be registered as a land charge Class D(ii). In registered land a restrictive covenant is a minor interest and should be entered on the register of title of the servient land either by a notice or a caution.

4   The common law rule that the burden of a freehold covenant cannot run with the servient land is one of obvious inconvenience. It may pass in equity but only if it is restrictive in substance. Positive burdens cannot run even in equity. The equitable principle 'he who enjoys the benefit must suffer the burden' was applied in *Halsall* v *Brizell* (1957).

In that case there was a covenant to contribute to the maintenance of a private road. A successor in title to the original covenantor claimed he was entitled to use the road but that, since the positive burden of contributing to its upkeep did not run with the land he had purchased, he was not liable for a contribution. Upjohn J held that if he wished to enjoy the benefit of using the road he must bear the burden of the maintenance contribution.

The application of the principle was examined by the House of Lords in *Rhone* v *Stephens* (1994). The relevant conveyance contained two clauses which were the basis of the litigation: clause 3 contained a covenant to repair a roof. The defendant who was the successor in title to the original covenantor argued that the covenant was not enforceable against her since a positive burden could not run with the land. The plaintiffs sought to enforce the covenant against the defendant and, basing their argument on clause 2 in the conveyance which imposed reciprocal benefits and burdens of support between the two properties, contended that since the defendant enjoyed a right of support under that clause, she was under an obligation to repair the roof.

The House of Lords distinguished the facts from those of *Halsall* v *Brizell*. Lord Templeman pointed out that in *Halsall* v *Brizell* there were reciprocal benefits and burdens. The condition, he said, must be relevant to the right. The right to use the road was interlinked to the obligation to contribute to its upkeep. The defendant could escape the obligation by surrendering his right to use the road. In the instant case that was not the position. The two clauses were independent of each other. If the defendant did not fulfil the obligation under clause 3 to repair the roof, she was still entitled to the benefit of the right to support conferred by clause 2. The plaintiffs' argument, that since the defendant enjoyed the benefits of clause 2 she was bound by the burden imposed by clause 3, could not be sustained.

5   Several methods are available to avoid the inconvenience that a positive covenant cannot run with the servient land:

a   The principle of *Halsall* v *Brizell* (1957) as explained above.

b   The benefits and burdens of leasehold covenants, whether positive or negative, may run with the reversion and the lease, although this must be now understood in the light of the Landlord and Tenant (Covenants) Act 1995 which applies to leases created on or after 1 January 1996. If a developer of an estate wishes to impose a positive covenant on his purchasers and their successors in title, say in respect of maintenance charges towards the upkeep of the common parts, the inconvenience of the rule becomes at once apparent if he is proposing to convey the freehold of each plot. If, however, instead of selling the freeholds, he grants long leases to his transferees then when they in turn assign their leases to their transferees the burden of the covenants in the leases, whether positive or negative, will pass and will be enforceable against the assignees by the reversioner and his successors in title providing certain conditions are satisfied.

c   Even after he has parted with the land the covenantor will remain liable to the original covenantee for the performance of covenants and damages for their breach. When the covenantor sells the land to a purchaser he can require that the purchaser enter into an indemnity covenant under which the purchaser agrees to indemnify the original covenantor if he is sued by the original covenantee. To cover himself, the purchaser in his turn should obtain an identical covenant from his purchaser so that over a period of time a chain of indemnity covenants is created. Thus, if a purchaser at the end of the chain breaks his covenant he cannot be sued by the original covenantor, because the burden being positive has not passed. The original covenantee may then sue the original covenantor. He in turn can then sue his purchaser on the indemnity covenant and he in his turn can then sue his purchaser and so on until the purchaser, in breach, at the end of the chain is finally reached.

This is not a satisfactory device. It only works if the chain remains unbroken. If one of the parties dies, disappears or goes bankrupt, then the chain is broken.

If the original covenantee wishes to sue the original covenantor and he cannot be located the chain is broken at the outset. By the time the covenant is broken by an ultimate purchaser, the original covenantor may have long since vanished.

d   Under s153 LPA 1925 a lease originally granted for not less than 300 years and which has not less than 200 years still to run may be enlarged into a fee simple provided it is not subject to a rent. Section 153(8) provides that 'the fee simple so acquired ... shall be subject to all the same trusts ... and to all the same covenants and provisions relating to user and enjoyment, and to all the same obligations of every kind, as the term would have been subject to it if had not been so enlarged.' This method does not appear to have been tested.

e   Although new rentcharges cannot be created after the Rentcharges Act 1977, the statute does contain a number of exceptions, one of which is an estate rentcharge. Section 2(4) defines an estate rentcharge as a rentcharge created for the purpose:

> '(a) of making covenants to be performed by the owner of the land affected by the rentcharge enforceable by the rent owner against the owner for the time being of the land; or
> (b) of meeting, or contributing towards, the cost of the performance by the rent owner of covenants for the provision of services, the carrying out of maintenance or repairs, the effecting of insurance or the making of any payment by him for the benefit of the land affected by the rentcharge or for the benefit of that and other land.'

A covenant to pay money or contribute to the upkeep of property may thus be construed to fall within this definition.

f)   The burden of a *covenant* by a covenantor to maintain and repair a fence cannot pass to his successor in title either at common law or in equity. However, the Court of Appeal in *Crow* v *Wood* (1971) held that it was possible for there to be an *easement* of fencing despite the imposition of a positive burden on the servient owner. This is clearly an exception to the rule that an easement must not impose an obligation on a servient owner to execute positive acts or spend money. The obligation must be drafted so as to create an easement and not a covenant.

6   The requirements for a building scheme were laid down by Parker J in *Elliston* v *Reacher* (1908):

a   the plaintiff and defendant must have derived their titles from a common vendor;
b   the common vendor must have laid out his estate in lots before selling commenced;

c   the plots must have been subject to restrictions which it was intended to impose on them all;

d   the common vendor must have intended that the restrictions were for the benefit of all of the plots.

In *Reid* v *Bickerstaff* (1909) it was held that the area of the scheme must be clearly defined. This was approved in *Emile Elias & Co Ltd* v *Pine Groves Ltd* (1993).

In *Reid* v *Bickerstaff* the scheme was described as 'the local law imposed by the vendors upon a definite area'.

In *White* v *Bijou Mansions* (1937) Sir Wilfred Green MR emphasised that every purchaser must know that there is a scheme of mutually enforceable restrictions.

The vendor must have

'… offered to sell to the purchaser a plot forming a part of that defined estate on the terms that the purchaser should enter into such restrictive covenants relating to his plot as the scheme contemplated upon the footing that the purchaser should reciprocally have the benefit of such restrictive covenants relating to the other plots on the estate as indicated by the scheme': *Reid* v *Bickerstaff* (1909) per Buckley LJ.

As Cozens-Hardy MR emphasised in the same case: 'reciprocity is the foundation of the idea of a scheme'.

At the root of the scheme is a common intention by all the parties that the covenants have been entered into for the mutual benefit of all the purchasers. This was expressed in the earlier case of *Nottingham Patent Brick and Tile Co* v *Butler* (1885). This common intention may be proved by a deed of mutual covenant between the parties or it may be deduced from the wording of the conveyances to the purchasers. If these methods of proof are not available then the requirements of *Elliston* v *Reacher* must be satisfied.

However, subsequent cases have modified the requirements of *Elliston* v *Reacher*. In *Re Dolphin's Conveyance* (1970), although the purchasers had not acquired their plots from a common vendor, the court held that nevertheless there was a building scheme. In 1965, in *Baxter* v *Four Oakes Properties Ltd* (1965) the owner did not lay out the estate in lots prior to sale, but again the court found there was a building scheme. In *Emile Elias & Co Ltd* v *Pine Groves Ltd* the attempt to establish a building scheme failed. There was no evidence of a common intention to enter into mutually enforceable covenants; nor had the area been defined.

7   Unless discharged, the life of a restrictive covenant is indefinite, which can cause major inconvenience many years after they have been created. However, they may be discharged as follows:

a   Release by the owner for the time being of the dominant land. Release may be by implication as well as by express means. If the dominant owner acquiesces in a breach to the extent that he represents to the servient owner that he is no longer interested in enforcing the covenant, this may amount to implied release: see *Chatsworth Estates Co* v *Fewell* (1931).

b   Discharge or modification by the Lands Tribunal: s84 LPA 1925 as amended by s28 LPA 1969. There are several grounds in these provisions under which an application may be made and in particular where the covenants have become obsolete due to changes in the neighbourhood. If the covenants are no longer of any substantial value or advantage or are contrary to the public interest the Lands Tribunal may discharge or modify them.

8   Planning controls and restrictive covenants exist side by side and sometimes overlap. It might be argued that the areas currently covered by restrictive covenants, which originate from the instigation of individuals operating in the private domain, should come within the planning control of public authorities. The Law Commission has resisted suggestions to that effect, pointing out that many matters with which restrictive covenants are concerned are too detailed to merit consideration by a planning authority. It also points out that in the cases of restrictive covenants the initiative in enforcing them is in the hands of the dominant owner. Were the same subject matter to be regulated by planning controls then the initiative would be with the local planning authority on whom the dominant owner would be dependent for enforcement: *Transfer of Land: The Law of Positive and Negative Covenants* (1984) (Law Com No 127).

Sometimes a conflict can arise between the two. In *Re Martin's Application* (1989) land was subject to a restrictive covenant prohibiting building on certain land. Planning permission was later obtained to build on it. An application was then made to the Lands Tribunal to have the covenant discharged, but it was dismissed. The rejection was confirmed by the Court of Appeal which pointed out that the grant of planning permission did not impose on the Tribunal an obligation to discharge the covenant. The granting of planning permission was merely a factor which the Tribunal must take into account when deciding whether or not to discharge the covenant.

SUGGESTED ANSWER TO QUESTION ONE

General Comment

This is a question concerning the enforcement of freehold covenants against successors in title of the original parties. The biggest problem in the question concerns Stella. As with most problem questions on this topic, the inclusion of a diagrammatical representation of the facts is advisable, not least because it should eliminate the possibility of a student confusing the various parties in the course of the answer.

Key Points

- Definition of a covenant
- Covenants and covenantees – dominant and servient tenements – positive and negative covenants
- A plaintiff wishing to enforce covenants must establish that he has the benefit and the defendant has the burden
- Burdens of covenants do not run at common law: *Austerberry* v *Oldham Corporation*

- Burden can only run in equity: *Tulk* v *Moxhay*
- Conditions for the running of the burden in equity
- If equity is invoked to ensure the transmission of the burden of a covenant then the common law rules cannot be relied upon to ensure that the benefit has passed: equity must be invoked
- The passing of the benefit in equity
- Application of the principles to the facts of the problem
- In Stella's case she may have to prove that a building scheme exists

Suggested Answer

A covenant, in the context of real property law, is an agreement by deed whereby one party (the covenantor) covenants with another party (the covenantee) that he will or will not engage in some stated activity on his land for the benefit of the covenantee's land. The land owned by the covenantee will have the benefit of the covenant and that owned by the covenantor will have the burden. The land benefiting from the covenant is the dominant tenement and the land subject to its burden is the servient tenement.

When Alex sold Plot B to Barry and Barry entered into the three covenants, Alex was the covenantee and Barry was the covenantor. The dominant tenement was Plot A and the servient tenement was Plot B. However, at that time Alex continued to own Plots C and D and it will be a question for consideration whether the benefits of the covenants was also conferred on them. The covenant is worded to the effect that it is for the benefit of 'Alex and his successors in title'. Carol and Diana became his successors in title when they later purchased Plots C and D from Alex, but the covenant does not refer to those plots themselves.

Carol and Diana are also covenantors since they too entered into the three covenants, and their respective plots must be regarded as servient tenements.

There are two kinds of freehold covenant – positive and negative. A positive covenant is one which obliges the owner to do something on his land (construct and maintain a fence) or to contribute money towards work to be done or services to be provided. A restrictive covenant is one which restrains a landowner in some respect in the use of his property, eg a covenant which prevents the covenantor from using his land for the purpose of conducting trade or business. On the facts, covenant (i) to use the house as a single dwelling-house is a restrictive one, covenant (ii) to use the house for residential purposes only is also a restrictive one, and covenant (iii) to maintain the house in a good state of repair is a positive one.

On the facts, Alex has sold Plot A to Paul (purchaser of original covenantee) and the three original covenantors Barry, Carol and Diana have sold their respective plots to Quentin, Rachel and Stella. These developments can be represented diagrammatically as follows:

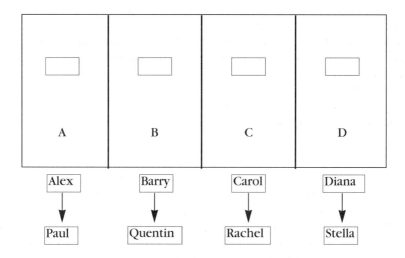

On the facts, Plot B is in disrepair (breach of covenant (iii)), Quentin is proposing to divide the house on Plot B into flats (breach of covenant (i)) and Rachel has started a massage business on Plot C (breach of covenants (i) and (ii)).

Paul and Stella want to enforce the three covenants against Quentin and Rachel. To do so they have to establish that the burdens of the covenants have passed to Quentin and Rachel and that the benefit of the covenants has passed to them under either the common law or equitable rules.

Turning first to the running of the burden of the covenants, the position at common law is that the the burden of a covenant, whether positive or negative, made between a vendor and purchaser cannot run directly with freehold land. This was decided in *Austerberry* v *Oldham Corporation* (1885) when the Court of Appeal held, that there was no authority in previous case law that, at common law, the burden of a freehold covenant could be annexed to land. In *Rhone* v *Stephens* (1994) the House of Lords was invited to overrule *Austerberry* but declined to do so on the grounds that the rule had been too long established. Thus, it is settled law that the burden of a covenant relating to freehold land cannot run in common law, whether positive or negative.

Paul and Stella must have recourse to equity in attempting to establish that the burdens of the covenants have passed to Quentin and Rachel. It is possible for the burdens of such covenants to run in equity under the doctrine of *Tulk* v *Moxhay* (1848). The decision in that case was based on notice. When Moxhay purchased the land in Leicester Square he had notice of the covenant entered into between Tulk and Elms in 1808 and was bound by it. In 1882 in *London and SW Railway* v *Gomm*, the Court of Appeal decided that the covenant must benefit the covenantee's land. The current position is that for the burden of a freehold covenant to pass in equity the following conditions must be satisfied:

1   The covenant must be negative in substance. Whether the wording is positive or negative is immaterial. It is the substance that matters. The wording of the covenant

in *Tulk* v *Moxhay* was positive, but was clearly negative in substance. A covenant not to allow a fence to fall into disrepair, although negative in wording, is positive because it imposes on the servient owner a positive obligation to repair the fence: see *Hayward* v *Brunswick Permanent Benefit Building Society* (1881).

2   At the time the covenant was made, the covenantee must have owned land which was capable of being benefited by the covenant and for the benefit of which the covenant was taken: *London County Council* v *Allen* (1914), following *Formby* v *Barker* (1903); *Re Nisbet and Pott's Contract* (1906).

A landlord holding the reversion of a lease will satisfy the requirement (*Hall* v *Ewin* (1887)), with the result that a landlord may sue a sub-tenant under the doctrine of *Tulk* v *Moxhay*, whereas he would normally be precluded from doing so because of the absence of privity of estate between him and the sub-tenant.

This requirement is indicative that equity is enforcing the covenant to protect land rather than its owner. It follows therefore that although the original covenantee may always sue the original covenantor, under their contractual relationship, once the covenantee has parted with the land he cannot sue a successor in title to the original covenantor. Equity will not assist the original covenantee because he no longer owns land to be protected: see *Formby* v *Barker*.

It further follows that a successor in title to the original covenantee can only enforce the covenant while he holds the land. Once he has parted with it he loses his right to sue.

3   At the time the covenant was made the original parties must have intended that the burden of the covenant should run with servient land. The wording of the covenant must be examined to see if such an intention has been expressed. If the covenantor covenants on behalf of himself, his heirs and assigns this will be indicative of that intention. In the absence of wording to that effect then s79 LPA 1925 may be applicable. Covenants relating to the land of the covenantor, if made after 1925, are deemed to be made on behalf of himself and his successors in title unless a contrary intention is expressed. Secton 79(2) enacts that in the case of restrictive covenants the phrase 'successors in title' includes owners and occupiers for the time being.

4   The covenant must 'touch and concern' the dominant land. In the words of Farwell J *Rogers* v *Hosegood* (1900) 'the covenant must either affect the land as regards mode of occupation, or it must be such as per se and not merely from collateral circumstances, affect the value of the land'. This is a further indication that the basis of equitable intervention is to protect land rather than the owner personally.

5   Restrictive covenants made on or after 1 January 1926 are registrable as a land charge, class D(ii): s2(5) Land Charges Act 1972. If not registered then it is void against a purchaser of the legal estate in the land for money or money's worth: s4(6) LCA 1972. If the covenant was made before that date then it is subject to the doctrine of notice. In the case of registered land, being a minor interest, it should be protected by an entry, notice or caution, on the register of title of the servient land. The entry should be made in the charges register.

It is clear that Paul and Stella must rely on equity to prove that the burdens of the respective covenants have passed to Quentin and Rachel. That being the case, they cannot invoke the common law rules to establish that the benefits of the covenants have passed to themselves. They must invoke equity to secure those transmissions. Benefits may pass in equity in three ways:

1   annexation of the benefits to the dominant land; or
2   express assignment of the benefits; or
3   a building scheme.

To take annexation first. Did the original parties to the covenant annex the benefit to the dominant land? This is a matter of this intention as expressed in the wording of the covenant,but the covenant must refer to the land to be benefited. In *Reid* v *Bickerstaff* (1909) the covenant was made with 'the vendors, their heirs and assignees'. This was held to be ineffective to annex the benefit to the dominant land because there was no reference to the land. A similar result was reached in *Renals* v *Cowlishaw* (1879). By contrast, in *Rogers* v *Hosegood* the covenant was made 'with the intent that they might enure to the benefit of the vendors, their heirs and assigns and others claiming under them to all or any of their lands adjoining'. This wording was held to be effective to annex the benefit to the dominant land.

If there is no wording expressing the original parties' intention then s78 LPA 1925, as contsrued by the Court of Appeal in *Federated Homes Ltd* v *Mill Lodge Properties Ltd* (1980) will be applicable. That case decided that s78 was no mere word saving section but actually of itself annexed the benefit of a covenantor's covenant to the dominant land and to each and every part thereof. However, it is thought that s78 can only apply if the covenant identifies the land to be benefited. The section contains no provision that it may be excluded, but in *Roake* v *Chadha* (1983) it was held that its application could be excluded by the parties.

Because of the construction put on s78 by the Court of Appeal decision, the second method of transmission – assignment – has considerably diminished in importance since in most cases the benefit will have been annexed to the dominant land thus obviating the necessity for it to be expressly assigned. When the dominant land is transferred the annexed benefit will automatically pass with it.

The application of the above principles may now be applied to the facts of the case. It is essential to identify the covenants, the enforcement of which is being sought. There are two plaintiffs: Paul and Stella. Paul is seeking to enforce the covenants made between Alex and Barry and Alex and Carol. He must establish that the burden of those covenants have passed to Quentin and Rachel respectively. Stella has to do the same.

The covenants relating to Plots B and C (respective covenantors Barry and Carol) may be considered together as they are identical. Covenant (iii) is disqualified for consideration at the outset since it is positive in substance.

Is the second requirement for the application of *Tulk* v *Moxhay* applicable? It is necessary to examine the state of affairs when the covenants were made. When Barry and Carol entered into their covenants with Alex (the covenantee) what land did Alex own? When Barry entered into his covenant with Alex, Alex owned Plots A, C and D. When Carol covenanted with Alex in respect of Plot C, Alex owned Plots A and D. Barry's covenant in respect of Plot B was capable of benefiting Plot A but probably not

Plot D since Plot B was separated from Plot D by Plot C. Carol's covenant could benefit Plot D next door but probably not Plot A which was separated from it by Plot B.

In respect of Plots B and C, did the respective covenanting parties (Plot B, Alex and Barry, and Plot C, Alex and Carol) intend that the burdens should run with Plots B and C. The covenants express no intention that the covenantors intended the burdens should run with the respective plots. Section 79 LPA 1925 will therefore be applicable: 'A covenant relating to any land of a covenantor ... shall, unless a contrary intention is expressed, be deemed to be made by the covenantor ... [and] his successors in title'. There is no evidence that the section has been excluded by the parties and it will accordingly apply.

The covenants must touch and concern dominant land. It is necessary to consider what is the dominant land in respect of the Plot B and Plot C covenants. When Barry covenanted with Alex in respect of Plot B, the benefited plots were Plot A and Plot C, next door. Plot D may be too far away to benefit, which may cause problems for Stella when she seeks to enforce the covenant in respect of Plot B, but for the moment we are advising Paul who is seeking to enforce the burdens of the covenant in respect of Plot B. The dominant land we are considering here is Plot A. It is a matter of evidence whether the covenants made by Barry in respect of Plot B 'touch and concern' Plot A.

Finally, to ensure that the burden of the covenants made between Alex and Barry in respect of Plot B have passed they must have been registered as a land charge class D(ii). If they have, Quentin will be deemed to have notice of them: s198 LPA 1925.

Whether Paul can establish that the burden of the covenant made between Alex and Carol (Plot C) has passed to Rachel is more problematic becuse it may not 'touch and concern' the dominant land (Plot A) because both plots are separated by Plot B.

Therefore, Paul may not be successful in enforcing the covenants against Rachel. He may not be able to prove that the burden of Carol's covenant has passed to her.

Stella is seeking to establish that the burdens of Barry's and Carol's covenants have passed to Quentin and Rachel respectively and the same principles as discussed in Paul's case must be applied. Just as Paul may experience the difficulties discussed in respect of Plot C, ie too far away from Plot A, Stella may encounter the same obstacles in respect of Plot B because it may be too far away from her Plot D. In that case she will be unable to prove that the burden of Barry's covenant has passed to Quentin.

If Paul and Stella can establish that the covenants' burdens have passed to Quentin and Rachel they must then proceed to establish that in equity the benefits of the respective covenants, ie those between Alex and Barry and those between Alex and Carol, have passed to them.

At the time those two sets of covenants were made in respect of Plots B and C, did the parties express any intention to annex the benefits to the dominant land? In Paul's case the dominant land is Plot A, in Stella's case it is Plot D, which again raises the problem indicated before. It may be too far away. Assume however for the purposes of argument it is not and consider the wording contained in the covenants. The covenants are made by Barry and Carol 'with Alex and his successors in title'. The difficulty here is that this wording contains no reference to any land and on the authority of *Renals* v *Cowlishaw* (above) it would not be sufficient to annex the benefit to any dominant land.

Section 78 LPA 1925 affects automatic annexation as explained in *Federated Homes Ltd* v *Mill Lodge Properties Ltd.* This section refers to a covenant relating to any land of the covenantee, but in the absence of any reference to the covenantee's land in the covenants the same difficulty may arise in the application of the section.

It may be that Stella could surmount these difficulties by showing that the land constituted a building scheme, which is a possibility because Alex had divided the land into four equally sized plots. The requirements for a scheme of development were first laid down in *Elliston* v *Reacher* (1908). For such a scheme to exist two basic requirements have to be satisfied. First, the area of the scheme must be defined. Second, those who purchase from the creator of the scheme do so on the footing that all purchasers should be mutually bound by, and mutually entitled to enforce, a defined set of restrictions. Clearly, if a scheme of development can be established it could also be pleaded by Paul, together with statutory annexation.

The essential feature of a building scheme is the common intention and in some instances this can be established without all the requirements of *Elliston* v *Reacher* being present. Thus in *Baxter* v *Four Oaks Properties Ltd* (1965) a scheme was found to exist even though the area had not been laid out in plots. In *Re Dolpin's Conveyance* (1970) a scheme was held to exist even though the purchasers had not purchased their plots from a common vendor. In both cases the common intention was deduced respectively from a mutual deed of covenant and from the conveyances to the purchasers, but in the absence such evidence the requirements of *Elliston* v *Reacher* will be necessary to establish a scheme.

In *Emile Elias & Co Ltd* v *Pine Groves Ltd* (1993) the area had not been defined and there was no evidence of a common intention to enter into mutually enforceable covenants. The covenants also lacked uniformity. It was held that no scheme existed.

Restrictive covenants in a building scheme must be registered under the LCA 1972.

Stella's best hope of success lies in attempting to prove the existence of a building scheme.

Both Paul and Stella, if they can establish their respective cases, should apply for injunctions to enforce the covenants.

SUGGESTED ANSWER TO QUESTION TWO

General Comment

This question is concerned with the enforcement of freehold covenants against the successors in title of the original parties. Although the question contains both a positive and a restrictive covenant more coverage should be afforded to the restrictive covenant because of the better enforcement regime applicable to such covenants, and thus there is more to deal with in relation to the restrictive covenant than the positive one. As with most problem questions on this topic, the inclusion of a diagrammatical representation of the facts is advisable, not least because it should eliminate the possibility of a student confusing the various parties in the course of an answer.

Key Points

- Definition of a covenant
- Distinguishing between positive and restrictive covenants
- Running of the burden of a restrictive covenant in equity
- Running of the benefit of a restrictive covenant in equity – express annexation, statutory annexation: *Federated Homes Ltd* v *Mill Lodge Properties Ltd*

Suggested Answer

A covenant in the context of real property law is an agreement by deed whereby one party (the covenantor) covenants with another party (the covenantee) that he will or will not engage in some stated activity on his land for the benefit of the covenantee's land. The land owned by the covenantee will have the benefit of the covenant and that owned by the covenantor will have the burden. Here there are two covenants to consider. In relation to Bertha's covenant to use Plot B only as a private residence Bertha is the original covenantor and Alice the original covenantee with Plot B being the burdened (servient) land and Plot A the benefited (dominant) land. However, the roles of the parties and the two plots of land are reversed in relation to Alice's covenant to maintain the wall separating the two plots in good repair.

There are two kinds of freehold covenant – positive and restrictive. A positive covenant is one which obliges the owner to do something on his land (eg a covenant to maintain a fence) or to contribute money towards work to be done. A restrictive covenant is one which restrains a landowner in some respect from the use of his property, eg a covenant which prevents the covenantor from using his land for the purpose of conducting trade and business. Here, Bertha's covenant to use Plot B only as a private residence is a restrictive one, while Alice's covenant with Bertha to maintain the wall separating Plots A and B in a good state of repair is positive.

The factual developments recounted in the question can be represented diagrammatically as follows:

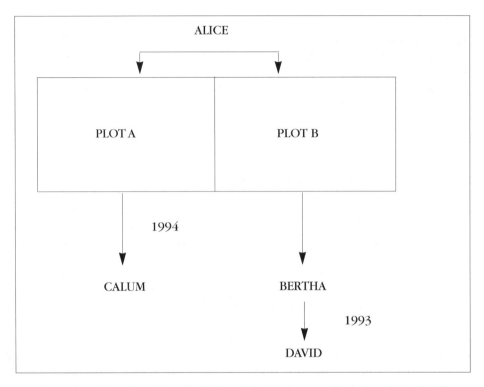

David needs to be advised in the light of the bad state of repair of the dividing wall and his proposed change of use of Plot B. The issues are twofold. First, can David enforce the positive covenant against Calum (ie can he make him repair the wall)? Second, is David bound by the restrictive covenant (ie is he prevented from converting his plot into a guest house with a restaurant)? The issues in respect of the positive covenant will be dealt with first.

For David to be able to enforce the positive covenant to maintain the wall separating the two pieces of land in a good state of repair against Calum he has to show that the benefit of the covenant has passed to him *and* the burden of it has passed to Calum under either the common law or equity rules. At common law, the benefit of a covenant can run with freehold land if certain conditions are satisfied. However, the main problem David has in relation to the positive covenant relates to the running of the burden (ie trying to show that Calum is bound by it). This is because the burden of a positive covenant cannot run directly with freehold land either at law or in equity: *Austerberry* v *Oldham Corporation* (1885). Accordingly, it would seem that David would be unable to enforce the positive covenant against Calum.

As to the restrictive covenant (to use Plot B as a private residence only) it is necessary to consider the *equitable* rules. For David to be able to convert Plot B into a guest house with a restaurant he has to show that the burden of the covenant has not run with the land so as to be binding on him or that the benefit of it has not run with Plot A to Calum.

David will only be bound by the covenant in equity if five conditions are satisfied.

First, the covenant must be negative in substance. This was laid down in *Haywood* v *Brunswick Permanent Benefit Building Society* (1881). Here it is, although worded positively (the house cannot be used for any purposes other than residential ones). Second, the covenant must have been made for the protection of land retained by the covenantee: *London County Council* v *Allen* (1914). Here it would seem that the covenant was made for the protection of Plot A, retained initially by Alice because where the covenantee has nearby land it will be presumed that the covenant does benefit the land unless the defendant can prove to the contrary: *Wrotham Park Estate Co Ltd* v *Parkside Homes Ltd* (1974). Third, the parties must have intended the burden of the covenant to run with the covenantor's (Bertha's) land. By virtue of s79 Law of Property Act (LPA) 1925 covenants relating to the covenantor's land which are made after 1925 are deemed to have been made by the covenantor on behalf of himself, his successors in title and the persons deriving title under him or them unless a contrary intention appears. Since here the covenant was entered into after 1925 and there is no such contrary intention, this third requirement is satisfied. Fourth, the covenant must 'touch and concern' the dominant land. Fifth, restrictive covenants made on or after 1 January 1926 are registrable as a land charges class D(ii) LCA 1972. The effect of registration is to give notice to the whole world: s198 LPA 1925.

Accordingly, it would seem David is bound by the covenant in equity assuming it has been registered.

Having shown that the burden of the restrictive covenant has probably passed to David in equity, it is necessary to consider whether the benefit of it has passed to Calum in equity. The issue is whether the benefit has passed to Calum in one or more of the ways recognised by equity: annexation; assignment; and building scheme.

Express annexation confers the benefit of the covenant upon the land, not individuals. Whether the benefit is so annexed to the land depends on the wording of the covenant. In particular, it must be possible to identify the land to be benefited from such wording. In *Rogers* v *Hosegood* (1900) the covenant was deemed to be annexed since it referred to the dominant land. However, in *Renals* v *Cowlishaw* (1879) the covenant was not annexed because it only referred to 'the vendors, their heirs, executors, administrators and assigns' (ie no reference was made to any land). Here the covenant was made 'with Alice and her successors in title'. This may not be enough to effect annexation because there is no identification of the benefited land.

In the absence of effective wording in the covenant, consider s78 LPA 1925 which states that a covenant relating to any land of the covenantee shall be deemed to be made with the covenantee and his successors in title. This was construed to effect a statutory annexation of the benefit of the dominant land in *Federated Homes Ltd* v *Mill Lodge Properties Ltd* (1980). However, it is suggested that the section would not be applicable here since the covenant does not refer to any land to be benefited. This would seem to follow from *Renals* v *Cowlishaw*.

Accordingly, it seems that the benefit of the restrictive covenant has not run with Plot A to Calum because there has been no annexation. Nor is there any evidence of an assignment or building scheme.

David should be advised, therefore, that although the burden has passed to him,

Calum cannot enforce the covenant against him because he has not acquired the benefit. He may therefore proceed with his plans since there is no-one to enforce the covenant against him.

SUGGESTED ANSWER TO QUESTION THREE

General Comment

Not a difficult question for the candidate who is well prepared. An understanding of how covenants affect successors in title other than purchasers is essential. The principles of registration must also be considered.

Key Points

Definition of a covenant – positive and negative covenants

a • Benefit of covenants running at common law
   • Benefit will run whether covenant is positive or negative
b • The effect of 12 years' adverse possession – Limitation Act 1980
   • Positive burden will run whether at common law or in equity
   • The negative covenant is registrable as a land charge D(ii)
   • If not registered a squatter cannot take advantage of non-registration as he has not given money or money's worth (LCA 1972)
c • Plaintiff must show he has acquired the benefit and the defendant the burden
   • Burden cannot run at common law
   • May run in equity under doctrine of *Tulk* v *Moxhay* – five conditions: benefits passing; equity; annexation; assignment; building scheme

Suggested Answer

A restrictive covenant is an agreement whereby one party (the covenantor) agrees with another party (the covenantee) that he (the covenantor) will, or will not, do certain acts on his land for the benefit of the covenantee's land. The land owned by the covenantee will have the benefit of the covenant and that owned by the covenantor will have the burden. On the facts Alan, who owns Whiteacre, is the covenantee and Douglas, who owns Blackacre, is the covenantor.

Covenant (a) is a positive covenant because it requires the covenantor, or his successors, to maintain and repair Blackacre. Covenant (b) is negative in that it simply prohibits the use of Blackacre for business purposes.

a) *Lessee of Whiteacre*

A lessee of Whiteacre is a successor in title to the original covenantee (Alan). In order to be able to enforce the covenants against Douglas (the original covenantor) the lessee must have obtained the benefit of the covenants. This he can do under the common law rules governing the running of the benefit. At common law four conditions have to be complied with in order for the benefit to run and they apply whether the covenant is positive or negative. First, the covenants must 'touch and concern' the dominant land. In *Smith & Snipes Hall Farm* v *River Douglas*

Catchment Board (1949) this was said to be satisfied if the covenants affected the mode of occupation, or directly affected the value of land. Covenant (b) clearly affects mode of occupation and (a) affects value. Second, the original covenantee must have had a legal estate in land. In this case Alan did have a legal estate in Whiteacre, the fee simple.

Third, the successor to the covenantee must have a legal estate in land, although not necessarily the same legal estate. This is also satisfied because the lessee would have a legal term. Before the enactment of s78 LPA 1925 the successor in title of the original covenantee had to own the same legal estate in the land as the original covenantee, but the wide wording of s78 changed that requirement, ie a covenant relating to land of the covenantee is deemed to be made with the covenantee and his successors in title and persons deriving title under him and this will include a legal lessee.

Fourth, at the time this covenant was made the covenantor and covenantee must have intended that the benefit of the covenant should run with the dominant land. However, in the absence of any expression of that intention in the covenant's wording s78 LPA 1925 may be applicable. The land of the covenantee, referred to in the section, must be identified by the covenant: *Rogers* v *Hosegood* (1900).

If the conditions are satisfied the benefit of both the positive covenant (a) and the negative one (b) will have run to the lessee enabling him to enforce them against Douglas, but the failure of the covenant to identify the dominant land means the fourth requirement is not satisfied.

It should be noted that it is not necessary to show that the burden of the covenants has run to Douglas as he is the original covenantor. Neither is it necessary to deal with registration because that would only be relevant when dealing with a purchaser of the burdened land (Blackacre).

b) *Adverse possessor of Blackacre*

The effect of 12 years' adverse possession of Blackacre by a squatter is to extinguish Douglas's title. This is the result of the Limitation Act 1980. The squatter does not acquire Douglas's title. 'His (the squatter's) title therefore, is never derived though but arises always in spite of the dispossessed owner': *Fairweather* v *St Marylebone Property Co Ltd* (1963) per Lord Radcliffe.

The burden of covenant (a) being positive can run neither at common law nor in equity and squatters will take free of it. The burden of covenant (b) is restrictive and may pass in equity. Restrictive covenants made on or after 1 January 1926 should be registered as a land charge class D(ii). If not they are void against a purchaser of the legal estate in the land for money or money's worth: s4(6) LCA 1972. Since a squatter pays neither money nor money's worth he cannot take advantage of non-registration of the covenant and he will be bound by it even if it is not registered.

The question of the benefit of the covenant does not arise since Alan is the original covenantee.

c) *A purchaser of Whiteacre and a purchaser of Blackacre*

In order for a purchaser of Whiteacre from Alan to enforce the covenants against a purchaser of Blackacre from Douglas, it must be shown that the benefit of the covenants has passed to the former and the burden to the latter.

The purchaser of Whiteacre will be a successor in title to the covenantee, and the benefit of the covenants can run to him at common law or in equity. The running of the benefit at common law has been dealt with in part (a) above.

However, in this case the original covenantor has transferred the servient land and it will be necessary to prove that the burdens of the covenants have passed to the purchaser. The burdens cannot run at common law: *Austerberry* v *Oldham Corporation* (1885); *Rhone* v *Stephens* (1994). It will be necessary to see if they will run according to the equitable rules. That being the case the common law rules cannot be used to effect the passing of the benefits. A successor in title to the owner of the dominant land must establish that the benefits have passed to him in equity.

It is advisable to begin by dealing with the burden first. Once it is established that the servient land has changed hands, then two consequences follow. Equity must be invoked to make the burdens pass and equity must be used to make the benefits pass.

The running of the burden of the covenants to the purchaser of Blackacre in equity is governed by the rule in *Tulk* v *Moxhay* (1848). Under *Tulk* and subsequent cases five conditions have to be satisfied. First, the covenants must touch and concern the dominant land. Second, the covenants must be negative in substance. Equity will not enforce positive covenants against a successor in title to the covenantor. The test to determine whether a covenant is negative is the 'hand in pocket test': *Haywood* v *Brunswick Permanent Benefit Building Society* (1881). If the covenant requires the covenantor to expend money it is positive and cannot be enforced against a successor in title. On the facts covenant (a) is positive and cannot be enforced against the purchaser of Blackacre from Douglas.

Third, at the time the covenant was made the original covenantee must have retained land capable of benefitting from it: *London County Council* v *Allen* 1914. On the facts when the covenant was made in 1960 Alan, the original covenantee, retained land capable of benefiting (Whiteacre). Fourth, there must have been an intention by the original parties that the burden should run. This is provided for by s79 LPA 1925; in the absence of contrary intention the covenantor is deemed to covenant on behalf of himself and successors in title.

Fifth, in order to be enforceable against the purchaser of Blackacre, it must be shown that covenant (b) was properly protected by the registration of a D(ii) land charge by Alan (the original covenantee) against the name of Douglas (the original covenantor). If it was, the purchaser of Blackacre will be bound by it; if not, then he will take free of it providing he is a purchaser of the legal estate and the land for money or money's worth (s4(6) LCA 1972) and this is so even if he has actual notice of it or in bad faith: *Midland Bank Trust Co Ltd* v *Green* (1981).

The benefit of the covenant may pass in equity to the purchaser of Whiteacre in three ways:

1   annexation of the benefit to the dominant land; or
2   express assignment of the benefit by covenantee of his successor; or
3   a building scheme.

As regards to (1) the original parties may have expressed that intention in the wording of the covenant itself. The intention may be expressed by being made with the covenantee and his successors in title. This demonstrates that the enjoyment of the benefit is not to be confined to the covenantee personally but it extends to whoever acquires the land after him. However, the covenant must also refer to the land to be benefited: *Rogers* v *Hosegood*.

In *Renals* v *Cowlishaw* (1879) no reference was made to the land to be benefited and it was held that there was no annexation.

If no expression of intention is found in the covenant's wording, s78 LPA 1925 will effect statutory annexation. This was the result of the construction placed on s78 by *Federated Homes Ltd* v *Mill Lodge Properties Ltd* (1980). There is no indication in the section that the application of the section can be excluded (unlike s79), but it was held in *Roake* v *Chadha* (1983) that it could be. Again the section will only apply if the covenant identifies the land to be benefited, ie the dominant land.

Subsequent to identification of the dominant land, the result of the *Federated Homes* case is that s78 will automatically apply unless excluded. Where it does not apply, it will be be necessary to consider express assignment. This is necessary where there has been no annexation and the benefit has been conferred on the covenantee personally. In those circumstances he may assign the benefit at the same time as he sells the dominant land to a purchaser.

In order for this to be achieved it has to be shown that the dominant land (Whiteacre) can be identified, directly or indirectly, in the assignment (see *Newton Abbot Co-operative Society* v *Williamson & Treadgold* (1952)), second, that the assignment was contemporaneous with the conveyance and, third, that there was a clear intention to assign the benefit.

There is no question of a building scheme in this case and it need not be considered in any detail. A building scheme or scheme of development is governed by the rules laid down in *Elliston* v *Reacher* (1908), and as later developed: see *Re Dolphin's Conveyance* (1970) and *Baxter* v *Four Oaks Properties Ltd* (1965). The rules require an intention on the part of the vendor to set up a building scheme in relation to a defined area of land. As long as that intention is manifest, the purchasers buy subject to the scheme of covenants which crystallises upon the first purchase. Under the scheme each purchaser can enforce, and have enforced against him, the negative covenants which make up the scheme. The covenants must be registered as land charge class D(ii).

Provided one of the three methods discussed above can be satisfied, the benefit of the covenants will have passed to the purchaser of Whiteacre in equity.

SUGGESTED ANSWER TO QUESTION FOUR

General Comment

The question is concerned with rights against third parties in respect of freehold covenants. A somewhat untypical and challenging question which gives a candidate well versed in the relevant law a good opportunity to demonstrate his knowledge and understanding.

Key Points

•   Definition of a covenant – positive and negative covenants
•   Section 56: LPA 1925
•   Positive burden cannot run either at common law or in equity
•   Passing of the burden of a negative covenant in equity
•   An inheritor cannot advantage of non-registration since he has given neither money nor money's worth
•   The three ways in which the benefit may pass in equity: annexation; assignment; and building scheme.

Suggested Answer

A covenant, in the context of real property law, has already been defined in the previous questions. The land owned by the covenantee has the benefit of the covenant and that owned by the covenantor has the burden. On the facts Jack, who owns the Alban Estate is the original covenantee and Priscilla who bought the plot, formerly part of that estate, is the original covenantor. Accordingly, the Alban Estate is the dominant (ie benefited) land and the plot sold off is the servient (ie burdened) land.

There are two kinds of freehold covenant – positive and restrictive. A positive covenant is one which obliges the owner to do something on his land. A restrictive covenant is one which restrains a landowner in some respect in the use of his property, eg a covenant which prevents the covenantor from using his land for the purpose of conducting trade and business. Here the covenant to use the land for residential purposes is a restrictive one while the covenant to maintain the house in a good state of repair is a positive one.

i   The scenario under consideration here can be represented diagrammatically as follows:

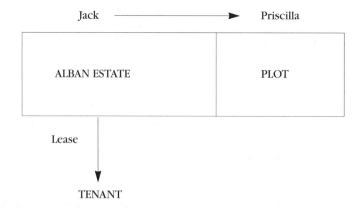

For the lessee of the Alban Estate to be able to enforce the covenants against Priscilla he must show that the benefit of them has passed to him. There are two possibilities in this regard.

First, he could seek to claim that he is entitled to the covenant's benefit by the application of s56 LPA 1925. The common law forbade any person who was not a party to a deed from suing on it. The rule was relaxed by s5 of the Real Property Act 1845. This was repealed and re-enacted by s56(1) LPA 1925 which now provides that 'a person may take … the benefit of any … covenant over or respecting land … although he may not be named as a party to the conveyance'. For the application of s56, a person who was not a party to the conveyance must establish the covenant of which he claims the benefit shows that it purported to be made with him and did not merely confer a benefit on him. The wording of the covenant must be such as to make him a covenantee even if he is not a party to the conveyance. It follows from this that at the time the covenant was made he must exist at that time and be identifiable at that time.

Thus, if in a conveyance of Blackacre to P, P covenanted with V, the vendor and with the owners for the time being of the adjoining plots of Whiteacre and Yellowacre, then whoever owned those plots at the time of the conveyance can sue P on the covenant even if they were not parties to it because the covenant was expressed to be made with them for the benefit of their plots. Thus, successors in title could not claim the benefit under s56 because they were not in existence at the time even if the covenant was expressed to be made with the successors in title to the owners of Whiteacre and Yellowacre. It will be noticed that to succeed under s56 a person does not have to be specifically named: the general description 'and with the owners for the time being of the adjoining plots of Whiteacre and Yellowacre' will be sufficient. Thus, for a tenant of the Alban Estate to claim the benefit under s56, he must show he was a tenant at the time the covenant was made and that is not the case here.

Second, he could claim that the benefit had passed to him at common law. The benefit of a freehold covenant may run at common law: *The Prior's Case* (1368). This has been the law for centuries and it applies whether the covenant is positive or negative. Thus a successor in title to the original covenantee may enforce it against the original covenantor. It is important to notice that it is only enforceable against the original covenantor, in this case Priscilla. It is not enforceable against her successors because the burden will not run at common law: *Austerberry* v *Oldham Corporation* (1885). However, for the benefit to run at common law the following conditions must be satisfied:

- The covenant must touch and concern the covenantee's land: *Rogers* v *Hosegood* (1900). In that case Farwell J stipulated that it must 'either affect the land as regards mode of occupation, or it must be such as per se, and not merely from collateral circumstances, affect the value of the land'.
- At the time the covenant was made the parties must have intended that the benefit of it should run with the covenantee's land. However, if this intention is not expressed in the wording of the covenant, then s78 LPA 1925 may apply: 'A covenant relating to any land of the covenantee shall be deemed to be made with the covenantee and his successors in title'.

The deed should identify the land of the covenantee which it is intended should be benefited, but in the absence of identification extrinsic evidence may be introduced to effect identification:

> 'As to the requirement that the deed containing the covenant must expressly identify the particular land to be benefited, no authority was cited to us and in the absence of such authority I can see no valid reason why the maxim "Id certum est quod certum reddi potest" should not apply so as to make admissible extrinsic evidence to prove the extent and situation of the lands': per Tucker LJ in *Smith and Snipes Hall Farm* v *River Douglas Catchment Board* (1949).

This view is not consistent with *Renals* v *Cowlishaw* (1879) nor, it would appear, with *J Sainsbury plc* v *Enfield London Borough Council* (1989).

• At the time the covenant was made the covenantee must have had a legal estate in the land. This was because the common law did not recognise equitable interests in land: *Webb* v *Russel* (1789). Moreover, the common law would only enforce the benefit on behalf of the covenantee's successor in title if he had the same legal estate in the land as the original covenantee. Thus, if the original owner held the fee simple estate and his successor was a lessee, the benefit did not pass to the lessee.

However, the requirement that the successor in title must enjoy the same legal estate as the original covenantee does not apply to covenants made after 1 January 1926. Section 78 LPA 1925 provides that a covenant relating to any land of the covenantee shall be deemed to be made with the covenantee and his successors in title. Thus, the benefit may pass to a tenant of a legal lease even though the original covenantee was the legal fee simple owner.

If these conditions are satisfied then the tenant in the problem may enforce the benefit of the covenant against Priscilla claiming the common law remedy of damages or the equitable remedy of an injunction.

ii The scenario under consideration here can be represented diagrammatically as follows:

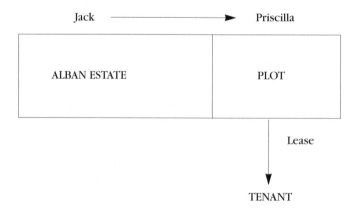

Jack as the original covenantee can enforce the covenants against a lessee of Priscilla's land if the burden of the covenants has passed to the lessee.

Dealing first with the positive covenant (to maintain the house in a good state of repair) the burden of such a covenant cannot run directly with freehold land either at law or in equity: *Austerberry* v *Corporation of Oldham* (1885); *Rhone* v *Stephens* (1994). However, certain devices (none of which are foolproof) are used to try to circumvent the rule. For example, there is the doctrine of *Halsall* v *Brizell* (1957) – a person who takes the benefit under a deed/agreement must also bear the burden (ie perform any obligation of a reciprocal nature). The lessee of Priscilla's land cannot be liable for any breach of the positive covenant unless the aforementioned doctrine applies which on the facts it does not because there is no reciprocal benefit.

Dealing, second, with the restrictive covenant, the burden of such a covenant cannot pass at law but can pass in equity: *Tulk* v *Moxhay* (1848). For the burden to run in equity five conditions have to be satisfied. First, the covenant must be a negative in substance. This was laid down in *Haywood* v *Brunswick Permanent Benefit Building Society* (1881). It is enough if the covenant is negative in substance, even if worded positively. Second, the covenant must have been made for the protection of land retained by the covenantee: *London County Council* v *Allen* (1914). Here, it would seem probable that the covenant was made for the protection of the Alban Estate retained by Jack: see *Wrotham Park Estate Co Ltd* v *Parkside Homes Ltd* (1974). Third, the burden of the covenant must have been intended to run with the covenantor's (Priscilla's) land. By virtue of s79 LPA 1925 covenants relating to the covenantor's land which are made after 1925 are deemed to have been made by the covenantor on behalf of himself, his successors in title and the persons deriving title under him unless a contrary intention is expressed. This will include a lessee. Since here the covenant was entered into after 1925, and there is no such contrary intention, this third requirement will be satisfied.

Fourth, the covenant must touch and concern the dominant land, in this case that part of the Alban Estate retained by Jack. In *Rogers* v *Hosegood* Farwell J stipulated that for a covenant to touch and concern the land it must either affect the land as regards mode of occupation or its value. Whether a covenant does touch and concern land is an issue of fact: *Re Ballard's Conveyance* (1937).

Fifth, the covenant must have been registered as a land charge class D(ii) under the Land Charges Act 1972. Failure to register will result in it being void against a purchaser of the legal estate in the land for money or money's worth.

Thus, if Priscilla's tenant was holding under a legal lease for money or money's worth (rent or a premium) and the covenant was not registered before the grant of the lease, he would take free of it even if he knew of it: *Hollington Bros Ltd* v *Rhodes* (1951).

In conclusion, if the covenant was registered it seems that Jack can enforce the restrictive covenant against Priscilla's tenant.

iii   The scenario under consideration here can be represented diagrammatically as follows:

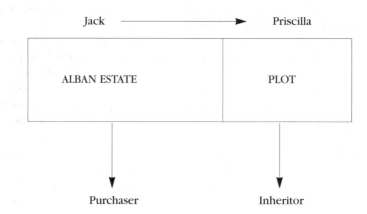

The issue here is whether the purchaser of the Alban Estate (the benefited land) can enforce the covenants against the person who has inherited Priscilla's land (the burdened land). To do so the purchaser has to show that the benefits of the covenants have passed to him and that the burdens of the covenants have passed to the person who inherited the servient land.

The burden can only pass in equity under the doctrine of *Tulk* v *Moxhay* as has been seen, and for the burden to pass to the person who inherited Priscilla's land the conditions enumerated before must be satisfied. One point should be noticed here in connection with the covenant's registration. If it is not registered the inheritor will not be able to take advantage of non-registration because he or she will not have provided money or money's worth and thus even if the covenant is not registered he or she will be bound by it assuming the other conditions are satisfied.

Since it is necessary to rely on equity to establish that the burden has passed it will be necessary to show that the benefit has passed according to the equitable rules. The common law rules cannot be invoked. There are three ways in which the benefit can pass in equity: annexation of the benefit to the dominant land; or express assignment of the benefit; or under a building scheme.

Annexation must be considered first. The burden of the positive covenant cannot run even in equity, but the restrictive covenant relating to residence may. Priscilla covenanted with Jack and his successors in title which is an indication that the covenant was not intended to benefit Jack alone. However, an intention to benefit Jack's land must also be expressed: *Rogers* v *Hosegood*. In *Renals* v *Cowlishaw* the covenant was expressed to be with 'the vendors, their heirs, executors, administrators and assigns' but that wording was held to be insufficient to annex the benefit to the land because it made no reference to the land. That is the position here. Priscilla's covenant does not refer to Jack's land and in the result there would be no annexation by the covenant itself.

Consideration must be given to s78 LPA 1925 as construed by *Federated Homes Ltd* v *Mill Lodge Properties Ltd* (1980). In that case the Court of Appeal decided that s78 was no mere word saving section but was effective in itself to annex the benefit of a covenant to the dominant land and each and every part of it. Despite the absence of any provision in the section 'unless a contrary intention is expressed' it was held n the subsequent case of *Roake* v *Chadha* (1983) that the operation of the section could be excluded by the parties. The section refers to 'A covenant relating to any land of the covenantee ...' which would seem to indicate that the covenant must refer to that land if the section is to be applicable. In *Federated Homes* the covenant did so refer: 'Clause 5(iv) shows clearly that the covenant is for the protection of the reclaimed land and that land is described in clause 2 as "any adjoining or adjacent property reclaimed by the vendor"': per Brightman LJ.

Because Priscilla's covenant does not refer to Jack's land it appears that s78 is not applicable.

If there has been no annexation, since there is no suggestion of a building scheme, then a purchaser would have to show that the benefit had been assigned to him. In *Re Union of London and Smith's Banks Ltd's Conveyance, Miles* v *Easter* (1933) the court enunciated the considerations to be satisfied for the benefit of a covenant to be expressly assigned in equity:

• the covenant must have been taken for the benefit of the covenantee's land and that land must have been indicated with reasonable certainty;
• the land, or part of it, must be retained by the plaintiff;
• the land must be capable of benefiting from the covenant;
• the assignment of the benefit must be contemporaneous with the conveyance of the land to which it relates.

There is no evidence that there has been an express assignment of the covenant's benefit and if that is the case then the purchaser of the Alban Estate would not be able to claim it.

It appears that the purchaser of the Alban Estate cannot establish that the benefit of the covenant between Jack and Priscilla has passed to him with the result that he cannot enforce the covenant against the inheritor of Priscilla's plot and this is so even if the burden of the covenant has passed to the latter.

7

Mortgages

Introduction

The selected questions aim to cover the areas of mortgage law likely to be of most interest to the examiner. Since the passing of the Law of Property (Miscellaneous Provisions) Act 1989 the traditional position on the creation of an equitable mortgage by deposit of title deeds has drastically altered, as illustrated by the case of *United Bank of Kuwait plc v Sahib and Others* (1996). Students should also be aware of the views of the Law Commission on the current methods of creating mortgages and its suggestion for reform.

In dealing with collateral advantages students should not omit to mention the common law position on restraint of trade and not confuse it with the equitable approach: see Question 2.

Questions

INTERROGRAMS

1 Define a mortgage.
2 What are the two methods of creating a legal mortgage?
3 What is the equitable right to redeem.
4 Define 'equity of redemption'.
5 What is foreclosure?
6 When may a mortgagee exercise his powers of sale?
7 What are the remedies of a legal mortgagee?
8 What are the remedies of an equitable mortgagee?

QUESTION ONE

Explain the ways in which legal and equitable mortgages of land may be created today, indicating any reforms you consider to be necessary.

London University LLB Examination
(for external students) Land Law June 1997 Q7

QUESTION TWO

Bill owned a baker's shop and an adjoining sandwich bar, and he mortgaged the shop to Gus, the local grocer. The mortgage deed provided that the mortgage should be paid off in 40 half-yearly instalments; that Bill should not sell biscuits or chocolates in the baker's shop so long as he owned it; that he should not sell biscuits or chocolates in the sandwich bar so long as he owned it; and that he would never sell either of his properties without giving Gus the chance of buying it for the best price that anyone else offered.

To what extent is Bill bound by these provisions?

London University LLB Examination
(for external students) Land Law June 1996 Q8

QUESTION THREE

'In recent times the courts have so elevated the standard of conduct expected of the selling mortgagee that the mortgagee's duty to his mortgagor has become analogous to a fiduciary duty.'

Discuss.

London University LLB Examination
(for external students) Land Law June 1994 Q5

QUESTION FOUR

In 1990 Henry bought a house to live in with his girlfriend, Joanna. The house was conveyed into Henry's sole name, but he agreed orally with Joanna that she was to have a 50 per cent beneficial interest in the house. The purchase price was £50,000; Henry provided £5,000 from his savings, Henry's father lent him a further £15,000 and Henry borrowed the remaining £30,000 from the Savewell Bank in whose favour he executed a charge of the property expressed to be by way of legal mortgage. In 1991 Henry lost his job and began to fall badly into arrears with his mortgage repayments. Joanna has now left him and the bank is pressing him to repay his debt even though he is confident that he will find a well paid job within the near future.

Henry would like to know:

a   what his position would be if the bank applied to the court for a possession order;
b   whether he would have any remedy if in the exercise of its power of sale the bank sold the house by private contract for less than its market value; and
c   how the proceeds of sale would be disposed of.

Advise Henry.

London University LLB Examination
(for external students) Land Law June 1992 Q4

Answers

ANSWERS TO INTERROGRAMS

1   'A mortgage is a conveyance of land or an assignment of chattels as a security for payment of a debt or the discharge of some other obligation for which it is given. This is the idea of a mortgage; and the security is redeemable on the payment or discharge of such debt or obligation, any provision to the contrary notwithstanding': *Santley* v *Wilde* (1899) per Lindley MR. It will be noticed, later on, that since 1

January 1926 a legal mortgage of land is no longer created by a conveyance of the legal fee simple to the mortgagee.

2   By s85 LPA 1925 a legal mortgage may be made in one of two ways:

a   by a demise for a term of years absolute;
b   by a charge by deed expressed to be by way of legal mortgage.

3   Originally a legal mortgage was created by the mortgagor conveying the legal estate to the mortgagee as security for the loan with provision for repayment of the loan, with interest, on a particular day in the future and with a further provision that if repayment was made on that date the mortgagee would re-convey the land to the mortgagor. At law the mortgagor could not repay the loan before that date; and if he allowed the date to pass he forfeited the right to redeem his property but remained liable for the repayments of the loan. The date in the mortgage for redemption was the legal, or contractual date, of redemption. Such an unfair state of affairs inevitably attracted the attention of equity which allowed a mortgagor to redeem after the legal date for redemption. That right conferred by equity was called the equitable right to redeem. It obviously could not arise until the legal date for redemption had passed.

4   This must be distinguished from the equitable right to redeem. At common law, before 1926, a legal mortgage was created by the conveyance of the fee simple to the mortgagee, and common law regarded him as the owner. Technically that was true, but equity took a broader view recognising that it was a rather qualified form of ownership. The land had only been conveyed to the mortgagee for a particular purpose, namely to provide security for a loan, and moreover the mortgagee was obliged to re-convey the property to the mortgagor on repayment of the loan. Equity regarded the mortgagor as the true owner of the land subject to the mortgage. This equitable ownership, as opposed to common law ownership, came to be known as the equity of redemption, and it could be transmitted by will or sale like any other interest in land. The equity of redemption therefore is a much wider concept than the equitable right to redeem. It is the totality of the mortgagor's equitable rights in the land of which the equitable right to redeem is but one. Whereas the equitable right to redeem only arose after the legal date for redemption, the equity of redemption arose as soon as the mortgage was created.

5   After the legal date for redemption had passed the mortgagor's interest in the land was purely equitable since at common law his legal estate had been forfeited. He remained, however, the owner in equity as signified by the phrase 'equity of redemption', which included his equitable right to redeem. A mortgagee can seek to extinguish the equity of redemption by a foreclosure action which has the effect of making him the owner in equity as well as at common law, although such an action cannot be commenced until the legal date for redemption has passed. This is a drastic remedy since its effect is to deprive the mortgagor of all of his interest in the land, including his right to redeem. Accordingly, it can only have been effected by a court action which is in two stages. The first stage is an order nisi which gives the mortgagor time to acquire sufficient funds to discharge the mortgage. If he does not do so in the time specified in the order the mortgagee can apply for an order

absolute. However, even after the order absolute has been made, the mortgagor can apply for the foreclosure to be re-opened and the court will do so if it considers it equitable. Moreover, on an application by the mortgagee to foreclose, the court has power under s91 LPA 1925 to order sale instead.

6   This must be considered in two stages:

a   Has the power of sale arisen? It will arise once the legal date for redemption has passed. If, however, which is the more likely case, the mortgage is repayable by instalments, then the legal date for redemption will not arise until one instalment is in arrears: *Payne* v *Cardiff Rural District Council* (1932).

b   It is not enough for the power of sale to have arisen. The mortgagee must then establish that it has become exercisable and this will not occur until certain conditions have been satisfied:

i   notice requiring repayment of the mortgage money has been served on the mortgagor and he has failed to repay in full within three months of service of the notice; or

ii   interest is at least two months in arrears; or

iii   there has been a breach of covenant in the mortgage deed (other than the covenant to pay the mortgage moneys).

These provisions are contained in ss101 and 103 LPA 1925 and only apply if the mortgage is by deed.

7   a   The mortgagee may sue the mortgagor on his personal covenant to repay the debt. The Limitation Act 1980 is applicable: the action is statute-barred after 12 years if the mortgage is by deed; if it is not by deed then the period is six years.

If, when the security is sold, the proceeds are not sufficient to cover the mortgage debt then the mortgagee is left with the remedy to sue for the remainder on the mortgagor's personal covenant.

b   Foreclosure. This is very rare nowadays. A mortgagee must apply to the court for foreclosure and the court has power to order a sale instead: s91 LPA 1925.

c   The mortgagee has a power of sale if the mortgage is by deed: s101 LPA 1925. The exercise of the power is governed by s103 LPA 1925. The duties of a mortgagee on sale should be noted: *Cuckmere Brick Co Ltd* v *Mutual Finance Ltd* (1971); *Parker-Tweedale* v *Dunbar Bank Ltd plc* (1990); *Tse Kwong Lam* v *Wong Chit Sen* (1983).

Building societies are under a statutory duty to obtain the best price reasonably obtainable when selling the mortgaged property.

d   The mortgagee has a right to take possession as soon as the mortgage is executed (*Four Maids Ltd* v *Dudley Marshall (Properties) Ltd* (1957)), and this is so without any default on the part of the mortgagor because where the mortgage is by demise its effect is to create the relationship of landlord and tenant, the mortgagee being the tenant. The mortgagee is in the same position if the mortgage is by legal charge: s87(1) LPA 1925.

Where the mortgagee seeks a court order for possession a measure of relief is available to the mortgagor under s36 Administration of Justice Act 1970, as amended by s8 Administration of Justice Act 1973. This relief, however, is only available if the mortgagee seeks possession by means of a court order. If he does not then the relief afforded by the statutory provisions to the mortgagor is not available. In *Ropaigelach* v *Barclays Bank plc* (1999), the mortgagee took possession of the mortgaged property while the mortgagors were temporarily absent, without first obtaining a court order. The Court of Appeal held it was entitled to do so and that since it had not proceeded through the court the mortgagors could not apply for statutory relief. The statutory relief was only available where the mortgagee sought possession by means of a court order.

Mortgagees taking possession are strictly accountable in equity for what income they should have received from the property: *White* v *City of London Brewery* (1889).

e   The mortgagee has a statutory power to appoint a receiver where the mortgage is by deed: s101 LPA 1925. No court order is required. It arises and becomes exercisable in the same circumstances as the statutory power of sale. The appointment of a receiver is an alternative to selling the property. The receiver's task is to collect the income yielded by the property, and to apply it in accordance with the provisions of s109(8) LPA 1925, ie after paying the outgoings and his commission, discharging the interest and capital of the mortgage. Subsection 2 provides that a receiver is deemed to be the agent of the mortgagor.

8   a   The mortgagee may sue the mortgagor on his personal covenant.
    b   The equitable mortgagee only has a statutory power of sale if the mortgage is by deed. However, if the mortgage is not by deed, the parties may agree to include in it a power of sale vested in the mortgagee but this power apparently only extends to the mortgagee's equitable interest. It is possible for a power of attorney to be included in the mortgage, giving the mortgagee powers to sell the legal estate.
    c   The equitable mortgagee has no right to possession of the mortgaged property but he may apply to the court for possession.
    d   If the mortgage is by deed, the mortgagee may appoint a receiver. If it is not by deed then he may apply to the court to appoint one.
    e   The main remedy used to be foreclosure but as has been stated this is now very rare. If a mortgagee applies to the court for foreclosure the court may make an order for sale instead.

SUGGESTED ANSWER TO QUESTION ONE

General Comment

A somewhat untypical essay question on mortgages which deals with a single aspect of the subject. It is essential to be fully conversant with the law on the creation of legal and equitable mortgages and to be able to identify its shortcomings. A good answer will include coverage of the Law Commission Report on Land Mortgages.

Key Points

- Definition of a mortgage
- *Samuel* v *Jarrah Timber & Wood Paving Corporation Ltd*
- Legal mortgage created by deed
- Two ways of creating a legal mortgage – by demise or by way of legal charge
- Methods of creating an equitable mortgage
- *United Bank of Kuwait* v *Sahib*
- Process of creation cumbersome
- Consequences of having legal and equitable mortgages – plethora of legal and equitable interests exisiting in same piece of land – two different schemes of protection – complex rules for determining priorities of mortgages
- Law Commission Report on *Land Mortgages*

Suggested Answer

A mortgage is essentially a transaction whereby an interest in property, be it land, housing or business, is transferred to a mortgagee (lender) as security for the loan, subject to a right of redemption vested in the mortgagor (borrower). However, unlike the definition, the practicalities of mortgages are rather complex. In *Samuel* v *Jarrah Timber and Wood Paving Corporation Ltd* (1904) Lord MacNaghten noted that 'no-one ever understood an English mortgage of real estate'.

A legal mortgage can only be created by deed and in one of two ways. Further, it can only be created in respect of a legal estate: s85 LPA 1925. First, a legal mortgage can be created by demise for a term of years absolute. The mortgage is made in the form of a lease of the mortgagor's property with a proviso (known as the proviso for cesser on redemption) that the lease should be determined when the mortgage is redeemed, that is, when all the capital and interest are paid off. If the mortgage is of a freehold the term of the lease is usually 3,000 years; if of a leasehold then the mortgage is a sublease for about ten days less than the mortgagor's unexpired term. Subsequent mortgages are created by granting a lease (or sublease in the case of mortgages of leaseholds) for at least one day longer than the previous mortgage. Second, a legal mortgage can be created by charge by deed expressed to be by way of legal mortgage: s87 LPA 1925. It is the more popular method of creation and is usually called a 'legal charge'. It is a simpler document than the mortgage by demise, but it confers exactly the same rights on both mortgagor and mortgagee. Its main advantage is that freeholds and leaseholds can be mortgaged together in one document, which is not possible when the mortgage is by demise. A legal charge is a legal interest within s1(2)(c) LPA 1925.

An equitable mortgage may be created in a number of ways.

If the interest which is being mortgaged is itself equitable then, even if the mortgage is created by deed, it is equitable. If no deed is employed then the requirements of s53(c) LPA 1925 must be observed:

> 'a disposition of an equitable interest … must be in writing signed by the person disposing of the same, or by his agent thereunto lawfully authorised in writing or by will.'

The written disposition will convey the equitable interest to the mortgagee with a proviso for its reconveyance by him when the mortgage is redeemed.

If the subject-matter of the mortgage is a legal estate but the mortgage is created by writing instead of by a deed, then the mortgage is not a legal one. However, equity may treat it as a contract to create a legal mortgage, but in that case the written document must comply with s2 Law of Property (Miscellaneous Provisions) Act 1989 which requires that contracts for the disposition of land must be made in writing, contain all the terms expressly agreed by the parties, and be signed by all the parties on their behalf. If the requirements of s2 are not observed the contract is void.

Another method of creating an equitable mortgage is by deposit of title deeds with the mortgagee, but the position has now been drastically altered by the Law of Property (Miscellaneous Provisions) Act 1989 as is illustrated by the case of *United Bank of Kuwait plc* v *Sahib and Others* (1996).

In this case the plaintiffs (UBK) and the defendants (SGA) were banks. In 1992 UBK was granted a charging order over S's interest in freehold property, jointly owned with his wife, to secure monies owing to UBK. SGA was owed money by S and it claimed to have an equitable mortgage over the same property. S and his wife had not granted a legal mortgage in favour of SGA but they had deposited the land certificate with their solicitors to be held by them to the order of SGA as security for the money owed to SGA, and the solicitors had confirmed that in writing to SGA.

UBK sued for a declaration to the effect that SGA did not hold an equitable mortgage over the property in its favour and that, if it did, it was postponed to UBK's charge. SGA argued that it did hold an equitable mortgage and that it took priority over UBK's charge by virtue of the deposit of the land certificate. UBK contended that since the alleged equitable mortgage had not been accompanied by a written memorandum there had been a failure to comply with s2 Law of Property (Miscellaneous Provisions) Act 1989 and that in the result no valid equitable mortgage had been created.

The Court of Appeal upheld UBK's contention. Before the 1989 Act it was possible to create an equitable mortgage by a deposit of title deeds unaccompanied by any written memorandum. Although s40 LPA 1925 required written evidence of an agreement for the disposition of land, failure to comply did not result in the transaction being void but merely unenforceable by court action. Equity took the view that in those circumstances, where one party had performed their part of the contract, eg by depositing the title deeds (or land certificate) with the mortgagee, then even though the contract was unenforceable at law, since there was still a valid contract and one party to it had performed its part, it would be inequitable for the other party to take advantage of non-compliance with the statutory requirements and refuse to perform his part. Accordingly, equity held that party to the contract. This was known as the doctrine of part performance.

The advent of the 1989 Act drastically altered the position. It repealed s40 and substituted in its place a requirement that a contract for the disposition of land must be made in writing, as opposed to being merely evidenced in writing, and with the provision that unless this requirement was satisfied the contract was void. The doctrine of part performance was applied on the basis that there was a contract. After the 1989

Act if there was no writing which complied with s2 then there was no contract at all, with the result that the application of the doctrine of part performance became impossible. In this case the deposit of the land certificate resulted in a contract to create a mortgage to which s2 applied. Since there was no written document the mere deposit of the land certificate by way of security could not create a mortgage and SGA's claim failed.

This case confirms that the repeal of s40 and its replacement by s2 has terminated the centuries old practice of creating an equitable mortgage by oral agreement, coupled with the deposit of title deeds with the mortgagee.

To summarise the current position, the mortgagor must deposit the title deeds or land certificate with the mortgagee with the intention that they are being deposited by way of security and for no other purpose, and be accompanied by a written memorandum complying with s2.

An express written agreement to create a legal mortgage to secure a loan will be recognised by equity as giving rise to an equitable mortgage which is enforceable by specific performance. However, the mortgage monies must actually have been advanced to the mortgagor before equity will enforce the agreement by specific performance: *Sichel* v *Mosenthal* (1862).

The written agreement must comply with s2 the Law of Property (Miscellaneous Provisions) Act 1989.

Finally, the parties may create an equitable charge and this occurs where property is designated as being available to satisfy an obligation to pay money owed in the event of default. It differs from a mortgage in that, whereas in the case of a mortgage the property is conveyed to the mortgagee with a provision for re-conveyance when the loan is discharged, a charge conveys no property to the chargee either at law or in equity. No formalities are required for its creation.

The remedies of an equitable chargee are limited to sale of the land and appointment of a receiver.

The method of creating mortgages was simplified by the 1925 legislation. However, the whole process is still cumbersome. Legal mortgages no longer involve a conveyance of the fee simple but instead, as noted above, are created either by a demise for a term of years or by a legal charge. However, the fact that English law still recognises the creation of equitable mortgages means that the law of mortgages suffers from the same defects which were apparent in land law prior to the 1925 legislation, namely a plethora of interests both legal and equitable which can exist in the same piece of land.

Other consequences of having legal and equitable mortgages are: (1) two different schemes of protection; and (2) complex rules for determining priorities of mortgages. Legal mortgagees either protect themselves by taking title deeds, or registering legal charges or puisne mortgagees (C(i) land charge), whereas equitable mortgagees have to register a general equitable charge: C(iii). Where registration is required for protection the normal rules apply making a mortgage void against a subsequent purchaser for want of registration. In consequence of the different types of mortgage, complex rules have evolved governing the determination of priorities between competing mortgages. Generally speaking, legal mortgages prevail over equitable, and the first in time has priority. Equitable mortgages are governed by the rule in *Dearle* v *Hall* (1828) (as amended by ss138 and 139 LPA 1925) which provides that priority depends upon the order in which notice of the mortgages is received by the owner of the legal estate.

The aforementioned criticisms of the law of mortgages led the Law Commission in its Working Paper (*Land Mortgages*: Working Paper No 99) published in 1986, and in its 1991 Report, to recommend that all the existing methods of creating mortgages be abolished and replaced by new forms of mortgage created by statute. Implementing the Commission's recommendation would have at least three main benefits. First, it would remedy the plethora of interests, both legal and equitable, which can exist at present in relation to the same piece of land. Second, the adoption of a single form of statutory mortgage would render the differing forms and methods of protection unnecessary. Third, the adoption of a single statutory mortgage which must be registered would eradicate many of the problems which currently arise as to priorities between competing mortgages.

SUGGESTED ANSWER TO QUESTION TWO

General Comment

The question raises a number of fairly standard examination issues in respect of commercial mortgages. It is crucial for students to note that the question deals solely with a commercial mortgage. A good answer would be well supported by reference to relevant case law.

Key Points

- Definition of a mortgage
- Domestic and commercial mortgages
- No clog or fetter on the equity of redemption
- Postponement of the right to redeem: *Fairclough* v *Swan Brewery Co Ltd*; *Knightsbridge Estates Trust Ltd* v *Byrne*
- Collateral advantages – surviving redemption: *Noakes* v *Rice*; *Kreglinger* v *New Patagonia Meat and Cold Storage Co Ltd*; *Esso Petroleum* v *Harper's Garage (Stourport) Ltd*; *Alec Lobb (Garages) Ltd* v *Total Oil (GB) Ltd*
- Option to purchase mortgaged property given to mortgagee: *Samuel* v *Jarrah Timber and Wood Paving Corp*; *Reeve* v *Lisle*

Suggested Answer

A mortgage is essentially a transaction whereby an interest in property be it land, house or business, is transferred to a mortgagee (lender) as security for the loan, subject to a right of redemption vested in the mortgagor (borrower).

Once a mortgage is entered into the equity of redemption comes into existence – this is the borrower's right of ownership of the property subject to the mortgage. Equity protects the borrower's equity of redemption through the maxim 'once a mortgage always a mortgage'. One of the ways in which this maxim is applied is that there must be no clog or fetter on the equity of redemption. This means that the borrower cannot be prevented from (a) ultimately redeeming his property, and (b) redeeming it free from any condition in the mortgage.

The basic purpose of a mortgage is to provide security for the repayment of the money lent by the mortgagee.

Here we are dealing with a commercial mortgage. Bill, the owner of a bakery shop, mortgages it to Gus, the local grocer. This is an important fact to note because the attitude of the courts to the terms of a mortgage seems to differ depending on whether they are dealing with a consumer/domestic mortgage or a business/commercial mortgage. The courts are more likely to intervene to prevent a lender taking advantage of a borrower in the former category of mortgage than in the case of the latter: see, eg, *Cityland and Property (Holdings) Ltd* v *Dabrah* (1968) and *Multiservice Bookbinding Ltd* v *Marden* (1978). This is because there is usually great disparity of bargaining power between the parties to a domestic mortgage than between the parties to a commercial mortgage.

The mortgage deed provides that the mortgage is to be paid off in 40 half-yearly instalments (ie, it is an attempt to postpone the right to redeem for 20 years). Equity allows the equitable right to redeem to be postponed provided the period of postponement is not so long as to render the right illusory: *Fairclough* v *Swan Brewery Co Ltd* (1912). In that case the subject-matter of the mortgage was a lease with seventeen-and-a-half years unexpired. The mortgage included a clause postponing redemption until the last six weeks of the term. The mortgagor also covenanted that while the mortgage remained unredeemed the mortgagor would not purchase his beer from anyone else other than the mortgagee. The mortgagor sought to redeem the mortgage and purchase his beer elsewhere, but the mortgagee insisted that he could not redeem until the last six weeks of the mortgage term. The Privy Council held that the postponement clause was void because its effect was to make the mortgage 'for all practical purposes irredeemable'.

In *Knightsbridge Estates Trust Ltd* v *Byrne* (1940) the period of postponement extended over 40 years but it must be distinguished from the *Fairclough* case. In *Knightsbridge* the subject-matter of the mortgage was freehold property, and the mortgagor agreed to repay the loan over 40 years by half-yearly instalments. Some six years later, finding it could borrow the monies at a lesser rate of interest, it sought to redeem the mortgage, claiming that the 40-year period in effect made it irredeemable and unreasonable. The Court of Appeal rejected the mortgagor's argument. In an important passage the Master of the Rolls explained equity's approach:

> 'Equity does not reform mortgage transactions because they are unreasonable. It is concerned to see two things: one that the essential requirements of a mortgage are observed, and the other, that oppressive and unconscionable terms are not enforced. Subject to this it does not, in our opinion, interfere.'

The test therefore is not 'reasonableness'. In *Multiservice Bookbinding Ltd* v *Marden* Browne-Wilkinson J made this very clear. In that case he regarded a number of important terms of the mortgage as unreasonable but went on to say:

'... the defendant made a hard bargain. But the test is not reasonableness. The parties made a bargain which the plaintiffs, who are businessmen, went into with their eyes open, with the benefit of independent advice, without any compelling necessity to accept a loan on these terms and without any sharp practice by the defendant. I cannot see that there was anything unfair or oppressive or morally reprehensible in such a bargain entered into in such circumstances.'

The mortgagor's claim was accordingly rejected. Likewise in *Knightsbridge* the Master of the Rolls found that the agreement was a commercial agreement between two companies experienced in such matters, and had none of the features of an oppressive bargain where the borrower was at the mercy of an unscrupulous lender.

Would the 20-year period of postponement be acceptable here? The property is apparently freehold as Bill is described as owning the shop. The facts bear a number of similarities with the *Knightsbridge* case.

In particular, it is a commercial mortgage affecting freehold property. Accordingly, there is much in favour of the period of postponement being upheld (the courts generally do not interfere with a bargain made between two parties of equal bargaining strength). There is, however, at least one important difference between the facts given and the *Knightsbridge* case. There the mortgagor was a large company, but here the mortgagor is a private individual and 20 years is a long period of time for an individual borrower. Accordingly, predicting the outcome of any challenge to the term is not without some difficulty.

As to the restrictions imposed by the mortgage on what Bill can sell in the baker's shop and the sandwich bar, they rank as collateral advantages. Although the basic purpose of a mortgage is to provide security for the repayment of the money lent by the mortgagee, in the case of commercial properties the lender may succeed in negotiating for some additional (collateral) advantage. For example, a brewery will often advance money on mortgage to the licensee of a public house, provided the borrower agrees to buy all his beer from the lending brewery. The orginal view of the courts was that all collateral advantages taken by a lender were void. This was because they were regarded as a disguised form of interest contravening the old usury laws: *Jennings* v *Ward* (1705). In 1854, the last of the statutes dealing with usury was repealed and thereafter the attitude of the courts to collateral advantages began to change.

Today there is no rule of equity which prevents a lender from stipulating for a collateral advantage. Rather, equity endeavours to 'hold the ring' so far as collateral advantages are concerned. The current law on collateral advantages can be summarised in the following two propositions. First, a collateral advantage which exists until redemption can be valid (*Biggs* v *Hoddinott* (1898)), but will be void if it is oppressive or unconscionable: *Cityland and Property Holdings Ltd* v *Dabrah*. Second, a collateral advantage which exists beyond redemption is void (*Noakes & Co Ltd* v *Rice* (1902)), unless it exists as an independent transaction: *Kreglinger* v *New Patagonia Meat and Cold Storage Co Ltd* (1914).

In *Noakes & Co Ltd* v *Rice* the subject matter of the mortgage was a lease which was due to expire in 1923. The mortgage taken out in 1897 contained a clause by which the mortgagor, Rice, would not, during the continuation of the *lease* 'whether any principal moneys or interest shall or shall not be owing', purchase his liquor from anyone else than the mortgagees. Some time later Rice wished to repay the loan and redeem the property free of the covenant. The mortgagees resisted his claim and the case went to the House of Lords. Lord Davey annunciated three equitable doctrines:

1 'once a mortgage, always a mortgage';
2 'a provision or stipulation which will have the effect of clogging or fettering the equity of redemption is void';
3 'the mortgagee shall not reserve himself any collateral advantage outside the mortgage contract'.

As he pointed out (1) and (2) go together, (2) being a corollary of (1). He explained (1): 'the mortgagee shall not make any stipulation which will prevent a mortgagor who has paid principal, interest and costs from getting back his property in the condition in which he parted with it'. As regards (2) he quoted the Master of the Rolls in *Santley* v *Wilde* (1899): 'a clog or fetter is something which is inconsistent with the idea of security, a clog or fetter is in the nature of a repugnant condition'.

What Lord Davey was emphasising was that the essential nature of a mortgage is that its purpose is to provide security for a loan with an inherent right vested in the mortgagor to redeem it on payment of the mortgage debt. He stated:

'A mortgage must not be converted into something else; and once you come to the conclusion that a stipulation for the benefit of a mortgagee is part of the mortgage transaction, it is but part of his security, and necessarily comes to an end on payment of the loan.'

In dealing with (3) Lord Davey explained that the origin of this doctrine lay in equity's attitude towards the laws against usury. When the usury laws were abolished equity revised its position and allowed mortgagees to stipulate for collateral advantages. Accordingly Rice was held to be entitled to redeem the mortgage and recover his property completely free of any obligation to purchase his liquor exclusively from the mortgagee.

Here Bill is required not to sell biscuits or chocolates in the baker's shop (the mortgaged property) 'so long as he owned it'. A collateral advantage which is limited in duration to the time of redemption is not inconsistent with the right to redeem and is therefore usually enforceable. However, here the collateral advantage is not so restricted because it is to apply so long as Bill owns the shop. Such a collateral advantage is void (*Noakes* v *Rice*) unless it exists as an *independent transaction*. A leading authority on this point is *Kreglinger* v *New Patagonia Meat and Cold Storage Co Ltd*. There a meat company mortgaged property to a firm of woolbrokers. The mortgage was for a period of five years, though the mortgagors were free to repay it within the five years if they wished. It was a term of the mortgage that the mortgagors would for a five-year period (irrespective of whether the mortgage ended within that time) offer their sheep's skins (a by-product of its meat business) to the mortgagees for purchase, who would offer the market price. The mortgagors redeemed after two years and they claimed to be able to offer their sheep's skins to persons other than the mortgagee. The House of Lords held that the mortgagors were still bound by the agreement as to the sheep's skins because the granting of the collateral advantage was a *separate contract* independent of the mortgage contract.

Whether in a given case a collateral advantage is the product of a separate transaction, despite being concluded at the same time as the mortgage, and in the same document, is a question of construction. Here it is submitted that the collateral advantage would not rank as an independent transaction – not least because it is to last so long as Bill owns the shop – whereas in *Kreglinger* it was only to last for five years from the creation of the mortgage. Further, the collateral advantage may also fail on the additional ground that it is an unreasonable restraint of trade: *Esso Petroleum* v *Harper's Garage (Stourport) Ltd* (1968).

Alec Lobb (Garages) Ltd v *Total Oil (GB) Ltd* (1985) was a complicated commercial case concerning a solus agreement in which the common law relating to restraint of trade and the equitable approach to oppressive and unconscionable bargains were examined. It is important that the two should not be confused. In the former, the question of reasonableness is relevant; in the latter it is not.

The findings of the Court of Appeal may be summarised thus:

1   As a general rule a covenant which required a petrol dealer to purchase his supply from one supplier alone was reasonable if it was to last for not more than five years; if it was to last significantly longer then it was to be regarded as unreasonable and invalid unless it could be established that the longer period was one of economic necessity, the burden of proof being on the supplier. Each case must be decided on its own facts. It was held that on the facts the covenant was not unreasonable.
2   If one party had acted oppressively as a general rule equity would set the transaction aside. However, the court would not find that the bargain was harsh and unconscionable solely because the parties were of unequal bargaining power, nor would it arrive at that conclusion simply because one party was compelled by economic necessity to make it. The court held that there was no unconscionable bargain. Although under economic pressure the plaintiffs had not been pressurised by the defendants and moreover had received independent advice although they had ignored that advice.

Further, Bill is required not to sell biscuits or chocolates in the sandwich bar 'so long as he owned it'. A point of distinction between this collateral advantage and the former one is that the sandwich bar is not subject to the mortgage. Such an agreement which restricts Bill's freedom in the way he carries on his trade is likely to be declared void on the basis that it is not necessary to protect the mortgagee's interest.

Finally, the mortgage in requiring Bill not to sell either property without giving Gus 'the chance of buying it for the best price that anyone else offered' is giving the mortgagee an option to buy both the mortgaged property and the non-mortgaged property. Equity will not allow a term which has the effect of preventing or limiting redemption. In *Samuel* v *Jarrah Timber and Wood Paving Corp* (1904) the court held that a term in a mortgage which gave the mortgagee an option to purchase the mortgaged property was void even if it was not oppressive. However, once the mortgage has been created, equity will not interfere if subsequently the mortgagor gives the mortgagee such an option. In *Reeve v Lisle* (1902) an option to buy which was granted to the mortgagee 12 days after the mortgage was entered into was upheld. Accordingly, on the authority of *Samuel v Jarrah Timber and Wood Paving Corp* Gus's option in respect of the mortgaged property is clearly void and is not saved by the fact that Gus has to give 'the best price that anyone else offered'. The result of the exercise of the option would be that the mortgagee becomes the owner of the land, a result that is inconsistent with the right to redeem.

As to Gus's option to buy the sandwich bar (the non-mortgaged property) the position is not so clear cut. If, as seems to be the case, Gus and Bill are of equal bargaining strengths, and if this option is deemed to be a separate agreement, it may be upheld. If on the other hand it is not so regarded then it would be void.

In conclusion, it is submitted that the court will uphold postponement of the redemption clause since there has been no unconscionable behaviour by Gus, and that Bill's obligation not to sell biscuits or chocolates in the shop would terminate on redemption unless Gus could estalish that it was an independent agreement, which seems unlikely. The agreement not to sell chocolates and biscuits in the sandwich bar would probably be declared by the court as being in restraint of trade. The agreement in relation to the sale of the shop would almost certainly be declared void by equity on the authority of *Samuel v Jarrah Timber*. The position as regards the sandwich bar is not so clear as it does not form part of the mortgage.

SUGGESTED ANSWER TO QUESTION THREE

General Comment

A somewhat challenging essay title because of its specific focus, which would give a student well versed in the relevant law a good opportunity to exhibit his knowledge and understanding. Not a question to be undertaken by a student with only an outline understanding of the relevant law.

Key Points

*   Definition of a mortgage
*   Power of sale – arising
*   Power of sale – exercisable
*   Mortgagee not a trustee of the power of sale
*   Duty to mortgagor to take reasonable care – *Cuckmere Brick Co Ltd v Mutual Finance Ltd*
*   *Parker-Tweedale v Dunbar Bank plc*
*   Sale by mortgagee to himself – *Tse Kwong Lam v Wong Chit Sen*
*   Section 13 Building Societies Act 1986
*   Section 105 LPA 1925

Suggested Answer

A mortgage is essentially a transaction whereby an interest in property, be it land, house or business, is transferred to a mortgagee (lender) as security for the loan, subject to a right of redemption vested in the mortgagor (borrower).

The most important rights enabling the mortgagee to recover the capital sum and/or interest are taking possession, sale, foreclosure and appointing a receiver. The question concerns the power of sale which is the remedy most commonly used as it enables a mortgagee to recover his capital speedily. It is usually combined with an action to obtain vacant possession to allow the best price to be obtained.

The power of sale arises when the mortgage has been made by deed and the legal date of redemption has passed and there is no contrary intention expressed in the mortgage deed: s101 Law of Property Act (LPA) 1925. Once the power of sale has arisen it becomes exercisable when one or more of the following conditions have been fulfilled: (1) default for three months after notice; or (2) interest two months in arrear; or (3) breach of some other term of the mortgage: s103 LPA 1925. The statutory power of sale is exercisable without a court order.

Over the last 25 years the responsibilities of a mortgagee to a mortgagor when selling mortgaged property have been considered by the courts on a number of occasions. In the first place it is important to note that a mortgagee has an absolute discretion as to the mode and time of sale. He can choose to sell by way of private treaty or by way of auction and is not required to wait until the market improves. Further, the mortgagee's motive for selling – spite against the mortgagor – has been held immaterial: see *Nash* v *Eads* (1880).

However, once the mortgagee decides to sell he is subject to certain duties. First and foremost, it was laid down in *Cuckmere Brick Co Ltd* v *Mutual Finance Ltd* (1971) that a mortgagee is not a trustee for the mortgagor in respect of the power of sale because the power is given to the mortgagee for his own benefit to enable him the better to realise his security.

However, the mortgagor is the person interested in the proceeds of sale in so far as they exceed the mortgage debt, and his interests must not be sacrificed. Accordingly, a mortgagee is under some duty to the mortgagor with regard to the sale. Originally the duty was considered to be no more than a duty to act in good faith: see *Kennedy* v *De Trafford* (1897). However, since the early 1970s it has been recognised that more than good faith is required, and the topic was examined in depth by the Court of Appeal in the leading case of *Cuckmere Brick Co Ltd* v *Mutual Finance Ltd.*

In that case the plaintiffs owned land near Maidstone, which they mortgaged to the defendants. The mortgagees, having decided to exercise its power of sale, advertised the property for sale by auction. Planning permission to erect 35 houses on the plot had been granted and this was stated in the advertisement. However, planning permission had also been granted for the construction of 100 flats and this was omitted from the advertisement. The land was sold for £44,000 and the plaintiffs argued that had the planning permission for the construction of the flats been included in the advertisement the property would have realised £75,000.

The court considered a mortgagee's duty to sell and held that the mortgagees owed a duty to take reasonable care to obtain the true market value and this the mortgagees had not done and in the result were liable in damages to the mortgagors. The judgment of Salmon LJ makes clear that:

1   a mortgagee is not a trustee of the power of sale for the mortgagor;
2   the mortgagee is under no obligation to 'nurse' the property in the sense that he is under no obligation to postpone sale if it appears that the market will become more favourable in the future; he may sell when he wishes;
3   however, when he does sell, he must obtain what Salmon LJ described as 'the true market value' at the time of the sale;
4   'if the mortgagee's interests conflict with those of the mortgagor, the mortgagee can give preference to his own interests, which of course he could not do were he a trustee of the power of sale for the mortgagor'.

He concluded that 'both on principle and authority, that a mortgagee in exercising his power of sale, does owe a duty to take reasonable precautions to obtain the true market value of the mortgaged property when he decides to sell it'.

The phraseology in the case seems to introduce the tort of negligence into this area of the law. In *Standard Chartered Bank* v *Walker* (1982) the duty was extended to the guarantor of a mortgage. Once the 'neighbour principle' expressed by Lord Atkin in *Donoghue* v *Stevenson* (1932) is introduced, it becomes necessary to pose Lord Atkin's question: 'Who is my neighbour?' In *Standard Chartered Bank* v *Walker* Lord Denning MR decided that a receiver owed the guarantor a duty of care on the basis of negligence. Discussing the mortgagee's duty on sale he stated that 'it is his duty to use reasonable care to obtain the best price which the circumstances permit' and that duty was owed to the mortgagor and to the guarantor, and he went on to explain the basis of that duty: 'the duty is only a particular application of the general duty of care to your neighbour which was stated by Lord Atkin in *Donoghue* v *Stevenson* (1932)'. The mortgagor and guarantor are clearly in very close 'proximity' to those who conduct the sale. The duty of care is owing to them – if not to the general body of the creditors of the mortgagor.

However, this drift towards the tort of negligence has been curtailed. An attempt was made to rely on it in *China and South Sea Bank Ltd* v *Tan Soon Gin* in 1989, and the Court of Appeal in Hong Kong approved it. The contention was, however, rejected by the Privy Council on appeal.

The tortious 'neighbour principle' which is the basis of a claim in negligence was invoked in *Parker-Tweedale* v *Dunbar Bank plc* (1991). In that case a separation agreement between husband and wife provided that the wife should become the sole owner of property and that the net surplus of monies on the sale of the property would vest in the husband as beneficial owner. He was, therefore, a beneficiary under a trust. The wife mortgaged the property but it was later repossessed by the mortgagees and sold. The husband claimed that they should have sold for a higher price and claimed damages from the mortgagees. The husband based his claim on the neighbour principle as applied in *Standard Chartered Bank Ltd* v *Walker*, and in particular on the judgment of Lord Denning MR.

Nourse LJ condemned that approach in no uncertain terms. 'It was,' he said, 'unnecessary and confusing for the duties owed by a mortgagee to a mortgagor and surety, if there is one, to be expressed in terms of the tort of negligence.' The duty, he explained, does not rest in tort, but is a 'duty owed by the mortgagee to the mortgagor, recognised by equity, as arising out of the particular relationship between them.' It followed, therefore, that the duty arising out of that particular relationship could not be extended to include a beneficiary of a trust of which the mortgagor was the trustee.

A sale by the mortgagee to himself either directly or through a third party may be set aside. In *Tse Kwong Lam* v *Wong Chit Sen* (1983) the matter was considered by the Privy Council. There it was held that there was no inflexible rule that a mortgagee exercising his power of sale under a mortgage could not sell to a company in which he had an interest. However, the mortgagee and the company had to show that the sale was made in good faith and that the mortgagee had taken reasonable precautions to obtain the best price reasonably obtainable at the time.

After paying off all prior mortgages, the money received from the purchase is held by the mortgagee on trust. This money must be used by the mortgagee, in the following order, to: (1) pay all expenses incidental to the sale; (2) pay himself the principal, interest and costs due under the mortgage; and (3) pay the surplus, if any, to the next mortgagee, or if none, to the mortgagor: see s105 LPA 1925. If there is a subsequent mortgagee he will hold the balance on trust to discharge the money owing to him and to pay the balance to the person next entitled.

The question of the mortgagee's responsibilities on sale to the mortgagor is an area of land law which has seen considerable development over the last 25 years. It is now clear that more than good faith is entailed. Rather, it is now clearly established that the mortgagee owes to the mortgagor a duty to take reasonable care. Given the view of the Court of Appeal in *Parker-Tweedale* v *Dunbar Bank plc* that the mortgagee's duty arises in equity and not in negligence it is true to say that the duty is now analogous to a fiduciary one.

SUGGESTED ANSWER TO QUESTION FOUR

General Comment

A question which couples the law of mortgages and trusts. As regards the bank seeking possession mention must be made of the Administration of Justice Acts. The case of *Cuckmere Brick* must be discussed in the context of the low sale price, and s105 Law of Property Act (LPA) 1925 as regards the distribution of proceeds. In dealing with the distribution of proceeds it is necessary to see whether Henry's father and Joanna can claim an interest in the house, and, consequently, in the proceeds. Constructive trusts, resulting trusts and proprietary estoppel should be considered in this context.

Key Points

- Definition of mortgage
- *Four Maids Ltd* v *Dudley Marshall (Properties) Ltd*
- Possession a prelude to sale – dwelling-house – s36 Administration of Justice Act 1970 – s8 Administration of Justice Act 1973
- *Cuckmere Brick Co Ltd* v *Mutual Finance Ltd* – mortgagee's duty of care on sale
- Section 101 LPA 1925 – s103 LPA 1925 – distribution of proceeds: s105 LPA 1925
- Father has no claim on the proceeds of sale
- Interest of Joanna – constructive or resulting trust

Suggested Answer

A mortgage is a security for a loan and can be either legal or equitable. In this case Savewell Bank have a legal mortgage in the form of a charge over the property. As legal mortgagee the bank have certain powers, namely of sale, to take possession, to foreclose and to appoint a receiver.

Possession

The bank is entitled to take possession of the house 'before the ink is dry on the mortgage' (*Four Maids Ltd* v *Dudley Marshall (Properties) Ltd* (1957)), unless it has expressly or impliedly excluded its right to do so: *Birmingham Citizens' Permanent Building Society* v *Caunt* (1962). In reality, however, possession is usually sought for two different reasons. First, if the mortgagee does not wish to realise his security he may seek possession of the land with a view to intercepting the rents and profits from the land, and applying them towards discharge of the mortgage debt. Such a move is attended by liability on the basis of wilful default, in the sense that the mortgagee will be liable to the mortgagor not for the income he actually generates from the land but for the income he could have generated from it: *White* v *City of London Brewery* (1889).

The second use of possession is as a prelude to sale, as the mortgagee will wish to obtain possession in order to sell with vacant possession. Henry should be advised as follows.

Where a mortgagee is seeking possession of a dwelling-house statutory provisions provide a measure of relief for mortgagors. Section 36 of the Administration of Justice Act 1970 provides that if it appears that the mortgagor 'is likely to be able within a reasonable period, to pay any sums due under the mortgage' the court may either adjourn the proceedings or suspend the possession order or postpone it. However, in some mortgages there is a provision that in the event of instalments being in arrears the whole of the principal sum shall forthwith become payable.

In *Halifax Building Society* v *Clark* (1973) the mortgage provided that if the mortgagor defaulted on payment of instalments then the whole principal immediately became payable. The court held that s36 had no application to that situation, being confined to default in the mortgage instalments, with the result that the mortgagor was unable to take advantage of the relief afforded by the section. In consequence the legislature enacted s8 of the Administration of Justice Act 1973 which enabled the court to approach the matter as if only the instalments in arrears were due.

The court's discretion to relieve the mortgagor is limited to those circumstances where it appears that there is a reasonable likelihood that he will be able to pay the arrears within a reasonable time.

Section 36(1) AJA 1970 applies where 'a mortgagee under a mortgage of land which consists of or includes a dwelling house brings an action in which he claims possession of the mortgaged property'.

In *Ropaigelach* v *Barclays Bank plc* (1999) the mortgagee sold the mortgaged property without first obtaining a court order for sale but the mortgagor challenged its right to do so. The Court of Appeal held that a mortgagee was not obliged to obtain a court order before sale because there was nothing in the section to that effect.

Henry LJ observed:

'Clarke LJ has drawn attention to the curious anomaly that mortgagors should have the protection afforded by s36 ... in cases in which the mortgagee chooses to enforce his right to possession through the court but should have no such protection where he chooses (and is able) to enter without first obtaining an order of the court.'

This decision enables mortgagees to deprive mortgagors of the relieving provisions of s36 and it remains to be seen if the legislature will respond to the suggestion of Henry LJ, expressed in his judgment, that reform is required.

As well as seeking statutory relief under s36 a mortgagor may be able to seek the assistance of equity to protect him against a mortgagee seeking possession against him: *Quennel* v *Maltby* (1979). In that case it was clear that the purpose of seeking possession was not to enforce the mortgage but to gain possession against a protected tenant of the house, but the Court of Appeal refused an order for possession. The Court held:

'The objective is plain. It was not to enforce the security or to obtain repayment or anything of the kind. It was in order to get possession of the house and to overcome the protection of the Rent Act ... Equity can step in so as to prevent a mortgagee or a successor from him, from getting possession of the house contrary to the justice of the case.'

In this case when the Savewell Bank applies to the court for a possession order Henry can request the court to exercise its statutory discretionary powers and possibly invoke equitable relief.

Sale at less than market value
In the first place the bank, as mortgagee, has an absolute discretion as to the mode and time of sale. It can choose to sell by way of private treaty (as in this case) or by way of auction, and it is not obliged to wait until the market improves. However, once the bank decides to sell it is subject to certain duties. First, and foremost, it is clear from *Cuckmere Brick Co Ltd* v *Mutual Finance Ltd* (1971) that a mortgagee is not a trustee for the mortgagor in respect of the power of sale.

Further, a mortgagee is under no obligation to 'nurse' the property, that is to say he is under no duty to wait for a more favourable market to develop. He may sell when he chooses to do so. However, when he does sell he must take reasonable care to obtain the true market value of the property at the time of the sale. At first sight this seems to be introducing the tort of negligence into this area of law, and in *Standard Chartered Bank* v *Walker* (1982) Lord Denning MR certainly thought that was the case, quoting Lord Atkin in *Donoghue* v *Stevenson* (1932). This view has been firmly rejected both by the Privy Council in *China and South Sea Bank Ltd* v *Tan Soon Gin* (1989) and the Court of Appeal in *Parker-Tweedale* v *Dunbar Bank plc* (1991), where Nourse LJ said that it was confusing and unnecessary to express the duty owed by a mortgagee to a mortgagor in terms of the tort of negligence. The basis of the mortgagee's duty to the mortgagor lay in the particular relationship between them imposed by equity.

If a mortgagee proves to be in breach of the duty arising from that relationship then he is liable in damages to the mortgagor. If the bank sold the house for less than the market value, the mortgagor would be entitled to the difference between the price actually obtained and that which it ought to have obtained.

Proceeds of sale

As the mortgage is by way of legal charge made by deed after 1881, there is power of sale in favour of the bank (s101 LPA 1925), and in view of the fact that Henry is badly in arrears, one of the conditions making the power exercisable under s103 LPA 1925 has been satisfied. Upon sale being concluded the proceeds of sale will be distributed in accordance with s105 LPA 1925. Under that section, in the absence of any prior encumbrance, the costs and expenses of sale will be defrayed first, then the bank will take the mortgage monies owing to it. Any balance will be paid to subsequent mortgagees if any, and if not, to the mortgagor (Henry).

Assuming the proceeds of sale are sufficient to satisfy the mortgage debt and leave a balance, that balance is paid to the mortgagor (Henry). The question is whether Henry's father and Joanna are entitled to a share of that balance.

Henry's father does not, on the facts as given, seem to have any claim against the proceeds of sale which remain after the mortgage debt has been discharged. His loan to Henry seems to have been a simple personal unsecured loan and there is nothing to suggest that the property should be a security for it nor that in return father should secure any form of equitable interest in the house.

It is unlikely that Joanna will be able to claim a share in the proceeds. In the first place she has not made any direct financial contribution to the purchase of the house either by way of deposit or mortgage instalments, so as to establish a beneficial interest in her favour under a resulting or constructive trust: *Lloyds Bank* v *Rosset* (1991). Second, although she may be able to point to the oral agreement that she should have a 50 per cent share in the house, she does not appear to have acted to her detriment upon that agreement so as to raise an interest in her favour under a constructive trust or by way of estoppel: *Lloyds Bank* v *Rosset* and *Grant* v *Edwards* (1986).

8

Licences

Introduction

This is a topic very much based on case law. The questions are not always capable of a definite answer and moreover the law is not always clear. The questions do, however, provide students with a good opportunity to demonstrate their skills of analysis and application, but an in-depth knowledge of cases is required. As the selected questions indicate, candidates must be prepared to argue alternative situations: leases; contractual licences; licences by estoppel; and constructive trusts.

Questions

INTERROGRAMS

1 How many types of licence exist today?
2 Is a licence revocable?
3 Is a licence enforceable against subsequent holders of the land?
4 Explain proprietary estoppel.
5 What are the differences between a constructive trust and proprietary estoppel?

QUESTION ONE

Old Mr Grant died in 1990 leaving his Hindley Manor estate to William, his elder son. William (who lived and worked in London) then entered into the following arrangements with members of the family. He executed a deed giving his mother, Alice, the exclusive right to occupy Hindley Manor House for the remainder of her life. He orally agreed to allow his sister, Sarah, to live rent-free in a disused barn on the understanding that she would be responsible for repairing the roof, installing electricity and making the barn generally more habitable. He agreed in writing to let a lodge on the estate to his brother, Ben, at a yearly rent until he (William) obtained planning permission to convert the lodge into a guest house. Recently William has retired from his job and he has written to Alice, Sarah and Ben indicating that he intends to live in the Manor House with his wife and that he wants the barn and the lodge to be vacated for occupation by his children.

Discuss.

London University LLB Examination
(for external students) Land Law June 1997 Q5

QUESTION TWO

When Tim married Janet, Barbara, Tim's mother, bought a house for the couple to live in. Barbara paid the whole of the purchase price and the house was registered in her sole name. The couple agreed to be responsible for repairs and other outgoings and they insisted, against Barbara's wishes, on paying her a token monthly 'rent'. A few years later the marriage broke down and Tim moved out of the house. Janet continued living in the house, doing the repairs and paying the rent. Finding herself short of cash, Barbara decided to sell the house and, while Janet was away on holiday, she sold it to a local building company. As the new registered proprietor, the company seeks possession of the house with a view to redeveloping the site.

Advise Janet.

London University LLB Examination
(for external students) Land Law June 1995 Q7

QUESTION THREE

In 1992 John and Karen met and became lovers. At the time they were both married and living with their spouses, but they both hoped to obtain divorces and then to marry each other. In 1993 Karen became pregnant by John and John purchased a flat for her to live in. Karen gave up her job, left her husband and moved into the flat. Shortly afterwards she gave birth to a daughter, Clare. The flat was conveyed into John's sole name and he paid both the deposit on the purchase price, all the bills and all the mortgage repayments. For three years John provided Karen with financial support for herself and Clare. In 1996 Karen found a good job and thereafter supported herself and her daughter as well as spending some money on maintaining and decorating the flat. On one or two occasions Karen asked John why he did not put the flat in their joint names, and he replied that it was because of his tax position, but that she had no reason to worry because she could stay in the flat for as long as she wished and because he was leaving her the flat in his will.

In 1999 John was killed in a car crash. In his will he left his entire estate to his wife, Wilma. His executors now seek possession of the flat with a view to selling it.

Advise Karen.

London University LLB Examination
(for external students) Land Law June 1991 Q5

QUESTION FOUR

Mr and Mrs Brown were the joint legal and beneficial owners of Magnolia House and when their son, Alan, married Diana in 1985, Mr Brown wrote to Alan inviting the couple to go and live with them. 'You could build an extension to the house so that you would be independent,' he wrote, 'you can live there rent-free for as long as you like and, of course, the house will be yours when we are dead.' Alan and Diana accepted the invitation; they built an extension at a cost of £20,000 and went to live with the Browns. Ten years later Mr Brown and his son Alan were killed in a car crash. Mrs Brown and

Diana have now quarrelled and Mrs Brown seeks possession of the house with a view to selling it. She wants to buy a small flat and she claims that Diana can well afford to buy accommodation elsewhere.

Advise Diana as to her rights.

London University LLB Examination
(for external students) Land Law June 1998 Q3

Answers

ANSWERS TO INTERROGRAMS

1   There are four basic types of licences:

   a   a bare licence;
   b   a licence coupled with an interest;
   c   a contractual licence;
   d   a licence by estoppel.

2   There are different rules for each type of licence:

   a   Bare licence. This is no more than a bare permission to be on land without any form of consideration furnished in return. It confers no interest in land on the licensee and is revocable at will at the instance of the licensor. He must, however, give the licensee a reasonable time to leave the land after which the licensee becomes a trespasser. When the licensor dies or sells the land the licence is automatically terminated because a bare licence is personal to the parties.
   b   Licence coupled with an interest. This is a licence coupled with a profit à prendre. A profit à prendre entitles the grantee to take something from the grantor's land, eg right of turbary: the right to take turf from the grantor's land. There is an implied licence for the grantee to enter the grantor's land in order to exercise the right. A profit à prendre is an interest in land which will bind a successor in title of the grantor. Since the licence is necessary for enjoyment of the profit à prendre it is irrevocable, and like the profit à prendre, will bind the successor in title to the grantor.
   c   Contractual licences. This is a licence arising out of contract, ie one granted in return for consideration. A ticket to enter a cinema is a classic example. The licensor's right to revoke the contract depends on the terms (express or implied) of the contract: *Winter Garden Theatre (London) Ltd* v *Millennium Productions Ltd* (1948). In that case there was no express term dealing with revocation and both the Court of Appeal and the House of Lords implied one but differed as to its terms. The Court of Appeal held that the licence was irrevocable while the House of Lords held that it was determinable by the giving of reasonable notice. That case also decided that a wrongful revocation of a licence could be restrained by an injunction.

   In *Chandler* v *Kerley* (1978), the Court of Appeal had to infer a contractual licence from the conduct of the parties and then further infer the terms of its revocability. It decided that the licence was revocable on the giving of 12 months' notice.

d Licence by estoppel. No direct answer can be given in the case of estoppel licences. The court has to decide in the first place whether there is a licence at all. It is only then that it must decide on its terms and that decision will depend on the facts of the particular case. The court is often concerned to decide the duration of the licence as in *Inwards* v *Baker* (1965) when it concluded that the claimant was entitled to remain in the bungalow for as long as he wished. In *Dodsworth* v *Dodsworth* (1973) it was held that the licencees could remain in the property until they had been compensated for the improvements they had made to it.

3 a Bare licences and licences coupled with a grant have already been discussed. Contractual licences and licences by estoppel (proprietary estoppel) must be considered separately.

b Contractual licences. In *King* v *David Allen & Sons Billposting Ltd* (1916) and *Clore* v *Theatrical Properties Ltd* (1936) it was held that a contractual licence does not confer an interest in land on the licensee and it cannot bind third parties. It is personal to the parties and the privity of contract rule applies. However, circumstances can arise when equity will impose a constructive trust on a third party to observe the terms of the licence. Lord Denning MR took that view in his minority judgment in *Binions* v *Evans* (1972). His reasoning was adopted by Dillon J in *Lyus* v *Prowsa Developments* (1982). In 1989 the Court of Appeal, in *Ashburn Anstalt* v *Arnold* (1988), confirmed that approach, but emphasised that it was only applicable if the conscience of the third party was affected. Mere notice was not sufficient to justify its imposition, nor was it sufficient of itself if the third party agreed to take 'subject to' the licence.

c Licences by estoppel (proprietary estoppel). The position here is rather more complex. In *Inwards* v *Baker* and *Ives (ER) Investments Ltd* v *High* (1967) (both unregistered land cases) the Court of Appeal confirmed that licences by estoppel conferred an equitable interest in land on the licensees which was capable of binding third parties. However, a claimant to a licence arising from proprietary estoppel does not know if he has such a licence, nor its extent, until the Court has ruled on those two issues. Once it has confirmed the existence of the licence and defined its terms there is no difficulty. In the case of unregistered land, not being registrable under the Land Charges Act 1972, it will bind the whole world except the bona fide purchaser (equity's darling). In the case of registered land, since it is not an overriding interest (s70(1)(g) LRA 1925 apart), it will be a minor interest and should be subject to an entry (either a notice or a caution) on the licensor's register of title. Failing that, it could fall within s70(1)(g) providing the requirements of that paragraph are satisfied.

The difficulty arises where the claimant has not reached the stage of securing a court order on the issues. Before that stage is reached the claimant cannot know if he has a valid claim at all, let alone its extent. It can be argued that until judicial adjudication he has no rights at all which can bind a third party. The position has been subject to much academic discussion and there is little judicial guidance available. The position remains to be clarified. In the case of registered land the claimant could perhaps enter a caution on the licensor's register of title.

4   This type of licence confers upon the licensee an equitable interest in land with the consequence that it is capable of binding third parties. In that respect it differs substantially from promissory estoppel as defined in *Central London Property Trust v High Trees House Ltd* (1947). Promissory estoppel is said to act as a shield not a sword. It can be used as a defence but it cannot found a cause of action. Proprietary estoppel can be both a shield and a sword because, as a sword it can be used to claim an equitable interest in land.

Proprietary estoppel arises when O, a landowner, allows E to spend money on his (O's) land or otherwise act to his detriment because of a belief that he has, or that he will later acquire (*Re Basham* (1986)), an interest in the land. The expectation in E's mind must have been created by O by a representation, encouragement or acquiescence (*Ives (ER) Investments Ltd v High* (1967)) so that it would be inequitable for O to act inconsistently with the expectation that he has created. In *Brinnand v Ewens* (1987) Nourse LJ stated the requirements to be satisfied to establish a claim by proprietary estoppel:

a   the claimant must show that he had prejudiced himself or acted to his detriment;
b   his conduct must arise from his belief that he had an interest in the property or would later acquire one;
c   that belief must have been instigated in some way by the land owner.

5   In *Lloyds Bank v Rosset* (1991) Lord Bridge said:

'If Mrs Rosset had, as pleaded, altered her position in reliance on the agreement, this could have given rise to an enforceable interest in her favour by way either of a constructive trust or of a proprietary estoppel.'

There is a suggestion here that the same facts may give rise to either a constructive trust or a proprietary estoppel. There are undeniable similarities between the two but the points of difference must be noted.

If a constructive trust is established then it will fall within the Trusts of Land and Appointment of Trustees Act 1996. Licences by proprietary estoppel do not come within the statute.

An equitable interest under a trust may be overreached. A licence by estoppel cannot.

A constructive trust is founded on a common intention of both parties. A proprietary estoppel arises out of representations made by one party.

In the case of proprietary estoppel the courts have a much more flexible approach in deciding what relief to afford the claimant. In constructive trusts the court is confined to establishing what is the value of the claimant's share in the property.

ANSWER TO QUESTION ONE

General Comment

The question concerns a number of issues in respect of leases and licences. The inclusion of a diagrammatical representation of the facts is advisable in order to eliminate the possibility of confusing the various parties and issues in the course of an answer. There are no third parties involved in the problem.

Key Points

- Legal lease
- Definition of a licence
- Types of licence
- Lease for 'life' (s149(6) LPA 1925)
- Trust of land
- Contractual licence
- Estoppel licence
- Periodic yearly tenancy: *Prudential Assurance Co Ltd* v *London Residuary Body*

Suggested Answer

It is necessary to consider the various interests which Alice, Sarah and Ben have in Hindley Manor, the barn and the lodge on the Hindley Manor Estate respectively. In particular, it is necessary to decide whether they have a lease or a licence. The facts of the question can be represented diagrammatically as follows:

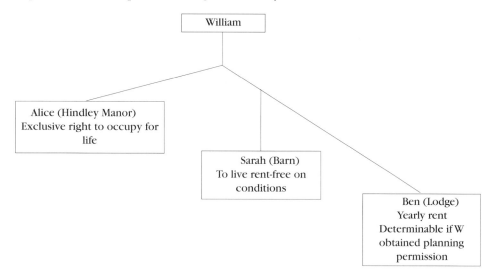

A lease is one of the two estates capable of existing at law – it gives rise to a proprietary right in land. For a lease to be a legal one it must either be made in accordance with s52 LPA 1925 if it is for more than three years duration or by parol if it is to take effect in possession for a term not exceeding three years at the best rent reasonably obtainable without taking a fine: s54 LPA 1925.

A licence is a permission given by the occupier of land which allows the licensee to do some act which would otherwise be a trespass. It does not usually give rise to an interest in land.

There are four main types of licence. First, there is the bare licence (mere personal permission to be on the licensor's land). Second, a licence may be coupled with the grant of an interest in land, eg a right to enter another man's land to hunt and take away the deer killed. Third, there is a contractual licence (a licence supported by consideration). Finally, there is the estoppel licence. In the context of this question, contractual and estoppel licences are particularly relevant.

William executed a deed giving his mother, Alice, the exclusive right of occupation of Hindley Manor House for the rest of her life. It is submitted that Alice may either have a 'lease for life' converted into a 90-year term by s149(6) LPA 1925 or a life interest under a trust of land. Each of these possibilities is considered in turn below.

There are several requirements for a valid lease of which two are relevant on the facts here. First, the lessor must confer upon the lessee the right to exclusive possession of land. Here Alice has exclusive possession of Hindley Manor. Second, there must be certainty of duration (ie the duration of the term must be certain or capable of being ascertained at the outset of the term – s205(1) (xxvii) LPA 1925). Accordingly, Alice would fall foul of this requirement since the Manor House has been granted to her for the rest of her life. However, by virtue of s149(6) LPA 1925 a lease at a rent or in consideration of a fine for life or determinable on life is converted into a term of 90 years, determinable by notice served after the termination of the life. Under this provision, provided Alice is paying rent or has paid a fine (premium) she would get a 90-year term but William could give notice to terminate after her death. There is no indication as to whether Alice is paying a rent or has paid a fine. Accordingly, it is doubtful whether she can take advantage of s149(6) LPA 1925.

Alternatively, William may be holding Hindley Manor House on a trust of land for Alice for life (presumably with the Manor House reverting back to him on her death). In order to create a trust of land the trust must be evidenced in writing: s53(1)(b) LPA 1925. Here William has executed a deed. Accordingly, the requirement of s53(1)(b) LPA 1925 would be satisfied.

Since the trust was created after 1 January 1997 it would not fall within s1 of the Settled Land Act 1925, because s2 of the Trusts of Land and Appointment of Trustees Act 1996 prohibits the creation of new settlements under the 1925 Act. Instead it is a trust of land as defined by s1 of the 1996 Act and subject to the provisions of that Act. Under the trust deed William holds on trust for Alice for life and he cannot terminate her life interest. However, Alice could lost her right to live in the Manor House if William were to sell it and overreach her interest by appointing another trustee to give a receipt for the proceeds of sale. In that event Alice would then be entitled to the income from the invested proceeds of sale for her life.

William has orally agreed to allow his sister Sarah to live rent-free in a disused barn subject to conditions. There is no lease since there is no indication as to how long Sarah can stay in the barn (ie there is no certainty of duration – see above). Accordingly, it is necessary to consider whether Sarah has a contractual licence or an estoppel licence. A contractual licence is one granted for valuable consideration (ie Sarah has to show that she has given value for it).

Clearly, in making the arrangement they did, William and Sarah have not applied their minds to any legal considerations. Basically a contractual licence is a contract to which the law of contract applies. Frequently people enter into loose and informal arrangements concerning the occupation of property and which work well enough providing they remain on friendly terms. Difficulties arise when they fall out and the occupant is told to leave. It is then open to the occupant to argue that occupancy is enjoyed as a result of a contractual licence, the terms of which confer either an irrevocable licence to occupy or for a period of time. All too frequently the parties have given little thought to the matter and it is then for the court to decide whether there is a contractual licence and, if there is, what are its terms. A classic example of this is found in *Chandler* v *Kerley* (1978).

Mr and Mrs K owned the matrimonial home. The marriage broke down and Mr K left. The plaintiff (Chandler) moved in and cohabited with Mrs K. The three parties then agreed that the plaintiff should purchase the house in his sole name and he did so, the cohabitation continuing but with Mrs K no longer having any legal rights in it. The relationship broke down and the plaintiff told Mrs K to leave. The question then arose as to what rights, if any, she had to occupy the house.

The Court of Appeal had to determine exactly what the arrangement was between Mrs K and the plaintiff. There was little concrete evidence. The court concluded that she had a contractual licence to occupy the house and that it contained an implied term that it was determinable by reasonable notice and that in the circumstances the period of notice to which she was entitled was 12 months.

Given the fact of a contractual licence two issues arise. What are the licensor's rights to revoke the licence and how does the licence stand in relation to third parties? In *Winter Garden (London) Ltd* v *Millennium Productions Ltd* (1948) the House of Lords held that the rights of revocability are governed by the terms of the contract and their construction. The difficulties of construction are illustrated by that case: the Court of Appeal construed the licence as being irrevocable; the House of Lords were of the opinion that it could be determined by the giving of a reasonable period of notice. Wrongful revocation may be restrained by an injunction.

A contractual licence of itself cannot bind third parties because of the privity of contract rule. Nor does it confer on the licensee an interest in land: *King* v *David Allen & Sons Billposting Ltd* (1916); *Clore* v *Theatrical Properties Ltd* (1936). However, in some circumstances a contractual licence can bind third parties through the vehicle of a constructive trust. In *Binions* v *Evans* (1972) Lord Denning MR, in a minority judgment, expressed that view and in *Lyus* v *Prowsa Developments Ltd* (1982) Dillon J adopted the same position. In *Ashburn Anstalt* v *Arnold* (1988) the Court of Appeal indicated the limits within which that solution can be applied. It confirmed that the imposition of a constructive trust on a purchaser to give effect to a contractual licence was permissible, but stressed that the court would not impose one unless it was satisfied that the conscience of the purchaser was affected. It emphasised that mere notice of itself was not sufficient: 'The mere fact that the land is expressed to be conveyed "subject to" a contract does not necessarily imply that the grantee is to be under an obligation, not otherwise existing, to give effect to the provision of the contract': per Fox LJ.

In this problem Sarah would have to show that in the first place a contract had been created in accordance with the normal contractual rules and in particular she must show that she has given consideration in return for William's permission to stay in the barn rent free. She appears to be able to satisfy this requirement because of the repairs and improvements she agreed to make to the barn. She must also prove that she and William intended to create a legal relationship and here she may experience difficulty. The law generally presumes that intention but in the case of domestic and social agreements the presumption does not apply. It would not apply here because William and Sarah are brother and sister and, accordingly, without the assistance of the presumption, Sarah would have to prove the intention which may well prove difficult for her. If she cannot do so then there is no contractual licence, but only a bare licence which William can revoke at will.

It there is a contractual licence then William's right to revoke it depends on its terms. Clearly no express terms to that effect have been agreed. It will be for the court to imply the terms of William's right to revoke, looking at all the circumstances of the case as was done in *Chandler* v *Kerley*, and it is very difficult to predict in this case what its decision would be. If it found that Sarah had an irrevocable licence to stay for as long as she wished, then if eventually William decided to sell the barn, the question would arise as to whether that licence bound a purchaser. That would depend on whether Sarah could successfully argue that the purchaser was subject to a constructive trust to give effect to her licence.

The arrangement between William and Sarah was an oral one but since a licence does not confer upon the licensee an interest in land it would not be void for want of compliance with s2 Law of Property (Miscellaneous Provisions) Act 1989.

Alternatively, Sarah may have an estoppel licence. Such a licence arises where an owner of land (William) allows another (Sarah) to spend money on that land or otherwise to act to her detriment under an expectation created or encouraged by the landowner (ie a representation or an assurance) that she will be allowed to remain on the land or acquire an interest in the land. In such circumstances the landowner will not be allowed to defeat that expectation and deny the other's right to remain or to have an interest in the land: *Ramsden* v *Dyson* (1866). In essence the requirements for an estoppel licence are representation, reliance and detriment. The facts are supportive of an estoppel licence. Here William has agreed that Sarah can live rent-free in the barn if she complies with a range of specified conditions (ie there is a representation). Sarah's repairs to the roof, installing electricity and making the barn generally habitable could be seen as detriment and evidence that she had acted in reliance on William's representation.

If, as seems likely, an estoppel licence arises in favour of Sarah, the task for the court will be to decide how best to satisfy it and the court will do the minimum necessary to do justice to the estoppel: *Crabb* v *Arun District Council* (1976). The courts have shown great flexibility in this regard. Remedies applied include transfer of the fee simple to the licensee (*Pascoe* v *Turner* (1979)), giving a life interest to the licensee (*Inwards* v *Baker* (1965)) and reimbursement of the licensee's expenses/outgoings: *Dodsworth* v *Dodsworth* (1973). However, this in turn has produced uncertainty because it is difficult for practitioners to anticipate how the equity will be satisfied in a given case. It seems that the remedy granted in cases of estoppel licence may be dependent on the representation made (ie the applicant gets what she has been promised). Here there is no indication as to what assurances, if any, William gave Sarah as to how long she could stay in the barn. It is submitted that any such assurance would greatly influence the court in deciding what remedy to grant in order to satisfy the equity. If there was no representation/assurance given by William as to duration, Sarah could expect to be given reasonable notice to vacate the barn and to be reimbursed the costs she incurred in repairing the roof, installing electricity and making the barn generally habitable.

Finally, William agreed in writing to let a lodge on the estate to his brother Ben at a yearly rent until William obtained planning permission to convert the lodge into a guest house. As previously noted, one of the requirements for a valid lease is certainty of duration (ie the duration of the lease must be certain or capable of being ascertained at the outset of the term – s205(1) (xxvii)). In *Lace* v *Chantler* (1944) a lease granted during the course of the 1939–45 war for the duration of the war was void. This principle was reaffirmed in *Prudential Assurance Co Ltd* v *London Residuary Body* (1992) where the House of Lords said that the principle in *Lace* v *Chantler* applies to all leases and tenancy agreements. Here Ben can occupy a lodge on the estate until William obtains 'planning permission to convert the lodge into a guest house'. Such a determinable clause is similar to the one in *Prudential Assurance Co Ltd* v *London Residuary Body*. There the tenancy was to continue until the land was wanted for road widening, but the House of Lords declared that a lease with such a clause was void because of uncertainty of duration, but went on to hold that the tenant held under a yearly lease arising from the tenants' possession and payment of a yearly rent.

Here Ben is in possession and paying a yearly rent, the lease having been expressly granted in writing. It is a legal periodic tenancy falling within s54 LPA 1925. A yearly tenancy is determinable by six months' notice from either party. The undertaking by William that he would not exercise his right of determination until he obtained planning permission is inconsistent with the right to terminate on the going of six months' notice and as such is void. In the result William may recover possession from Ben by giving him six months' notice.

SUGGESTED ANSWER TO QUESTION TWO

General Comment

A mixed question which touches upon several areas of land law, including matrimonial property, licences, leases and aspects of registration. It provides students well versed in the relevant areas with an opportunity to display their knowledge and understanding. Not a question for students who had only revised some of, but not all, the areas covered.

Key Points

- Legal estate in one party
- Acquisition of a beneficial interest – constructive trusts
- Periodic tenancy
- Contractual licence – *Ashburn Anstalt* v *Arnold*
- Estoppel licence – effect on third parties; LPA 1925 s70(1)(g) – difficulties before court order

Suggested Answer

In view of the fact that Barbara provided all the purchase money for the house, and had it registered in her sole name, it is necessary to see if Janet can establish an interest in the property which will be binding on the building company to which Barbara subsequently sold the house. Having regard to the facts of the question, it would seem appropriate to consider whether Janet has acquired a beneficial interest, a periodic tenancy or a licence.

A person not on the legal title can acquire a beneficial interest in a variety of ways, including by way of resulting or constructive trust. For example, a direct contribution to acquisition of the property (contribution to the purchase price or mortgage instalments, paying legal costs, etc) will give rise to a resulting trust with the size of the share being proportionate to the party's contribution. Here, since Barbara paid the whole of the purchase price, this rules out any form of direct financial contribution by Janet to the acquisition of the house. While a direct contribution to acquisition is clearly sufficient to acquire a beneficial interest, the position as to indirect contributions is much more difficult. In essence Janet is relying upon indirect contributions, ie 'repairs and other outgoings' which necessitates consideration of the possibility of a constructive trust.

In *Lloyds Bank* v *Rosset* (1991) Lord Bridge laid down the requirements for the establishment of a constructive trust. First, has there been at any time prior to acquisition or, exceptionally at some later date, any agreement, arrangement, or understanding reached between the parties that the property is to be shared beneficially? This may be based on evidence of express discussions however imperfectly remembered. Once such a common intention has been proved then the party who is not on the title, and who is claiming a beneficial interest, must show that she has acted to her detriment or significantly altered her position in reliance on that common intention in order to give rise to a constructive trust.

If no express common intention can be established then the court must rely on the conduct of the parties to infer a common intention that the property should be shared beneficially:

> 'In this situation direct contributions to the purchase price by the party who is not the legal owner, whether initially or by payment of mortgage instalments, will readily justify the inference necessary to the creation of a constructive trust. But, as I read the authorities, it is at least extremely doubtful whether anything less will do': per Lord Bridge.

Mrs Rosset's contribution consisted of her doing some interior decorating and supervising the builders who were carrying out renovation work. Lord Bridge said that

Mrs Rosset's contribution, when set against the property value of over £70,000, was 'so trifling as to be almost de minimus' and her claim failed.

This reference to direct contributions seems to denote some confusion with resulting trusts since that is the way a resulting trust may be created, but his words make it quite clear that he had a constructive trust in mind.

In his judgment he also pointed out that where conduct is relied upon to prove common intention and detrimental reliance, conduct which establishes detrimental reliance may not be sufficient to prove common intention. In his view the detrimental conduct relied upon in *Eves* v *Eves* (1975) and *Grant* v *Edwards* (1986) could not have been relied upon to prove common intention. Fortunately for the claimants in those cases there was express oral evidence of common intention.

In this problem it appears unlikely that Janet will be able to successfully argue that she has a beneficial interest under a constructive trust. There is no written declaration of trust to satisfy s53(1)(b) LPA 1925 *nor* is there evidence of an oral expression of common intention. Nor does it appear that contribution to the costs of repairs and payment of the outgoings will justify the inference of common intention or constitute detrimental reliance. In *Grant* v *Edwards* Nourse LJ explained that for conduct to amount to detrimental reliance it must be 'sufficient to constitute conduct on which she (the claimant) could not have been reasonably expected to embark unless she believed she had a beneficial interest in the house'.

Next, it is necessary to see if Janet has a lease as she is paying a token monthly rent and after the marriage breaks down she continues to do so. A periodic tenancy (from week to week or month to month) can be created, either by express agreement or by inference – such as that arising from the payment and acceptance of rent measured by reference to the period in question (week or month, etc). In this case there is obviously no express agreement as the payments are against Barbara's wishes. Nevertheless, as Barbara accepted these payments from Janet, then it is submitted that Janet could have a monthly periodic tenancy by inference. However, a monthly periodic tenancy is not very advantageous to Janet vis-à-vis the new registered proprietor, since such a tenancy can be brought to an end by the tenant being given a month's notice to quit.

Consideration must now be given to the question as to whether Janet has a contractual licence which would be binding on the building company.

Janet must first prove the necessary ingredients for a contract and in particular that she gave consideration and that the parties intended to enter into legal relations. Tim and Janet provided consideration in undertaking the responsibility for repairs and paying the outgoings. Generally, the law presumes an intention to create legal relations but this does not apply to domestic and social agreements. Seeing that this is a family arrangement the presumption will not apply with the result that the intention must be positively proved. On the facts this would probably present no difficulty.

The more difficult question is whether the contractual licence would bind the building company since because of the privity of contract rule contracts do not bind third parties. They are personal transactions which do not confer upon the licensee any interest in the land: *King* v *David Allen & Sons Billposting Ltd* (1916); *Clore* v *Theatrical Properties Ltd* (1936). In *Ashburn Anstalt* v *Arnold* (1988) Fox LJ confirmed this view:

'A mere contractual licence to occupy land is not binding on a purchaser of land even although he has notice of the licence.'

Nevertheless, in limited circumstances a contractual licence, although of itself not binding on a purchaser, may be made to bind him through the medium of a constructive trust. Lord Denning MR was of that view in *Binion* v *Evans* (1972) and his reasoning was adopted by Dillon J in *Lyus* v *Prowsa Developments Ltd* (1982). In *Ashburn Anstalt* v *Arnold* the Court of Appeal confirmed that possibility but warned that caution must be employed in adopting that course: 'a constructive trust will not be imposed unless the conscience of the estate owner (the purchaser) is affected': per Fox LJ. Mere notice of the contract is not enough to bind a purchaser.

Fox LJ added: '... we do not think it desirable that constructive trusts of land should be imposed in reliance on or inferences from slender materials'.

There is nothing in this problem to justify the imposition of a constructive trust on the building company.

The other possibility for Janet in respect of licences is to try to show that she has an estoppel licence. Such a licence arises as follows. If a landowner (Barbara) allows another person (Janet) to spend money or alter her position to her detriment in the expectation that she will enjoy some privilege or interest in the land, then the owner will be prevented (ie estopped) from acting inconsistently with that expectation. In essence the requirements of an estoppel licence are representation, reliance and detriment.

The difficulty here is that Barbara does not appear to have made any express representations to Tim and Janet. It is said she bought them a house to live in and some kind of promise may be inferred from that, but it is not clear exactly what she was promising or for how long the arrangement was to continue.

The most likely inference is that they could continue to live there provided that they did the repairs and paid the outgoings. It is probable that Janet has a claim in proprietary estoppel on the facts, but the difficult question is to assess its extent. The court's answer to the question 'How is the equity to be satisfied?' varies very considerably and each case is decided on its merits. Nor is there a consistent approach. On the one hand the court may attempt to fulfil the expectation created in the claimant's mind or, on the other, it may value the claim according to the detriment which the claimant has suffered.

Assuming that Janet is entitled to a claim founded on proprietary estoppel, will it be binding on a purchaser – in this case the building company? Consideration must be given to whether it constitutes an overriding interest under s70(1)(g) LRA 1925 since title to the land is registered. Overriding interests bind a purchaser without appearing on the register and even though he has no knowledge of them. There are three aspects to establishing an overriding interest under s70(1)(g). First, the claimant must have a proprietary interest in the property (an equitable interest).

If Janet does have an interest founded in proprietary estoppel then it does constitute an equitable interest in land: *Inwards* v *Baker* (1965) and *Ives (ER) Investments* v *High* (1967) (both of which were unregistered land cases). Being an equitable interest in land it is eligible for inclusion in s70(1)(g) LRA 1925 and subject to the provisions of that section it will bind a purchaser.

Second, the claimant must be in actual occupation of the land prior to completion of the transaction: *Abbey National Building Society* v *Cann* (1990). Whether a person is in actual occupation is a question of fact and degree. There must be some degree of permanence and continuity, not a mere fleeting presence. It is submitted that Janet could show a degree of permanence and continuity of occupation, and this would not be destroyed just because she was temporarily absent on holiday at the time Barbara sold the house to the building company. Third, if an enquiry is made by a prospective purchaser and the right is not disclosed (because of active concealment on the part of the person claiming an overriding interest under para (g)), then the purchaser will take free of that right.

However, there are difficulties in applying s70(1)(g) to proprietary estoppel. Janet cannot know if she has an interest arising from proprietary estoppel, nor its extent, until a court decides those issues. Once it does, if Barbara then sells the house, Janet's interest would bind the purchaser providing the requirements of s70(1)(g) were satisfied. The difficulties arise when there is a sale before the position has been crystallised by a court order. Before an order is made the rights of a claimant under s70(1)(g), if they exist at all, are undefined and the question must be posed as to whether undefined rights can fall within that section. The courts have not yet resolved this issue and in the meantime the problem can be but noted.

Before an order is made the best Janet could do would be to enter a caution on Barbara's register of title. It is difficult to see how she could enter a notice because of the difficulties in drafting its terms.

Thus, it is difficult to advise Janet with any certainty on the issue of proprietary estoppel. If she has an interest, how the court would define its extent must be a matter of speculation. If she obtained a court order in her favour then her rights would be binding on the building company under s70(1)(g). If a sale occurred before that then her position would be very uncertain.

SUGGESTED ANSWER TO QUESTION THREE

General Comment

Another topical question on the area of licences and proprietary estoppel which demands a good knowledge of case law for a satisfactory answer. Students need to be careful with this type of question that they do not spend time setting out their views on how this type of situation should be dealt with and not spending sufficient time on the law as it stands today.

Key Points

* Legal title passes to executors and Wilma entitled to estate under will
* What claims does Karen have?
* Constructive trust: was there an agreement between the parties?
* Has Karen acted to her detriment in reliance?
* Contractual licence?
* Proprietary estoppel: consider *Coombes* v *Smith, Re Basham*

- Has Karen relied on any promise?
- Flexibility of doctrine
- Conclusion: looks unpromising but perhaps has a right to stay until daughter is older

Suggested Answer

Legal title in the flat has passed to John's executors and Wilma is entitled to John's estate under his will. Karen must try to establish some claim which will be binding on the executors. There are a number of possibilities. She could argue that she is entitled to some form of equitable proprietary interest in the flat; that she has some form of licence entitling her to remain there; and that she is entitled to some remedy under the doctrine of proprietary estoppel. There is no indication that John ever gave her the deeds of the flat and no possibility on the facts as set out in the question of making a claim to a valid donatio mortis causa under *Sen* v *Headley* (1991). The various possible claims will be examined in turn.

John had sole legal title to the flat and in order for Karen to claim a property interest in it she may show that she is entitled under some form of trust, a constructive trust being the most appropriate. The decision of the House of Lords in *Lloyds Bank* v *Rosset* (1991) attempted to clarify the law relating to the circumstances in which the court will impose a constructive trust. If there has been an express agreement between the parties, either prior to acquisition or exceptionally at some later date, the court will impose a constructive trust if the party claiming an equitable interest has acted to his detriment or changed his position in reliance on that agreement. If there has been no such agreement, the court relies on conduct to infer the existence of a common intention to share and Lord Bridge doubted whether anything other than a direct contribution to the purchase price would be sufficient to justify that inference. There does not seem to have been any express agreement between the parties prior to the acquisition that it would be shared beneficially and Karen has not made any direct contribution to the purchase price, either initially or by contributing to the mortgage repayments. The work which she did in decorating the flat would surely be disregarded as in *Rosset* itself and *Burns* v *Burns* (1984).

There is some evidence that, at a later stage, John led Karen to believe that she would have a share in the flat as he said to her that he did not put the flat into joint names because of his tax position. This sounds like *Eves* v *Eves* (1975), where the man said that the only reason the property was being put in his name alone was that his female partner was under 21, and *Grant* v *Edwards* (1986), where the man told his female partner that the only reason the property was not being acquired in joint names was because of her divorce proceedings. Both ladies acted to their detriment in reliance on those assurances and a constructive trust was imposed in their favour. The difficulty for Karen is that John's statement to her was made some time after the actual acquisition, but Lord Bridge did indicate that in exceptional circumstances a later agreement might be sufficient. He did not, however, give any guidance as to what would constitute exceptional circumstances. In any event, has Karen acted to her detriment or changed her position in reliance on what John said to her?

It is not clear whether the claimant's conduct in any given case is such that it can be said that it was done on the reliance of a belief in the common intention nor whether it can be described as detrimental. Browne-Wilkinson VC recognised this in *Grant* v *Edwards* in 1986:

> 'Setting up house together, having a baby, making payments to general housekeeping expenses … may all be referable to the mutual love and affection of the parties and not specifically referable to the claimant's belief that she has an interest in land.'

This appears to be the case here. Further, although Karen acted to her detriment in initially giving up her job and leaving her husband, thereafter, for three years, she enjoyed the benefit of rent free accommodation and financial support. This would present problems for a court in trying to decide whether overall she had acted to her detriment.

In 1996 she found work and was able to support herself and her daughter. She also spent an unspecified amount on maintaining and decorating the flat. On one or two occasions John told her that he did not put the flat in their joint names because of his tax position but we are not told if this was said before or after Karen's contribution to maintaining and decorating the flat. To establish a claim under a constructive trust she would have to prove that the expenditure was incurred as a result of her belief in a common intention that she was to have a beneficial share in the flat. If John's statement constitutes an oral expression of that intention, her expenditure, if it was to constitute detrimental reliance, must have been incurred after those expressions of intention, and because of the absence of information about the times he made the statements, we are unable to say whether this was so. In any event, it is probable that the amount spent would not be sufficient to amount to detrimental conduct. In *Lloyds Bank* v *Rosset*, where Mrs Rosset did some interior decorating and supervised building work, Lord Bridge, in comparing the value of her contribution against the house's value of £70,000, described it as 'so trifling as to be almost de minimus'.

Karen could argue that she has a contractual licence to live in the flat. There is no express contractual agreement between her and John but the courts are sometimes prepared to infer one in these types of arrangements. *Hardwick* v *Johnson* (1978) was one such case. Lord Denning MR outlined the problem:

> '… these family arrangements do have legal consequences, and, time and time again, the courts are called upon to determine what is the true legal relationship resulting from them … so many things undecided, undiscussed and unprovided for that it is the task of the courts to fill in the blanks.'

The Court of Appeal acknowledged that the parties had not applied their minds as to what might happen in the future and consequently had formulated no intention to cover the situation which in fact later arose.

What the court appears to have done is to construct a contract, not based on the parties' intention, because there wasn't one, and then gone further and implied a term into it to cover the subsequent events based on speculation, deduced from the circumstances of that case, about what the parties would have agreed had they thought about the matter. In that case Lord Denning differed from his two judicial colleagues as to the contents of that term which demonstrates the difficulties involved in this kind of exercise. There is an element of artificiality about this form of judicial activity but at least the courts are attempting to find a constructive solution to the problems produced by these informal arrangements.

Another example is to be found in *Chandler* v *Kerley* (1978). It does appear from these cases that the courts are readily prepared to find that the parties intended to create legal relations. Generally, the intention to create legal relations is presumed in contract law, except in the cases of social and domestic agreements when it must be specifically proved. However, in the cases referred to the courts seem to have been readily prepared to find that proof.

If Karen could persuade the court to find a contractual licence she would then have to further persuade it to imply a term defining the rights of the licensor (John) to revoke it. She should not experience too much difficulty in achieving that objective since John has assured her she could stay in the flat as long as she wished, adding that she was being left it in his will. This would appear to give her an irrevocable licence to stay as long as she wished to remain.

This may look promising from Karen's point of view but a difficulty arises after John's death since contractual licences only bind the parties themselves. They do not confer upon licensees an interest in land and nor do they, of themselves, bind third parties: *King* v *David Allen & Sons Billposting Ltd* (1916). They can, however, in limited circumstances, bind third parties through the imposition of a constructive trust. But, as was made clear in *Ashburn Anstalt* v *Arnold* (1998), this will only be done if the conscience of that third party is affected and that mere notice will not be enough.

There are no grounds for deciding that the licence, if it exists, would bind Wilma through a constructive trust.

Can Karen establish a claim arising from proprietary estoppel? She would have to show that John had made representations to her that she has, or would at some future time have, an interest in the house and that in reliance on that representation she had acted to her detriment. John promised that she could stay in the flat as long as she wished and that he would leave it to her when he died. *Re Basham* (1986) decided that proprietary estoppel includes cases where the claimant has been led to believe he will acquire a right in property at some future time. Karen would have to show also that her detrimental conduct followed John's assurances and resulted from them. The difficulty here is one of timing. We do not know which came first: John's assurances or Karen's conduct.

If John's assurances preceded Karen's conduct, it will be necessary for Karen to show that she acted to her detriment or altered her position on the faith of her belief. In *Coombes* v *Smith* (1986) it was held that having a child, moving away from her husband, redecorating and not trying to provide otherwise for herself did not show acting to one's detriment. The actions were either due simply to a desire to live with the defendant, or done as occupier of the property. By contrast, in *Re Basham*, a long history of working without pay, foregoing opportunities to move, caring for the deceased and spending her own money to resolve a boundary dispute were sufficient for a claim based on proprietary estoppel when coupled with frequent promises by the deceased that his property would pass to the plaintiff on his death. Karen's situation looks closer to that in *Coombes* v *Smith*.

The problems that she would experience in establishing a claim under a constructive trust as regards detrimental relevance have been discussed in that context and it is submitted that the same problems would be present in attempting to establish a claim in proprietary estoppel.

Karen's position is not a strong one. It seems very unlikely that she can establish a claim by means of a constructive trust. There may be a contractual licence but it would not bind Wilma and a claim founded on propriety estoppel seems unlikely to succeed because of the difficulties in proving detrimental conduct and reliance on John's promises.

SUGGESTED ANSWER TO QUESTION FOUR

General Comment

A searching question which requires detailed analysis and application of the principles of proprietary estoppel. Notice in particular the position of claimants relying on testamentary promises; the possibility of a claimant's right being exhausted as illustrated by *Sledmore* v *Dalby*; and the difficulties relating to the binding effect of a licence by proprietary estoppel on third parties before judicial adjudication.

Key Points

*   Proprietary estoppel – definition – *Wilmott* v *Barber*; *Electrolux Ltd* v *Electrix Ltd*; *Taylor Fashions Ltd* v *Liverpool Victoria Trustees Co Ltd*
*   The requirements for the establishment of propreitary estoppel
*   The necessity for detrimental reliance by the claimant: *Greasley* v *Cooke*
*   Application to the facts of the problem – difficulties in relying on testamentary promises: *Gillett* v *Holt*; *Taylor* v *Dickens*
*   Once proprietary estoppel established, how is the equity to be satisfied?
*   *Sledmore* v *Dalby* – Diana may have exhausted her equity
*   The position of third parties in proprietary estoppel

Suggested Answer

The first issue to explore is whether the facts of the case can give rise to a claim in Diana's favour based on proprietary estoppel.

The doctrine may be summarised in these terms: where an owner of land (O) allows another (E) to spend money on that land or otherwise act to his detriment under an expectation created or encouraged, or acquiesced in by O, that he will be allowed to remain on the land or later acquire an interest in it, then equity will restrain O from defeating that expectation and deny E's right to remain on the land or acquire an interest in it.

It differs from promissory estoppel in that promissory estoppel is a defence, or as it has been described, a shield. It is not a cause of action entitling a plaintiff to assert a claim. Proprietary estoppel by contrast, although it too can be employed as a defence, may form the basis of an assertion of a claim, resulting in the plaintiff acquiring proprietary rights in land. It can be used as a sword as well as a shield: *Pascoe* v *Turner* (1979).

In *Willmott* v *Barber* (1880) the requirements necessary for the establishment of estoppel were expressed by Fry J in the form of five probandi, but these are no longer strictly applied, the courts having adopted a more flexible approach: *Electrolux Ltd* v *Electrix Ltd* (1953). In that case Evershed MR observed:

> 'I think it is clear that it is not essential to find all the five tests set out by Fry J literally applicable and satisfied in every particular case.
>
> The real test, I think, must be whether upon the facts of the particular case, the situation has become such that it would be dishonest or unconscionable of the person having the right sought to be enforced, to continue to seek to enforce it.'

Goff LJ expressed agreement and went on to say 'the test is whether, in the circumstances, it has become unconscionable for the plaintiff to rely on his legal right'.

In *Taylor Fashions Ltd* v *Liverpool Victoria Trustees Co Ltd* (1982) Oliver J, after an extensive review of the authorities, adopted the same approach.

The basis of a claim under the doctrine of proprietary estoppel must now be analysed. What must a claimant establish? The following requirements can be deduced from the authorities:

1   In relation to claims in respect of land, there must be some conduct by the owner, either taking the form of a positive representation or acquiescence, which induces the claimant to believe that he has rights in the land or will acquire rights in it at some time in the future. *Inwards* v *Baker* (1965) was an illustrative case. A father owned land and when told by his son that he (the son) was contemplating purchasing land on which to erect a bungalow, suggested that the son should build the bungalow on his (the father's) land instead. The son accepted that suggestion and did so. Several points should be noted: there was no contract between the parties; it was an informal family arrangement consisting of the father's promise and the son's acceptance. Nor did the father convey any land to his son. The son built the bungalow on his father's land, and in law the ownership of it vested in the landowner father.

The son clearly acted to his detriment in spending money on the construction of the bungalow.

Many years before the events occurred, the father had made a will leaving the land to a third party. The father died in 1951. The third party could have ordereed the son to leave but she did not do so. When, however, she died, her trustees did. The son claimed a licence by estoppel and the Court of Appeal agreed. The son was allowed to remain in the bungalow for the remainder of his life. In his judgment Lord Denning MR said:

> 'If the owner of land requests another, or indeed allows another, to expend money on the land under an expectation created or encouraged by the land owner that he will be able to remain there, that raises an equity in the licensee such as to entitle him to stay.'

Ives (ER) Investments Ltd v *High* (1967) furnishes an illustration of passive conduct giving rise to an 'equity arising out or acquiescence'. Lord Denning MR described how that came about.

> 'The right arises out of the expense incurred by Mr High in building his garage, as it is now with access only over the yard, and the Wrights standing by and acquiescing, knowing that he believed he had a right of way over the yard. By so doing the Wrights created in Mr High's mind, a reasonable expectation that his access over the yard would not be disturbed. That gives rise to "an equity arising out of acquiescence".'

The expectation created in the claimant's land is not confined to existing rights but may relate to an expectation to acquire rights in the future. Such was the case in *Re Basham (Deceased)* (1986). In that case the claimant acted as she did, without payment on the belief, induced by the promise, that she would inherit the promisor's land. He died intestate and she had no claim on the estate. It was held that she had acted to her detriment in reliance on the promisor's promise that she would acquire his estate when he died and that she was therefore entitled to the whole estate.

2   The claimant, relying on the representation or promise must have acted to his detriment. The detriment need not involve the expenditure of money. In *Greasley* v *Cooke* (1980) the claimant (in 1938) went to work in the household of a widower, his three sons and a handicapped daughter as a maidservant. In 1946 she commenced living with one of the sons, K, as man and wife. From 1948 onwards she ceased to be paid any wages, but she neverthess continued to look after the household. From time to time she had been given assurances by K, although expressed in vague terms, that she could live in the house as long as she wished. K died in 1975. The house then vested in one of the other sons and the daughters of another son, and they claimed possession of the house. In resisting the claim, the claimant claimed a licence by estoppel and she succeeded. The Court of Appeal held that:

a   the assurances she had been given were sufficient to found a claim in proprietary estoppel; and

b   that gave rise to a rebuttable presumption, that the claimant acted as she did on reliance of those assurances; the burden of proof of rebutting that presumption passed to those who contended that there was no proprietary estoppel; and

c   although the claimant must establish detriment in reliance on the assurances that need not consist of the expenditure of money.

The Court of Appeal held she could stay in the house as long as she wished.

In *Brinnand* v *Ewens* (1987) Nourse LJ summarised the requirements necessary to establish a claim under the doctrine:

a   the claimant must show that he had prejudiced himself or acted to his detriment; and

b   he must have acted in the way he did because he believed he had an interest in the property or would acquire one at some future time; and

c   the belief must have been induced by the landowner.

Whether the claimant has acted to his or her detriment is a question of fact which it is not always easy to decide. If a claimant gives up her flat and job to move into rent-free accommodation provided by her boyfriend, can she be said to be acting to her detriment? In *Coombes* v *Smith* (1986) it was held that the claimant, on having a child, moving away from her husband, redecorating and not trying to provide otherwise for herself, did not show that she was acting to her detriment. Her actions were either due simply to a desire to live with the defendant or done as an occupier of the property.

In this problem, Mr Brown made various written promises to Alan and Diana including one that they would eventually inherit the house. Contained in that letter was the suggestion that they could build an extension to the house if they wished. There is no doubt that the promises were intended to be acted upon by Alan and Diana and that they did act upon them. To some extent there is a parallel with *Inwards* v *Baker* where father encouraged his son to build a bungalow on his (the father's) land. In this case the promises are more extensive in that they offer rent-free accommodation and the prospect of future ownership in the house.

It is important to notice that there appears to be no contractual arrangement between the parties. It is an informal family arrangement without any intention to enter into legal relations.

When Mr Brown and Alan were killed Mrs Brown became sole owner of Magnolia House, being the survivor of the joint tenancy. Diana has no kind of legal interest in the house at all. Faced now with the prospect of eviction, Diana must consider whether she has acquired an equitable interest in the house arising out of proprietary estoppel which is binding on Mrs Brown. If such an interest can be established it will then be necessary to consider its extent.

The promises made are clear enough. The question is the response of Diana acting in conjunction with Alan. She must show she and Alan acted to their detriment. Although this does not necessarily involve the expenditure of money (*Greasley* v *Cooke* (1980)) in this case there was the expenditure of £20,000 for the extension. According to the same case the promises gave rise to a rebuttable presumption that Diana and Alan acted as they did in reliance on those promises. It is presumed that the expenditure of £20,000 was the result of Mr Brown's assurances. This presumption will stand unless Mrs Brown can rebut it and on the facts it would appear that she would not be able to. In enjoying rent-free accommodation Alan and Diana cannot be said to have been acting to their detriment but in view of their considerable financial outlay this factor may be discounted. However, the rent-free accommodation may be relevant later on in a different context.

Although the promise in relation to future ownership of the house is clear and unambiguous, it can present difficulties. *Re Basham* leaves no doubt that proprietary estoppel can embrace the expectation of acquiring rights in land at a future time and in that case the claim succeeded. However, the difficulties may occur when a promise is made that the claimant will be left property by will because a will has no effect until the testator's death. If a testator promises to make a will in a claimant's favour, he is free to change his mind. Likewise, if he actually makes the will, he is free to revoke it. A claimant, invoking the doctrine of proprietary estoppel in those circumstances, should be wary. The point arose in *Gillett* v *Holt* in 1998. In that case Gillett (G) claimed that he had spent all his working life working for Holt (H) on the understanding encouraged by H, that H would leave him his estate in his will. The defendant, H, resiled on that promise, dismissed G from his employment and altered his will in favour of a third party, to the total exclusion of G.

G sued H in proprietary estoppel but his claim failed at first instance. Carnwath J pointed out that under English law it was a fundamental right of a testator to choose the destination of his estate and that a promise by a testator to leave his estate to a beneficiary would only be enforced if it would have been unconscionable for him to resile from it. Persons in G's position should always be aware of a testator's right to change his mind. For a claimant to succeed it is not enough merely to prove the testator's promise. He must go further and prove that the testator had made an irrevocable promise and G was unable to establish such a promise. Carnwath J held that G's claim must fail.

The case went to appeal and the Court of Appeal reversed the decision of Carnwath J, holding the assurances given by H 'were repeated over a very long period' and that they were 'completely unambiguous'. In two wills, in 1976 and 1977, H had left all his estate to G and in 1984 H told G and his wife that they 'had a very secure future'. Walker LJ noted that G and his wife had 'shaped their lives to H's convenience' and that detriment had been amply established. H was ordered to transfer the farm on which G had worked to G together with the sum of £100,000.

The decision is based on a finding of fact by the Court of Appeal but it does not alter the basic principle of law expounded by Carnwath J.

The point was considered by Weeks J sitting in the High Court in *Taylor* v *Dickens* (1998), when he said:

> 'It is not sufficient for A to believe that he is going to be given a right over B's property if he knows that B has reserved the right to change his mind. In that case, A must also show that B created or encouraged a belief on A's part that B would not exercise that right.'

In that case the testator told the claimant she would make a will in his favour and she did so. She later revoked it. The claimant was always aware that a will could be revoked and the testatrix never gave him any undertaking that she would not do so. The claimant's contention that the promise should be upheld, failed.

Weeks and Carnwath JJ were expressing the same views. Carnwath J also said that he could see no difference between the cases where there was a promise to make a will which was not fulfilled and those cases where it had been fulfilled but was followed by a revocation, and that for a claimant to succeed in proprietary estoppel he must show that the promises of a testator went beyond mere statements of intention and amount to, in effect, what a reasonable person would regard as an irrevocable promise by a testator.

These cases could present a problem for Diana. That Mr Brown, in his letter, had expressed an intention to leave the property to Alan and Diana, cannot be doubted, but Diana has to go on to prove that it amounted to an irrevocable promise and that it would be unconscionable to allow that promise to be resiled from. There is, on the facts, no evidence to that effect and it would seem, therefore, that she would be unable to claim the house on the basis of that promise.

Further, it is difficult to see how Mr Brown was in a position to make the promise. He and Mrs Brown were joint tenants in law and equity of the house with the result that Mrs. Brown automatically acquired Mr Brown's share in his death by right of survivorship. Mr Brown was not in a position to make the promise he did. The most he could have done would have been to sever the equitable joint tenancy, converting his share into a tenancy in common and willed that half share to Alan and Diana. This additional factor should have impressed upon Alan and Diana the realisation that they could not rely on that particular promise.

Diana must base her claim in proprietary estoppel on the expenditure of money encouraged by Mr Brown. She cannot claim the whole house based on Mr Brown's promise that both she and Alan would eventually inherit the house but must be content with a lesser claim based on the expenditure of £20,000. That claim appears to be well founded and the next question is: 'what is the extent of that claim?' That, as in all cases of proprietary estoppel, is the next step when a claim has been established. The courts frequently pose the question in the form 'How is the equity to be satisfied?'

In answering this question, equity can be seen at its most flexible, with the courts adopting whatever solution the justice of the case demands. Each case depends on its own facts. However, an analysis of the courts' approaches in answering this question, reveal differences. One approach is that the expectations created in the claimant's mind should be the criterion for deciding the extent of the claim; another approach places the emphasis on compensating for the detriment suffered. As yet the courts have not adopted a settled approach; some decisions are based on the former, some on the latter, and some decisions do not reflect either. In *Inwards* v *Baker* the Court of Appeal awarded the son a life interest in the property which seems inadequate. The transfer of the fee simple in the plot on which the bungalow was built seems the more appropriate solution. In *Pascoe* v *Turner* (1979) the claimant was awarded the fee simple which seems excessive when her comparatively modest expenditure is considered. In awarding her the fee simple, the court was motivated by a desire to protect her security in the property bearing in mind that an estoppel interest is not registrable under the Land Charges Act.

Since the appropriate remedy is at the discretion of the court to be applied to the facts of individual cases, the decisions can at best only provide guidelines.

The court, in deciding the extent of Diana's claim must necessarily base its decision on the sum of £20,000 which was spent in constructing the extension. Since this inevitably increased the value of the house, it would appear that Diana could expect to receive, not just the return of the £20,000, but a proportionate share in the house's value which the £20,000 bore in relation to the house's value at the time. Thus, if the house was valued at £100,000 before the extension, then £20,000 would represent one-fifth of that value, with the result that the court would award Diana one-fifth of its current price.

However, the case of *Sledmore* v *Dalby* (1996) could present Diana with a problem because Mrs Brown, relying on that case, could argue that any gain to which Diana might be prima facie entitled to should be reduced because she had enjoyed 10 years' rent-free accommodation.

In 1962 Mr and Mrs Sledmore purchased a house and in 1965, when their daughter married Dalby, they granted a leasehold joint tenancy to them both. When the daughter became ill and Dalby unemployed in 1976, the Sledmores told them they need no longer pay any rent. At first instance the judge found that the tenancy then ended. Mr Sledmore encouraged Dalby to carry out substantial improvements to the house having told Dalby and his wife that he intended that eventually they would acquire it. Mrs Sledmore was aware of that. In 1979 Mr Sledmore conveyed his share in the house to Mrs Sledmore, who then changed her will to give the house exclusively to her daughter. Mr Sledmore died in 1980 and the daughter in 1983. Thereafter Dalby continued to live in the house paying no rent. In 1990 Mrs Sledmore gave Dalby notice to quit. By then he had found employment and was living in another house, although he did spend one or two nights per week in Mrs Sledmore's house. Mrs Sledmore's position, by contrast, had deteriorated. She was living on social security and the house was in need of repairs.

On appeal, the Court of Appeal made an order for possession in Mrs Sledmore's favour but had to deal with Dalby's claim that he was entitled to live in the house for the rest of his life rent free since he had been led to believe that by Mr Sledmore and with his encouragement had made substantial improvements to the house. The court considered that although Dalby had justifiably entertained his expectations and performed works in reliance of them, bearing in mind that he had enjoyed 17 years' rent-free accommodation and the respective current situations of the parties it was now not inequitable to hold that Dalby's equity had expired. Whatever equity Dalby had was now exhausted by the enjoyment of the rent-free accommodation.

In Diana's case, the financial situation of Mrs Brown is not known. Nor do we know anything about Diana's finances apart from Mrs Brown's assertions. The court would decide the case on what it conceived to be its merits, but it would doubtless take into account the fact that Diana had enjoyed 10 years' rent-free accommodation, as did the court in *Sledmore v Dalby*. It could either decide that it had extinguished Diana's claim entirely or reduced it.

Mrs Brown has indicated that she wishes to sell the house and then the question will arise as to whether Diana's equitable interest, assuming she has one, will bind a purchaser if Mrs Brown and Diana have not settled the matter between them.

This is a different issue. It seems certain that an interest acquired under the doctrine of proprietary estoppel constitutes an interest in land, binding on a successor in title of the person who made the promise or gave the assurance. Lord Denning MR made this clear in his judgments in *Inwards v Baker* and *Ives (ER) Investments v High* (1967), but in those cases Lord Denning was speaking after the court had decided that an equitable interest had arisen and its extent. Such an interest is not registrable under the LCA 1972. It would be binding on the whole world except the bona fide purchaser for value of the legal estate in the land without notice. It was to safeguard the claimant against such a purchaser that the court in *Pascoe v Turner* ordered that the fee simple in the house be transferred to her.

The major difficulty arises from the situation before the court has adjudicated. Before that occurs, a claimant, in this case Diana, cannot know for sure if she has an estoppel interest let alone its extent. If Mrs Brown sold the house before Diana's interest had been decided then the position seems very uncertain.

Diana could sue a purchaser claiming that her rights arose before the sale to the purchaser and that the court, if it gave judgment in her favour, would be doing no more than articulate already existing rights. It is difficult to imagine a purchaser contemplating buying property subject to the possibility of potential undefined rights, although if a purchaser had no knowledge of those potential rights he could claim to be a bona fide purchaser. At present it seems to be still an open question whether estoppel interests existing before judicial definition will bind a purchaser.

Diana's position therefore is tenuous. She probably has an estoppel interest arising from the expenditure of £20,000, but there is the distinct possibility that the court could regard that interest as having been exhausted by the enjoyment of 10 years' rent-free accommodation. If Mrs Brown sold the property before Diana had obtained a court order defining her interest the difficulties are even more acute. If the court did rule in her favour before sale then Diana's rights would be lost to a purchaser who fell within the definition of a bona fide purchaser.

9

Adverse Possession

Introduction

The problem questions in this area may be set in the context of either unregistered or registered land, and students should therefore note the points of difference in the two systems insofar as they relate to adverse possession. As regards registered land, attention should focus on registration of possessory titles, the rectification provisions and s70(1)(f) LRA 1925.

Students are advised to read in full the judgments in *Buckinghamshire County Council* v *Moran* (1990) and *Hounslow London Borough Council* v *Minchinton* (1997).

Questions

INTERROGRAMS

1 Explain the relativity of titles in English law.
2 What rights does an adverse possessor enjoy in the land before the statutory period of 12 years has elapsed?
3 What is the nature of a possessory title?
4 What is the meaning of adverse possession?
5 What is the difference between prescription and limitation?

QUESTION ONE

In 1980 Miss Twigg purchased a house. The house had a rectangular garden that was 30 feet wide and stretched 70 feet behind the house. The property was bounded on both sides by brick walls and at the end of the garden by a broken-down fence. Beyond the fence there was a plot of land, 30 foot square, which belonged to the local council. This plot abutted on the highway and the council intended to convert it into a lay-by. In 1980 the plot was bounded on three sides by hedges and trees and it consisted largely of bracken, rough grass and rubbish thrown over the hedge from the road. In 1984 Miss Twigg removed the broken-down fence, cleared away the rubbish and began to get rid of the bracken and rough grass. In 1985 Miss Twigg died, leaving the house to her cousin, Molly. In 1986 Molly moved into the house and she immediately built a fence along three sides of the plot (including the side adjoining the highway) as she wanted both to prevent her dogs running out into the road at the back and to deter people throwing rubbish into the plot from the road. Late in 1997 the council decided to proceed with its lay-by plan and it wrote to inform Molly of its decision.

Advise Molly.

London University LLB Examination
(for external students) Land Law June 1998 Q7

195

QUESTION TWO

In 1984 Miss Sprigg purchased Oaktree Cottage (registered land). The garden of the cottage backed on to a field from which it was separated by an old wooden fence. The field formed part of the Blackacre Estate whose owner, Lord Blacktown, intended to develop it as a caravan site for summer tourists. In 1985 Miss Sprigg removed part of the fence and began cultivating vegetables on part of the field; in 1986 she built a chicken coop on the field and reared chickens there; in 1987 she fenced in that part of the field that she was using to protect her chickens and vegetables from thieves and animals. In 1989 Miss Sprigg died leaving the cottage to her sister, Maud. Maud continued to grow vegetables and keep chickens on the enclosed part of the field. In 1991 Lord Blacktown sold the field to Sunshine Caravans and in 1996 they wrote to Maud informing her that they proposed to develop the field as a caravan site and requiring her to vacate the field. Maud ignored the letter and in 1999 Sunshine Caravans commenced proceedings for possession.

Advise Maud.

London University LLB Examination
(for external students) Land Law June 1994 Q3

Answers

ANSWERS TO INTERROGRAMS

1   It is important to appreciate that no-one can own land in English law. It is held on socage tenure of the Crown. Title has always depended on possession. The person in possession is presumed to have a better right to the land than anyone else. Moreover, that person has an estate in fee simple absolute in possession. The relativity of titles can be illustrated as follows. Suppose A is in possession of land and is then adversely dispossessed by B. A is entitled to recover possession from B. Under the Limitation Act 1980 he must do so within 12 years after which his title is extinguished (s17), leaving B with the paramount title. It is important to note that B does not acquire A's title. In *Fairweather* v *St Marylebone Property Co Ltd* (1963) Lord Radcliffe, explaining the squatters' title, said:

> 'He is not at any stage of his possession a successor in title to the man he has disposed. He comes in and remains in always by right of possession, which in due course, becomes incapable of disturbance as time exhausts the one or more periods allowed by statute for successful intervention. This title, therefore, is never derived through but arises always in spite of the dispossessed owner.'

Supposing B, before the statutory period has elapsed, is in his turn dispossessed by C, he can recover possession from C since he has a better title to the land than C and C cannot contend that B has no right to the land because of A's prior right. A has a better title to the land than B, but B has a better right to the land than C.

It is against this background the adverse possession under the Limitation Act must be understood.

2   Since title in English law is based on possession an adverse possessor will have a fee simple absolute in possession but the paper owner will also have that estate. Although he has been dispossessed his title will remain the superior one until it is extinguished. In the meantime the squatter, because he has a fee simple estate, may dispose of it by sale or gift or devise it by will. In the event of him dying intestate it will pass to those entitled on his intestacy. If he is dispossessed himself he may sue to recover his estate from his dispossessor but he must do so within the statutory period and if he does not he loses his right of recovery and his title will be extinguished. Throughout the statutory period he is always liable to an action for recovery of the land by the person with a better title than his own, eg the paper owner whom he has dispossessed.

3   Once the statutory period of 12 years has elapsed, the squatter acquires a possessory title. It will be appreciated that it is in the nature of a negative title insomuch that he acquires it because the paper owner's superior title has been extinguished leaving the dispossessor with the paramount title. Since he has acquired it by possession he has no conveyance to prove his title, and this absence of documentary proof inevitably causes complications as far as unregistered land is concerned, should he attempt to sell it. He will have to satisfy a purchaser that he has indeed acquired a possessory title.

   His position is different where the land in question is registered. In registered land the source of title is the register, and once the 12-year period has elapsed the adverse possessor is entitled to be registered as proprietor of the land with a possessory title in place of the proprietor he has dispossessed. Until that is done the paper owner will continue to be the registered proprietor. As soon as the 12-year period has expired, s75 LRA imposes on the registered proprietor a trust to hold the land on trust for the adverse possessor until he has effected registration of himself as registered proprietor. This trust confers on the adverse possessor an equitable interest in land and is an overriding interest under s70(1)(f) LRA 1925: 'rights acquired or in the course of being acquired under the Limitation Acts.'

   Where the adverse possessor has acquired a part of the paper owner's land by adverse possession, it will also be necessary to rectify the paper owner's title to remove from it the area acquired by the adverse possessor. The court and the land registrar have wide powers of rectification (s82 LRA 1925) but s82(3) and s24 Administration of Justice Act 1977 provide that rectification may only be made against a registered proprietor in possession in limited circumstances, eg where rectification gives effect to an overriding interest: see *Chowood v Lyall* (1930); *Re Chowood's Registered Land* (1933).

   In the situation referred to, this restriction would not apply because the registered proprietor (the paper owner) would not have been in possession because of the dispossessor's adverse possession.

   In the case of unregistered land, once the adverse possessor has acquired title he will take subject to all rights to which the land was already subject. He will be bound by all legal estates and rights and also equitable rights. In the case of any unregistered LCA 1972 land charges he cannot take advantage of the non-registration since he will be neither a purchaser of any interest in the land for valuable consideration, nor a purchaser of the legal estate in the land for money or money's worth. In the case of unregistrable equitable interests he will be unable to claim he is a bona fide purchaser for value of the legal estate in the land without notice since he will have given no value.

As regards registered land he will take subject to overriding interests and minor interests even where the latter are not protected by an entry on the register of title.

4   Adverse possession means possession inconsistent with the title of the paper owner. For a claim to a possessory title under the Limitation Act, it is not enough that the paper owner has discontinued possession or has been dispossessed. The claimant must then take adverse possession of the land and only then will time begin to run against the paper owner. Adverse possession is a matter of fact and whether possession of land is adverse depends on the circumstances of each case and in particular on the nature of the land itself. The adverse possessor must establish physical control of the land, with the intention of possessing the land (animus possidendi).

Whether physical control has been established is a matter of fact. What may be physical control in one case may not be in another. In *Buckinghamshire County Council* v *Moran* (1989) the adverse possessor had secured a gate leading to the land with a lock and chain and that was held to be good evidence of physical control. It was said in *Seddon* v *Smith* (1877) that enclosure was the strongest possible evidence of adverse possession.

The adverse possessor must intend to exclude the whole world from possession, including the paper owner and this intention must be manifest and clear.

It is not necessary for the claimant to have an intention to acquire ownership nor is it necessary to exclude the owner at all future times:

> '... what is required ... is not an intention to own or even an intention to acquire ownership but an intention to possess – that is to say an intention for the time being to possess the land to the exclusion of all other persons, including the owner with the proper title': per Slade LJ in *Buckinghamshire County Council* v *Moran*.

In considering whether the possession is adverse the acts of the squatter must be examined in relation to the nature of the land. This is not always an easy matter.

One must take account of the natural way of using that particular land and its character. In *Powell* v *McFarlane* (1977) the plaintiff claimed possession of three acres of land and the manner of exercising possession included grazing a cow, cutting of hay, repairing the boundary fences and cutting brambles. Slade J held that those acts were insufficient to constitute adverse possession. In *Hounslow London Borough Council* v *Minchinton* (1997) Millett LJ took the view that the acts relied upon were 'not substantial' but he held them to be sufficient to constitute adverse possession because that was the only sensible use of that particular piece of land because of its rough nature.

5   In prescription the claim must be made as of right: neither by force, nor in secret, nor must it be based on permission. Moreover, prescription is based on the acquiescence of the servient owner to the user of his land by the dominant owner:

Dalton v *Angus* (1881) per Fry J. Limitation on the other hand may be described as possession 'as of wrong'. In prescription the servient owner's predecessor in title is presumed to have granted an easement by deed of grant.

In limitation there is no presumption that the paper owner has granted anything. The emphasis in limitation is on the intention of the adverse possessor. He must intend to possess the paper owner's land to the exclusion of the whole world including the paper owner.

The grant of an easement is presumed from long use as of right. Limitation works in a negative way. The adverse possession raises no presumption of user as of right. The adverse possessor is a trespasser against whom the paper owner is entitled to recover possession of his land. Under the Limitation Act he must commence his action for recovery within 12 years. If he does not his title is extinguished (s17), leaving the trespasser with the paramount title. That title is not derived from the dispossessed owner but 'arises always in spite of the dispossessed owner': per Lord Radcliffe in *Fairweather* v *St Marylebone Property Co Ltd* (1963).

SUGGESTED ANSWER TO QUESTION ONE

General Comment

This problem embraces a considerable number of factors relating to adverse possession and serves as a reminder of the need to be thoroughly familiar with *Buckinghamshire County Council* v *Moran*. Candidates should note that there was a gap between Miss Twigg's death and Molly's assumption of occupation, and be prepared to deal with it. Potentially that gap could be fatal to Molly's claim.

Key Points

- The basic principles of adverse possession - the claimant must prove three matters:
  - possession of the land
  - animus possidendi
  - adverse possession
- Once 12 years' adverse possession is proved, the paper owner's title is extinguished: s17 LA 1980
- Time begins to run against the paper owner when the three matters are established
- Molly herself can only prove 11 years' adverse possession - needs to seek to include Miss Twigg's activities
- The relevance of the local council's future plans for the land
- Did Miss Twigg have physical control of the land? - *Hounslow London Borough Council* v *Minchinton*
- There does not have to be an intention to exclude the owner in all future circumstances
- Did Miss Twigg have the requisite intention?
- Was Miss Twigg's possession adverse?
- Probable that Miss Twigg was in adverse possession since 1984
- Molly must prove that she too was in adverse possession

- The effect of the council's letter asserting ownership
- On the facts it appears Molly can prove 13 years' adverse possession with the result that the council's claim is statute-barred and its title extinguished

Suggested Answer

The question here is: can Molly claim title to the council's land under the Limitation Act 1980?

Before embarking on that enquiry, it is necessary to examine the basic principles behind adverse possession claims. Section 15(1) of the Limitation Act 1980 provides:

> 'No action shall be brought by any person to recover any land after the expiration of 12 years from the date on which the right of action accrued to him or, if it first accrued to some person through whom he claims, to that person.'

Time begins to run against the paper owner when the right of action accrues to him and the statute contains provisions for determining the date of accrual of the right of action to recover the land. Part I of Schedule I provides:

> 'Where the person bringing an action to recover land, or some person through whom he claims, has been in possession of the land, and has while entitled to the land been dispossessed or discontinued his possession, the right of action shall be treated as having accrued on the date of the dispossession or discontinuance.'

A person claiming a title by adverse possession under the statute, must prove:

1 factual possession of the land; and
2 that in enjoying factual possession he intended to possess it (animus possidendi); and
3 that his possession is 'adverse'

Once the 12-year limit has expired the paper owner's title is extinguished: s17.

The first fact which must be established is 'when did time begin to run against the paper owner?' The answer to that question is the date on which the owner was dispossessed or had discontinued his possession and adverse possession was assumed by a stranger.

The law was fully considered by the Court of Appeal in *Buckinghamshire County Council v Moran* (1989). In this case the council purchased a plot of land in 1955 with the intention that it should be developed to provide a road diversion but it did not proceed with the plan. In 1967 the defendant's predecessors in title bought adjoining land (Dolphin Place) and treated the council's land as an annex of their own property. They cultivated the plot from time to time and parked a horse box there. No-one challenged their activities.

In 1971 the defendant purchased Dolphin Place and he too treated the council's land as an annex of Dolphin Place. The evidence was that by October 1973 the defendant had enclosed the plot so that access to it could only be gained through Dolphin Place. There was a gate to the plot fronting the highway and the defendant had secured it with a lock and chain. The defendant treated the land as a garden of Dolphin Place and planted daffodils there and trimmed the hedges. Slade LJ quoted his own previous judgment in *Powell v McFarlane* (1979):

'Factual possession signifies an appropriate degree of physical control. It must be single and exclusive possession … The question what acts constitute a sufficient degree of exclusive physical control must depend on the circumstances, in particular the nature of the land and the manner in which land of that nature is commonly used or enjoyed.'

Slade LJ had no difficulty in concluding that by October 1973 the defendant had acquired physical possession of the land. In dealing with animus possidendi, Slade LJ again referred to his judgment in *Powell* v *McFarlane*:

'… the animus possidendi involves the intention, in one's own name and on one's own behalf, to exclude the world at large, excluding the owner with the proper title.'

Quoting too from *Seddon* v *Smith* (1877) that 'enclosure is the strongest possible evidence of adverse possession' (per Cockburn LJ), he concluded that the defendant had the necessary animus possidendi. In the result Moran's claim to title by adverse possession succeeded.

Turning now to the facts of the problem. If Molly is to resist the council's intention to proceed with its lay-by plan, she must be able to assert that the council's land had been adversely occupied for 12 years. The most she can assert on her own behalf is a claim to 11 years' adverse possession. If she is to succeed, she must be able to prove that Miss Twigg was in adverse possession for at least a year and be able to add that period to her own. If Miss Twigg was in adverse possession then she will have acquired a fee simple actual in possession since possession is good evidence of title even though there was no conveyance of the fee simple to her by the council. Where one squatter succeeds another, providing there is no discontinuance of possession, the two periods may be added together to compute the 12-year period. On the facts there seems to have been a delay before Molly entered into possession in the year following Miss Twigg's death, but it could probably be argued that Miss Twigg's executors stood in her shoes until Molly's assumption of possession.

Molly's first task will be to prove the date when adverse possession commenced, which necessitates an examination of Miss Twigg's conduct in 1984. She must prove that Miss Twigg entered into possession, took physical control of it with the requisite intention to possess and that the possession was adverse.

In this type of case it is not always clear if the paper owner has abandoned possession leaving the squatter to enter land which is in effect vacant, or whether the paper owner is still in possession and the entry of the squatter amounts to an ouster. That question arises here. On the face of it the local council vacated the land but the fact that it had future plans for its use may indicate that it had not. In *Buckinghamshire County Council* v *Moran* Slade LJ stated that it was incorrect to say a paper owner, who retains land with a view to using it in a particular way at some future time, can never be dispossessed. It was still possible for him to be subject to a successful claim by an adverse possessor. But he went on to quote from his judgment in *Powell* v *McFarlane*:

'… that in circumstances where the owner has no present use for his land but has future plans for the use, then the court will, on the facts, readily treat a trespasser whose acts have not been inconsistent with those plans, as having not manifested the requisite animus possidendi or alternatively, as not have acquired a sufficient degree of exclusive occupation to constitute possession.'

He expanded on this further in dealing with the situation where the squatter is aware of the owner's plans:

> 'If in any given case the land in dispute is unbuilt land and the squatter is aware that the owner, while having no present use for it, has a purpose in mind for its use in the future, the court is likely to require very clear evidence before it can be satisfied that the squatter who claims a possessory title has not only established factual possession of the land, but also the requisite intention to exclude the world at large, including the owner with the proper title ... In the absence of clear evidence of this nature, the court is likely to infer that the squatter neither had nor had claimed any intention of asserting a right to possession of the land.'

To summarise, even though the council has future plans for its land which may be evidence that it has not abandoned it, it may still be liable to be dispossessed but the onus of proof is on the squatter to prove an intention to possess which is not to be readily inferred, particularly where the squatter is aware of the owner's future plans for the land. There is no evidence that Miss Twigg was aware of the council's plans.

Can Miss Twigg be said to have taken physical control of the land? There is a question of fact which was explained by Slade LJ in *Powell* v *McFarlane*.

The land in this case was waste land in that the council was not at the time using it for any particular purpose, and, given its nature, Miss Twigg's acts would probably be sufficient to enable a court to infer that she had taken physical control. In *Hounslow London Borough Council* v *Minchinton* (1997) Millett LJ assessed the acts in that case as 'not substantial' but 'that was the only available use for the land, given its rough nature'. The position is similar in Miss Twigg's case, but there is additional evidence to support that conclusion by her removal of the broken-down fence.

Was there the requisite intention on Miss Twigg's part to take possession? In *Powell* v *McFarlane* Slade LJ explained that the burden of proof was on the adverse possessor:

> '... the courts will require clear and affirmative evidence that the trespasser, claiming he has acquired possession, not only had the requisite intention to possess, but made such intention clear to the whole world.'

There does not have to be an intention to own the land nor one to exclude the owner in all future circumstances. All that is necessary is that there is 'an intention for the time being to possess the land to the exclusion of all other persons': per Slade LJ in *Buckinghamshire County Council* v *Moran*.

Is such an intention manifested here? On the facts, that appears to be the case.

Can Miss Twigg's possession be described as adverse?

Adverse possession means that the possession must be of such a nature that it is inconsistent with the paper owner's title. Whether the acts in question are sufficient to constitute adverse possession depends again on the nature of the land. Trivial acts will not be enough as illustrated in *Tecbuild Ltd* v *Chamberlain* (1969). Basically, the squatter must treat the land as though he owns it, eg enclosing it by a fence. This latter activity is also evidence of physical possession and intention to possess: *Seddon* v *Smith* (1877).

In *Buckinghamshire County Council* v *Moran* the claimant treated the council's plot as though it were his own garden.

The facts indicate that Miss Twigg's possession was adverse. She removed the broken-down fence separating her garden from the council's plot and then entered it, cleared away the rubbish and began to get rid of the bracken and grass. She was behaving as though she owned the plot. It may be concluded that time began to run against the council in 1984 when Miss Twigg commenced her activities.

In 1985 Molly inherited Miss Twigg's house and moved into it in 1986. Miss Twigg's adverse possession would have invested her with the fee simple absolute in possession, since in English law possession is evidence of title. Molly would have inherited that fee simple as well as Miss Twigg's period of adverse possession, thus enabling her to include that period of time in eventually calculating the 12-year period.

She too must prove adverse possession from 1986 to 1996 on the same principles. If any, her claim is stronger because of her construction of the fence: *Seddon* v *Smith* (1877).

It writing to Molly the council was asserting its ownership but that would not negative Molly's adverse possession unless that claim was acknowledged by Molly and there is no evidence that she did so. Thus, on the facts, Molly can in all probability, claim 13 years' adverse possession with the result that under the Limitation Act 1980 the council would find itself statute-barred and its title extinguished.

SUGGESTED ANSWER TO QUESTION TWO

General Comment

This question serves as a reminder that questions on adverse possession can be set in a registered title context and cannot be answered fully without a knowledge of that branch of land law. Although not arising in this problem, sometimes it is necessary to discuss the provisions in the Land Registration Act relating to rectification.

Key Points

- Meaning of adverse possession
- Section 15 Limitation Act 1980
- Significance of fencing
- Successive squatters – aggregation of periods of adverse possession by different owners
- Significance of communication from paper owner – *Buckinghamshire County Council* v *Moran*
- Registering a caution – s70(1)(f) Land Registration Act 1925
- What action should squatter take in face of possession proceedings?

Suggested Answer

Adverse possession, with which this question is concerned, means possession inconsistent with the title of the true owner. Section 15 of the Limitation Act 1980 sets a 12-year period for the recovery of land. It provides that 'No action shall be brought to recover land after the expiration of 12 years from the date on which the right of action accrued.' Here it will be necessary to consider the following main issues: (a) when did adverse possession by Miss Sprigg commence?; (b) successive periods of adverse possession, ie that of Miss Sprigg first and then Maud; (c) the significance of the communication from Sunshine Caravans who bought the field from Lord Blacktown; and (d) what action Maud can take in the face of possession proceedings commenced by Sunshine Caravans? Each of these issues will be considered in turn.

In 1984, Miss Sprigg purchased Oaktree Cottage which is registered land. Evidence of title takes the form of a register and filed plan issued by the Land Registry which will mirror the documentary title prior to first registration. On the facts given, the registered title will include the back garden up to the adjoining field. When, in 1985, Miss Sprigg removed part of the fence and went onto part of the field to cultivate vegetables she went onto land beyond her registered title and began to treat it as her own. As previously mentioned, s15 Limitation Act 1980 provides that no action can be brought by the true owner to recover any land after the expiration of 12 years from the date on which the right of action accrued to the plaintiff or the person through whom he claims. Time begins to run as soon as: (a) the owner has been dispossessed or has discontinued his possession; and (b) adverse possession has been taken by some other person. Miss Sprigg must have had an intention to exclude the owner as well as other people: see *Powell* v *McFarlane* (1979). Adverse possession is a question of fact in which circumstances such as the nature of the land and the way in which the land is enjoyed, must be taken into account. In *Wallis's Cayton Bay Holiday Camp* v *Shell-Mex and BP Ltd* (1975) Lord Denning said that just because some other person enters onto land and uses it for some seasonal purpose like growing vegetables that action was not adverse to the owner. Accordingly, on the facts it is doubtful, before the fencing in 1987, that acts sufficient to show and establish factual possession and an intention to possess to the exclusion of all others existed. Enclosure is the strongest possible evidence of adverse possession but it is not indispensable: see *Seddon* v *Smith* (1877). It is submitted therefore that on the facts time began to run in 1987.

In 1989 Miss Sprigg died leaving Oaktree Cottage to her sister Maud. If a squatter who has not barred the true owner sells the land he can give the purchaser a right to the land which is as good as his own. This rule also applies to devises or gifts of the land by the squatter. In each case the person taking the squatter's interest can add the squatter's period of possession to his own. Here, Maud can add Miss Sprigg's two-year adverse possession to her own.

Turning to the position of the paper owner, it would seem that in 1999 12 years have elapsed since 1987 when the fencing was carried out by Miss Sprigg. However, in 1996 – before 12 years had elapsed – Maud received a letter from Sunshine Caravans informing her that they propose to develop the field as a caravan site and requiring her to vacate the field. It must be shown that the claimant has accepted the assertion of the right by the paper owner and the mere assertion alone by the true paper owner of a claim to possession in land, contained in a letter sent to the squatter, is not sufficient to prevent the squatter obtaining title by adverse possession. Accordingly, if Maud continued to use the land in spite of her knowledge of Sunshine Caravans' intentions this would not be a bar to her continuing to acquire title by adverse possession, provided she maintained her intention to possess the land: see *Buckinghamshire County Council* v *Moran* (1989).

What action should Maud take in the face of the possession proceedings? If Maud is confident that she has established factual possession and intention she could defend the possession proceedings and assert her squatter's title. She is in possession and should not move off the land unless she is willing to do so. Sunshine Caravans may wish to settle the proceedings and purchase her interest in the land. Maud could make application to the Land Registry for a possessory title to the land on the basis of her adverse possession. However, in view of the commencement of proceedings by Sunshine Caravans the Land Registry would not proceed with her application until the outcome of the court proceedings were known.

Finally, it is important to note the raison d'etre of the Limitation Act 1980. It is that those who go to sleep upon their claims should not be helped by the courts in recovering their property and that there should be an end to litigation.

Old Bailey Press

The Old Bailey Press integrated student law library is tailor-made to help you at every stage of your studies from the preliminaries of each subject through to the final examination. The series of Textbooks, Revision WorkBooks, 150 Leading Cases/Casebooks and Cracknell's Statutes are interrelated to provide you with a comprehensive set of study materials.

You can buy Old Bailey Press books from your University Bookshop, your local Bookshop, direct using this form, or you can order a free catalogue of our titles from the address shown overleaf.

The following subjects each have a Textbook, 150 Leading Cases/Casebook, Revision WorkBook and Cracknell's Statutes unless otherwise stated.

Administrative Law
Commercial Law
Company Law
Conflict of Laws
Constitutional Law
Conveyancing (Textbook and Casebook)
Criminal Law
Criminology (Textbook and Sourcebook)
English and European Legal Systems
Equity and Trusts
Evidence
Family Law
Jurisprudence: The Philosophy of Law (Textbook, Sourcebook and Revision WorkBook)
Land: The Law of Real Property
Law of International Trade
Law of the European Union
Legal Skills and System
Obligations: Contract Law
Obligations: The Law of Tort
Public International Law
Revenue Law (Textbook, Sourcebook and Revision WorkBook)
Succession

Mail order prices:	
Textbook	£14.95
150 Leading Cases/Casebook	£9.95
Revision WorkBook	£7.95
Cracknell's Statutes	£9.95
Suggested Solutions 1998–1999	£6.95
Law Update 2001	£9.95

To complete your order, please fill in the form below:

Module	Books required	Quantity	Price	Cost
		Postage		
		TOTAL		

For Europe, add 15% postage and packing (£20 maximum).
For the rest of the world, add 40% for airmail.

ORDERING

By telephone to Mail Order at 020 7381 7407, with your credit card to hand.

By fax to 020 7386 0952 (giving your credit card details).

Website: www.oldbaileypress.co.uk

By post to: Mail Order, Old Bailey Press, 200 Greyhound Road, London W14 9RY.

When ordering by post, please enclose full payment by cheque or banker's draft, or complete the credit card details below. You may also order a free catalogue of our complete range of titles from this address.

We aim to despatch your books within 3 working days of receiving your order.

Name

Address

Postcode   Telephone

Total value of order, including postage: £

I enclose a cheque/banker's draft for the above sum, or

charge my   ☐ Access/Mastercard   ☐ Visa   ☐ American Express
Card number

☐☐☐☐ ☐☐☐☐ ☐☐☐☐ ☐☐☐☐

Expiry date   ☐☐☐☐

Signature: ....Date: ....